PAULIE STEWART
All the Rage

PAULIE STEWART
All the Rage

M
MELBOURNE BOOKS

This book is dedicated to the unknown Australian who decided to register as an organ donor. Thanks for your liver which has allowed me to write this and for all the new stories you helped make happen. Special thanks to my mum June Veronica Stewart.

This book wouldn't have happened without the support, prodding and many hours of editing and encouragement from Peter Wilson and the tireless help of Maggie Miles, Annie and Janie Stewart, Kathy Watt, Brendan Fitzgerald, Kate Cuthbert, Oliver Johnson, Max Johnson, Mick Reid, Frances Le Plastrier-Stewart and Aretha Brown.

For invaluable medical support a massive shout out to Dr Greg Stewart and Dr Beth Quinn.

WARNING: a large amount of this material was written under the influence of morphine and oxycodone in Ward 8 at the Austin Hospital Heidelberg so don't take it all as gospel.

INTRODUCTION
(1989)

'You are communists? You are spies? Who are you?'

I am up in East Timor in the border hamlet of Balibo. Late 1980s and I have just been stopped in the street by an Indonesian policeman after getting off a bus.

Frogmarched to a police station with my travelling companion Colin Buckler from our band the Painters & Dockers, we now stand and watch ten young Indonesian army recruits, all stripped to the waist, finishing a strenuous drill.

Two older Indonesian army officers appear and summon the recruits together and they soon encircle us.

The officers want to know who the hell we are and what we are doing there.

We desperately try to explain that despite the accusations being flung at us, we are not communists or political agitators.

'No, no really! In Australia we are entertainers,' I proclaim as if our paisley shirts, long hair and eyeliner don't give us away.

They don't believe us.

'Sing "Cotton Fields" then,' barks one of the senior-looking chaps.

'Pardon?,' I meekly reply.

'Yeah, sing "Cotton Fields" or else,' smirks one of his subordinates.

Colin and I look at each other and it dawns on us that there is really only one way out of here. So we start up on the old Minstrel classic!

'When I was a little biddy baby my mama come and rock me in the cradle,' we throw in some bum wiggles and hand gestures—anything really to brighten up the act, 'in those old cotton fields back home.'

We sing the whole tune. At the finish, the two older Indonesians reluctantly look at each other.

'Get out of this place right now,' says the boss man.

Shaken, we beat a hasty retreat back to the bus and get out of town.

This was my first visit to East Timor, which is now known as Timor-Leste, but it would not be my last. The small village of Balibo would have a huge impact on my life.

1

HAVE YOU MADE OUT A WILL?
(2006)

In 2006, at the age of forty-six, I went into hospital for a small hernia operation. Afterwards in the recovery room the doctor said, 'There is quite a bit of liquid there in your gut mate, you need to get it looked at.'

'Sure pal. Whatever.' And with typical male health denial, I headed out that night for beers with my journalist colleagues.

I felt terrible the next morning but still did nothing. A few days later I was due to meet my little sister Janie for a slap-up Japanese lunch and I told her that she may have to wait twenty minutes or so because I had a follow-up consultation with the doctor before our sushi.

The doctor was a liver expert and the second we walked in he looked aghast at my yellow appearance. He examined my eyes and chest and instructed my startled little sister to take me 'directly to the emergency department' at the Western and General Hospital in Footscray, saying he would let them know we were coming.

I was examined there by a young doctor who recommended emergency surgery. Suddenly I was on a trolley with nurses rushing me to the operating theatre, and the young doctor asked, 'Have you made out a will?'

'Why?'

He changed the subject. 'Have you had a good life?'

'You are kidding, right?'

In a matter-of-fact way, the young doctor told me that I needed immediate surgery because my liver was packing it in. He produced a document for me to sign, to confirm that I realised the seriousness of my condition and that if I died on the operating table the hospital couldn't be held responsible.

'So much for the sushi,' I told Janie.

After an eight-hour wait and much prodding and poking, the medical staff determined that things were so serious there was nothing they could do immediately because I needed a liver transplant. It could take up to a year, even longer, to get a new one. Without being too melodramatic, that meant I could die waiting.

It freaked me out to learn that only 500 liver transplants up until then had ever been performed in Australia and that our rate of organ donation was among the lowest in the Western world.

One side effect of liver disease is a condition called encephalopathy or as I call it, 'brain drain'. Basically, the liver normally cleans the bloodstream and when it's not functioning properly a lot of toxins build up in the brain, which collects it like a big sponge. That disrupts your ability to think clearly, concentrate and remember stuff. You do crazy things, say crazy things and have crazy thoughts, delusions of grandeur, flights of fantasy, depression, sleeplessness ... you name it.

The encephalopathy kicked in and hit me in waves.

On one occasion, I spent a maddening half-hour repeatedly asking my younger daughter Aretha how to put my glasses on. I asked her sister Frances, 'Have you got a pet blue lizard?' I was sure I had seen one crawling around the house. At one point I thought I was buried alive in Caulfield cemetery, another time that I had been sent for medical attention in Chicago. I dreamt that I ran into Rupert Murdoch at my letterbox and asked him, 'Are you coming to Australia or what?' He looked horrified and I woke up laughing my head off.

It took me half an hour to walk to the nearby shops and back, which used to take five minutes.

During one hospital visit, a young trainee doctor informed me that she would have to give me a rectal examination. I pulled a mock sad face.

'Is that too uncomfortable for you, sir?' she asked.

'No but I thought you might take me out for Yum Cha and the movies first.'

Her laughter made my day. One of the doctors turned out to be a transvestite. Aretha had painted my toenails bright pink and this doctor noticed and gave me a wink. I was grateful for the extra loving care and cups of tea that came my way.

Another doctor suggested that to help me stay positive I should write my thoughts down. Keep the old brain active and keep the brain drain away. He put me in contact with renowned Australian author and historian Inge Clendinnen, herself the recipient of a liver transplant back in 1994 when the procedure was still in its infancy.

Clendinnen was wonderfully supportive and during some of her visits to the Austin for her own treatment she sat down and explained how writing kept her sane. Now is the time for contemplation, she suggested. So, slowly, I began to jot things down.

Stories jumbled around in my brain as I recalled some of the more unusual events in my life. I've been in rock bands and worked as a newspaper reporter my whole life and I now realised what an odd career it was. I had an editor at the *Sunday Herald Sun* in Melbourne who would often walk past my desk and say, 'You can't write, can't sing, can't play a musical instrument. How do you survive?'

Good question, really. But survive I did.

Don't get me wrong, I'm not after sympathy. My illness was self-inflicted, mostly fuelled by alcohol and drug abuse. I started writing because I was scared and I had no choice but to think about death.

Now, the bands I have played in were never huge commercial successes or Top of the Pops-type acts. I have been more like a travelling carnival man doing countless shows with neither the support nor the constraints of a major record contract.

I'd always been happy to charge into all manner of crazy situations, and lying bored in hospital wards for lengthy stays the memories poured out of me.

However, the first story that tumbled onto my notepad was my run home from school in 1975.

* * *

Everyone experiences the death of a loved one but when a death in the family is famous, never forgotten by the country you live in, it lingers like a spiteful ghoul wanting attention at the most inappropriate times.

I still vividly remember the run home from school on that day, 16 October 1975.

I lived in a safe, secure and predictable bubble with my parents, two brothers and two sisters in our leafy suburban home in inner Melbourne. My world was school, the footy, surfing, playing tennis, the Sunday roast, riding my bike, doing a paper round, television shows like *World of Sport, Get Smart, Hogan's Heroes* and *Epic Theatre* and endless barbecues.

The fact that my two older brothers went to my school gave me some kind of protection there and having both an older and a younger sister meant I was surrounded by girls of all shapes and sizes unlike many others at my Catholic boys' school. Life was pretty chilled.

The walk home from school on that unforgettable day took a familiar route. A posse of schoolmates and I meandered through the laneways of Malvern up to the nearby railway station. One was Peter Drummond, who'd explained the facts of life to me during an earlier walk. Sex education was unheard of at my school so my eager friend outlined all the 'ins and outs' in the fifteen minutes it took to walk to the station. He even showed me his prize possession, a photo of a woman with massive mammaries ripped from a *Playboy* magazine that he carefully folded and protected as if it were the Mona Lisa.

On this particular walk home, we discussed all the important issues: the cutest candidates at the nearby girls' school who would be at the school dance that night, our favourite football stars and the latest act we'd seen on weekly TV music show *Countdown*. We shared notes about which of the De La Salle brothers who taught at our school were best to be avoided, especially one brother who everyone knew never to be alone with, Frank Keating. He was eventually jailed after pleading guilty to sexually abusing several of the boys at my school during my time there.

At Malvern railway station I farewelled my pals who toot-tooted off to their homes in the bayside suburbs on the red rattler trains, then I walked through the station towards the tram that would take me to my home in North Caulfield.

The tiny newspaper stand at the station caught my eye with the poster for that afternoon's *Melbourne Herald*.

'FIVE NEWSMEN MISSING IN EAST TIMOR'

A shadow passed over my heart. 'Hang on ... East Timor!'

I had no idea where the country was. Was it in Africa, perhaps? Or South America? But what I *did* know was that my brother Tony was one of those newsmen. He had excitedly phoned Mum a few days before, proudly proclaiming, 'I'm off to cover my first war, Mum, off to East Timor.'

I didn't wait for the tram but ran the last two kilometres down Alma Road as fast as I could. As each stride got me closer to home my anxiety rose. My mind was racing, my heart pounding and I knew Mum would be freaking out.

About a year earlier Tony, never the academic, had been thrilled to get a job at television station HSV7 Melbourne as a sound man attached to the news crew. He loved being under the wing of experienced cameraman Gary Cunningham, who had gone with him to East Timor.

Mum, a school teacher for thirty years, had been worried about Tony's job prospects and helped him get the gig by approaching a neighbour who happened to be Channel 7's news director, John Maher.

Tony loved his new job and it gave him enough pay to leave the home nest. He did hate it though when Mum talked me and my little sister Jane into singing Rolf Harris' 'Two Little Boys' at the Channel 7 Christmas party. It was my first ever public performance and while I enjoyed it, I could see Tony blushing with embarrassment as he stood among his workmates in the audience.

At home I made my way straight to the kitchen where, sure enough, Mum was surrounded by aunties who had seemingly endless pots of tea on the boil.

She was in tears. 'Paulie, your brother is missing.'

'I know, Mum.'

'They say nothing is definite up there but he should be safe.'

'He'll be right, Mum. It's okay.'

'We are just waiting to hear from the authorities. They said they would update us.'

'Great, Mum.'

'They said the journalists may have been captured by Indonesian forces up at a little border village. They wouldn't hurt them would they?'

'I don't think they would risk upsetting us,' replied one aunt.

'I mean the Indonesians are our friends, aren't they?' asked another.

"I'm sure they will be fine Mum."

That night we didn't hear a word from the Australian Government or Channel 7. The nasty truth is that the only call Mum ever got from the Australian Government was from a lowly official at our embassy in Jakarta who contacted her weeks after Tony went missing to say, 'Where do we send the bill for the coffin?'

It was later revealed by several sources, including the daughter of the then Australian Foreign Affairs Minister Senator Don Willesee, that Canberra knew of the murder of the journalists almost immediately, a full week before they informed us.

Seven agonising days.

It was an unnecessary pain inflicted for the sake of diplomatic relations. In the decades that followed my brother's death I wrote to the Prime Minister, Gough Whitlam and pleaded with him to contact Mum and offer his sympathies. After all, he was in charge when it happened. 'Gough the Great' couldn't bring himself to offer any comfort to my mum and will always be tainted in my eyes by his cruel indifference.

While Mum was distressed and teary over Tony's disappearance, Dad was angry.

Reports came through that six days after the Channel 7 crew arrived in East Timor, Australian journalist Jill Jolliffe and a media spokesman for the East Timor independence movement José Ramos-Horta, later to become the nation's president, had run into the newsmen and warned them not to go to the border hamlet of Balibo.

They told them the Indonesians and their local militia allies were preparing to invade the town, and Jakarta was determined to stop the world knowing about its activities.

Those who warned the journalists said later that Greg Shackleton, the 29-year-old reporter who was leading the Channel 7 news team, had dismissed their concerns. This was Shackleton's first time in a conflict zone and his final assignment before he was due to go to New York to study journalism, so it was his last chance to get a big scoop under his belt before heading off to the US.

'I hope they followed that advice and left in time. They are bloody stupid if they didn't,' growled Dad. 'Channel 7 had no right to send such an inexperienced crew into the thick of it.'

East Timor was just an hour's flight from Darwin but Tony had never even left Australia before and the dangers of reporting in a war zone should have been obvious.

Dad scoffed at the report that the journalists had hand-painted an Australian flag on their house in Balibo as a means of identifying themselves.

'As if that is going to stop them from being shot at,' Dad hissed. Several days later, HSV7 supremo Ron Casey came to our house to talk to Dad. I knew who he was because we never missed his

Sunday program *World of Sport*. The two disappeared to the lounge room and even though Mum bustled us outside we could hear the muffled shouting.

My dad had had a hard life and had no reason to be soft on anyone. He lost his mum in his early teens and grew up with a father who was notorious for his temper, epileptic fits and throwing his weight around.

Dad went bankrupt in an early business venture with his father, Jack, and found himself facing financial ruin with five children to feed, so he swallowed his pride, bought an old ute and became the local 'bottle-o' in St Kilda. This was the guy who would pick up your empty beer bottles and return them to Carlton & United Breweries for the small refund. Many of the guys who worked for him were fresh out of prison doing the only job they could find.

It was dirty work but Dad sucked it up and got on with it to make sure we were comfortable, well-educated and secure. He built the business from the ground up. We were all proud when years later he was described as one of the country's first true "Greenies" after becoming an innovative recycler setting up practices across Australia and Malaysia.

The only time I ever saw Dad cry was the day Tony went missing. Discovering him softly sobbing in a back room far away from everyone left me rattled. I had never seen him so vulnerable, so hurt and so scared. In fact, over the next few days, I also saw my other brother Greg and sisters Annie and Jane all weeping. Mum of course was inconsolable. I was totally thrown by all this grief. I am not for one moment saying I was braver than anyone else but I took it upon myself to cheer them up by acting the buffoon. It was soon my role in the family. I can now see how I extended that attitude to my whole life and everyone I dealt with.

I also lost my religion that day. I had been a keen altar boy before Tony's death. Mum, aunties and sisters were in tears when a Roman Catholic nun, who was a family friend, dropped in to offer support. At one stage I was outside with her and under her breath she said to me, 'I don't know why everyone is crying, they should be happy that

Jesus has taken your brother to live with him.' I looked at the nun, so angry I couldn't speak.

What crap. How could a benevolent God allow so much pain to be inflicted on us?

That was me done with religion.

On that terrible day, more relatives, friends and neighbours came and went with endless cakes, curries and casseroles and the question of my Year 9 school dance that night came up.

I didn't want to go but Mum insisted. She wanted everything to be predictable and normal, as though Tony wasn't missing. She spent the rest of her life wanting that.

To keep Mum happy, I turned up at the school hall and moped about as the students made the usual embarrassed introductions to each other and shuffled nervously around the dance floor. The night dragged on to its conclusion and was just about to finish up when an announcement crackled through the loudspeakers calling me to the centre of the dance floor with my dance partner. Bewildered, I took her by the hand and moved to the centre of the room. The voice continued, 'Okay everybody, let's hear it for Paul because we have just heard his brother has been found alive and well in East Timor. It's time for the last dance. Take it away.'

You beauty. Deep breath. What a relief. Spontaneous applause and everyone smiling.

I jumped around with my dance partner with a grin from ear to ear. As I left the hall I was patted on the back and congratulated as if I had actually done something worthwhile.

I made my way home with wings on my feet. I couldn't wait to see the family back to their old happy selves but the looks around the table upon my entry told me something was up.

'False report,' said an aunty, 'they're still missing.'

Mum started sobbing uncontrollably.

It was then and there that I learned life doesn't always go according to plan. And that it can really hurt. I resolved at that moment to never take it for granted. I would never plan more than a month ahead and

I promised myself to live every minute like it counted. Yep, I wouldn't burn the candle at both ends. I would set the whole thing on fire with a blowtorch.

The killing of the Balibo Five is now part of Australian folklore. While it will never attract the same scale of remembrance as Gallipoli or Vietnam, I have travelled the length and breadth of Australia and when I tell people of a certain age I am a brother of one of the journalists killed in East Timor they all know the tale.

I thought after my brother's death that it would all fade away over time and yet, for almost half a century, there haven't been too many days when I haven't spoken about it.

Years later Bryan Dawe, one part of famed Australian comedy duo Clarke and Dawe, approached me in a bar. Tears came to his eyes as he told me that he had been a friend of Tony. 'I have always felt terrible about your brother's death because when he told me was being sent to East Timor I laughed and said, "So, what kind of flowers do you want on your coffin?"' Dawe and Tony were at a party on Tony's last night in Australia and Dawe made his smartarse remark when Tony drove him home.

'No one thought for a second that they were going into a real danger zone or I would never have said such a thing,' Dawe confessed. 'What I said was meant to be ironic. You can imagine the guilt I felt days later.'

My mother never got over Tony's death. It made her prone to anxiety and nervousness all her life. She never completely dropped the ball because she had four other children to raise but in the last few years of her life she spoke of Tony more than ever.

It was only when my liver problems prompted me to start writing about my experiences that I came to see how much my own life was shaped by the tragedy in Balibo.

October 16, 1975 was the day my life changed forever.

2

MY MOB
(1960–75)

A story that did the rounds on many family occasions was how my sisters dressed me as a little girl and gave me the name Betty Martin.

The girls and I would then go skipping down the street singing their made-up little ditty, 'Hey Betty Martin tippy-toe, tippy-toe.'

I was more than happy to dress up and make a fool of myself. Some things never change!

As the fourth child of five, I learned to fight for airtime within the family and was encouraged by both parents.

Dad would drag me out at barbecues to sing songs and put on little shows and Mum dragged me along to the school where she taught to play my primitive trumpet bleatings for her class.

Growing up in my Melbourne neighbourhood of North Caulfield there was one thing that never sat quite right with me as many of my neighbours carried a haunted look about them.

I didn't understand the strange tattoos some wore on their arms or why they would quickly cover them up if they saw me staring at their unusual scrawlings. One of my first childhood memories was of the old lady who lived across the road who would scream all night if an ambulance ever went through our suburb.

Mum explained that many of our neighbours were Jewish Holocaust survivors, including the old woman opposite us who had been arrested by the Nazis. The wail of the ambulance siren would bring back horrifying memories for her of the Gestapo when they came to arrest her.

There always seemed to be minorities living in the shadows around us. The people who live close but out of sight.

Our Dad was St Kilda boy Noel John Stewart who fascinated me with his stories of growing up in the bayside suburb like, for example, the time thousands of US servicemen camped in The Peanut Reserve opposite his house during World War II.

Dad said some of the heaviest fighting of the war took place in the laneways of St Kilda between the visiting Americans and the locals.

It is comforting to think that before he died, I had rebuilt bridges with my dad, who was unimpressed by my punk music career.

Dad and I differed in so many ways. He shunned attention, I craved it. Mum said he never liked to stand out in a crowd mainly because of the actions of his own father.

Grandad Jack, a former vice president of the St Kilda Football Club, worked for a long time as "security" for Melbourne powerbroker John Wren, who shot to fame after the novel *Power Without Glory* by author Frank Hardy portrayed him as an unsavoury character.

While many praised author Hardy, in our house he was considered a traitor for attacking a working class boy like Wren who had made good.

I wonder what Grandad Jack would have thought of me when years later I became a friend of Hardy's granddaughter Marieke, at whose invitation I appeared at the Melbourne's Writers Festival in 2018.

My parents even got to meet the infamous Wren, joining him on many occasions for boxing matches at his Festival Hall in West Melbourne, and pride of place in our lounge room was an ornate tea set that he gave them when they wed.

I can remember meeting an old lady at a party once who said she knew Granddad Jack and then introduced me to her friends as, 'Paul, grandson of one of John Wren's bodyguards.'

A story often told about Granddad Jack—a fiery character and staunch supporter of the Democratic Labor Party, the Catholic-led breakaway from the Australian Labor Party—was the time he tangled with notorious local gangsters and original Painters and Dockers Union heavyweights Norman Bradshaw and Freddie 'the Frog' Harrison.

These two chaps petrified many people but not my granddad. Apparently, Jack and my dad (who was about ten at the time) were driving down a one-way St Kilda street when the two heavies came driving up the same street the wrong way.

The two cars drew up to one another and stopped. Stalemate.

According to Dad, the two gangsters motioned to Jack to back up but much to their surprise, he didn't budge. One of the gangsters had had enough and got out and walked up to Jack's car window and angrily gestured to him to move along.

Jack apparently wound down his window, motioned to the thug to come closer and then leaned out of his car and floored the guy with one punch.

His companion was so startled by this he got out of the car and put his semi-conscious mate in the back seat and reversed up the street.

Dad knew the gangsters by reputation and was terrified. Grandad Jack didn't flinch.

Jack had been on his way to Gallipoli with other ANZAC troops early in World War I but suffered several epileptic fits and was sent home. Relatives said he never really got over the shame. Mum's view was that he was a perfectly balanced guy with a big chip on each shoulder.

My dad went out of his way to avoid confrontation. His two favourite sayings were 'When in doubt, do nothing' and 'Let it go through to the keeper'.

I clearly remember performing at a Painters & Dockers gig on Mordialloc Pier where we had hundreds of young punters jumping around like crazy. From the stage I saw Dad up the back with his arms crossed and a look of disdain on his face.

No, not a fan.

I am grateful for two incidents that happened later in life. Dad told me that he had once stopped at the Standard Hotel in Fitzroy for a quiet beer and upon noticing all the band posters on the wall mentioned to the barman, 'My son plays in a band.'

'What are they called?' he asked.

'The Painters & Dockers,' said Dad.

'The Dockers are awesome mate; that beer is free.'

To Dad, that was more impressive than winning an ARIA Award (which I later did). Likewise, in retirement Dad hired a couple of workers to do some repairs at the family home.

After work one day, one of the workers sheepishly knocked on the back door and asked him, 'Sorry to be a pest but can I ask why you have a photo of Paulie Stewart on your mantelpiece?'

'He is my son,' he said.

'We love The Dockers and never miss a gig,' was the reply.

It took many years but Dad came around in the end and we became very close in the last years of his life.

Dad may have shunned the limelight but Mum was a show-off and a frustrated performer. I would often come home from school to find her prancing around the kitchen singing Gilbert and Sullivan or some operatic verse. I would slot straight in as one of the 'three little maids from school' or one of the prancing sailors from the *HMS Pinafore*.

As a teacher she always just happened to end up in the annual school productions at the places she taught. Dad wouldn't be seen dead in a theatre but Mum loved it. She and my brother Greg never missed a Barry Humphries Melbourne performance.

She also had a bizarre sense of humour and shared with Tony a love of Monty Python. Her favourite Python skit was the scene in which an Arab with a translation book walks up to an English policeman and cheerfully says, 'My hovercraft is full of eels.'

It was family legend that after meeting through tennis club friends, Elwood-born June fancied Noel, who loved his tennis, squash and golf. We often heard the story that on one of their first dates Dad was impressed to find her standing outside her home practising her golf swing. She had never played golf in her life.

Dad had a running gag when he would sit around the table looking at his five children. 'All I ever did was ask her to go to the pictures,' he would sigh before laughing.

When I complained to him at eighteen that I found it restrictive living at home, he went to the garage and came back with two suitcases.

'Which one?' he asked.

Now I thought I had just been expressing an opinion, but he said, 'Here, take the blue one and make sure you drop in every now and then to see your mother.'

I was out of the family home quick smart with his blessing.

Mum was never the same after Tony's death and it broke Dad's heart to see her anguish. She only ever did one major interview about his murder after which Shirley Shackleton, the estranged wife of Greg Shackleton rang her and abused her for daring to speak on behalf of the families, even accusing Mum of getting her information wrong over some detail.

Years later my brothers and sisters took out an intervention order against Shirley, who would ring Mum (then eighty-three) and badger her for support against June's own children, me and my siblings, on issues relating to the Balibo murders.

Mum never wanted revenge against the Indonesians, just the truth about her boy's death. She was left with a heightened anxiety about the welfare of her children, and towards the end of her life the old wounds about Tony's loss reopened.

It didn't help when she picked up a newspaper one day to find politician Nick Xenophon saying he was going to bring the remains of the journalists from Jakarta to Australia, no matter what the families thought.

I spent many hours talking about Tony with Mum over the years—on the quiet, of course, because Dad forbade it.

It was cruel timing that on the day we buried Mum the Australian Federal Police contacted us to say they were dropping their investigation into the Balibo murders.

Mum's parents were the tiny Vera, nicknamed 'Trill' and trombone-playing Tax Office worker Francis King Hewitson.

I was always impressed that 'Kingie' had worked for a stint at Luna Park on the boats in the River Caves ride. I also remember constant trips to Luna Park and rides on the Rotor and visits to the Giggle Palace.

Trill was fiery and opinionated. Dad called her 'Frank Nitty' after Al Capone's feared right-hand man.

At just fourteen, she had to take over as head chef at the country pub her father ran when her mother died early. Used to dealing with drunks, she could more than hold her own with older men and bullshitters.

Staunch ALP supporters, the Hewitsons' first meeting with their future son-in-law's DLP-loving father Jack almost ended in fisticuffs.

Trill was the greatest cook ever, thrifty, and never wasted a single piece of food. Her homemade pasties and her pork crackling were fought over and lusted after.

There may have been divisions in the family but Tony's death brought as all together. Family tussles were minor stuff compared to the savage murder of a loved one.

As a fifteen-year-old I was in awe of Tony, twenty-one, and missed him badly but years later I started to get a little embarrassed when I first spoke at rallies and protests as the brother of one of the dead journalists.

East Timorese refugees would approach me after a speech and say how sorry they were for my loss. I would ask them in return if they had lost any relatives.

'Yes, seven members of my immediate family,' or nine members etc. etc., would be their reply.

It was ingrained in me early that while six white newsmen died in 1975 (eight weeks after the Balibo murders Roger East was shot on the wharf in Dili by Indonesian troops), there were hundreds of thousands of East Timorese killed during the Indonesian occupation of the former Portuguese colony.

One of the few ways the Australian media would focus on East Timor and the murdered journalists for many years was when a new witness was supposedly found. Honestly, so many "eyewitnesses" have come forward you could fill the MCG with them.

I have been asked questions like, 'A new report suggests the journalists were killed after they were wrapped in barbed wire then set on fire. What is your view on that?'

Or, 'A new report says the journalists were hanged and then had their genitals cut off and put in their mouths. Care to make a comment?'

'Latest eyewitness says all five were shot in the back as they ran away,' etc., etc., on and on.

These stories would appear from nowhere and I always felt bad for Mum and Dad, who had to constantly relive the shocking moment over and again and re-imagine Tony's final moments.

Not knowing the truth about what happened has left us all to fill in the horrible blanks with our own imaginations. Most people I know have lost a family member or close friend but not many have had to face five decades of hearing different stories of how their loved ones supposedly met their deaths.

To be honest, the families have always been divided in our responses and have even been critical of each other.

Shirley Shackleton has often behaved as if she were the only one of the family members who really cared about the fate of the journalists. That was nonsense of course.

Dad went to the Thorn Television awards when the local TV industry held a ceremony marking the journalists' deaths. Shirley was also invited and rightly or wrongly, wrangled a free colour TV set from the organisers. Dad was startled by this and really upset. No free TV would ever compensate him for Tony's death. He vowed to never attend such an event again. That didn't mean he didn't care. It meant he cared too much.

3

COPY BOY
(1979)

One of the most important turning points in my life came when I was weeks out of high school. In January 1979 at the age of eighteen, I was hired by Australia's biggest newspaper company, The Herald and Weekly Times as a copy boy, the lowest rung of the journalism ladder.

There were several hundred applicants for a handful of jobs every year and I got one.

Let's not make any mistake about how I got it. It was because the company, (which also controlled television station HSV7 Melbourne) "owed my family".

My academic history after all was nothing of note. But Mum had given me good advice before my job interview: 'Make sure you mention your brother!'

The interview with prominent journalist Peter Game was proceeding badly, especially when he looked at my not-so-flash final results. Finally he let out a sigh and said, 'So why do you want to be a journalist anyway?'

His attitude changed when I explained that his organisation's former employee Tony Stewart, killed in Balibo, was in fact my big brother and that I wanted to follow in his footsteps.

He immediately sparked up and excused himself for a few minutes, saying, 'I just need to ring someone.'

I knew the gig was mine.

Sure enough, he soon returned and rather than risking any embarrassment to the company he recommended me for a job.

That is how I found myself in my dad's old suit walking nervously up Flinders Street to the imposing five-storey Herald and Weekly Times building on Monday, 22 January 1979.

I was with the company for the next thirty years.

Right from the get-go, I realised that Tony's death was why I got the job and to be truthful, I always felt very guilty about it. On the other hand, I was thrilled as it was like winning the gold pass to visit Willy Wonka's Chocolate Factory.

The H&WT published Melbourne's two biggest-selling and hugely influential newspapers, *The Herald* in the afternoon and the *Sun News-Pictorial* in the morning, and it was the thriving breeding ground of many of the country's top journalists.

That year happened to see the company's biggest ever intake of cadets and I scraped in at the bottom of that eighteen-strong group as a copy boy, meaning I had missed out on a prestigious cadetship and needed to spend a year doing menial office tasks before becoming a cadet.

There were six copy boys and copy girls, including two other products of Catholic boy schools, Peter Wilson and Robert Thomson.

I had most in common with Peter because we both came from hard-working small business families with no sense of entitlement and we were only too happy to start off running office errands.

We had actually met months earlier at a Lou Reed concert where he was hugely unimpressed with me for wearing make-up. We were both assigned to *The Sun* and he quickly became one of my dearest friends and would later become an award-winning journalist who has worked all over the globe.

My mum often told the story about our first day on staff at *The Sun* when we had come home and sat in the garden outside her kitchen window. Peter had big dreams and said, 'One day I am going to be one of Australia's leading journalists and make my name as a foreign correspondent.'

I was just as excited: 'Gee, this job is great,' I said, 'We get to wear long pants every day!'

Peter and I worked hard but also threw ourselves into the social life of young journalists. We were not guaranteed weekends off so every night was potentially Saturday night, especially if you had the late-night adrenalin hit of getting a good story in the paper.

Robert Thomson became the most senior Australian journalist in history. He would eventually be the first Colonial to be editor of prestigious London-based *The Times* and then *The Wall Street Journal* in the US, and reach the dizziest heights of leadership at Rupert Murdoch's News Corporation. He became a top executive at the worldwide organisation alongside the Murdochs.

I mean, even US President Donald Trump referred to him in 2020 as the world's leading 'media man'. One story I later read about him in a US magazine called him 'Rupert Murdoch's only friend'.

But that's not his biggest claim to fame in my book. Trying out with the St Kilda AFL Under-19s side is Robert's real glory story. I became close friends with his youngest brother Johnny who went on to establish a prestigious Art Gallery in New York.

Nowadays you have to be a B-grade reality soap star or sporting icon to be noticed by the *Herald Sun*, the successor to those two great newspapers, and its stories are often one-sided and written with a clear political bias.

But when I started at *The Sun* it was the glorious old days of real news journalism where both sides of the story got a hearing. It was this fair and balanced reporting that made the paper one of the most successful in the world, with a huge readership throughout Victoria.

My dad started each day with a cup of tea, a cigarette and *The Sun*, as did countless others. It was years before the rise of the shrill fascists and racist columnists.

No mention of a life in newspapers would be complete without mentioning the photographers who were so vital to delivering the finished story. I learned early in the piece that they were their own breed and heaven help the young journalist who ever referred to one of them as 'my photographer' when out on a job.

'No, arsehole, you are my journalist,' was a typical reply.

Nowadays, anyone can take a photo, but to be a great news photographer is certainly a gift. It takes a special something.

Most people might think the winning photo, when covering an Olympic running race, is the athlete successfully crossing the finishing line. No. True genius is getting the shot of the competitor who stops to help a fellow racer up when he falls over. That was a classic newspaper photograph published in the *Melbourne Herald*.

One of the first stories I ever covered went well enough, getting an interview completed and snaps taken in good time. However, on the way back to the office the photographer, Colin Bull, insisted we stop at a pub near work for a beer.

The fact that it was only 10.30am and I hadn't eaten any breakfast didn't really register with me as I downed four large pots of beer in twenty minutes.

As anyone who knows me will confirm, I have never been a great one for holding my liquor and so I arrived back at work pissed as a fart.

Thank God the chief-of-staff's secretary Marilyn Rawadi spotted my condition and sent me straight home in a cab before any boss could see me. It wasn't the last time she saved my butt over the next three decades, bless her.

I spent a lot of time doing the bottom-rung jobs, like getting the boss his lunch and picking up his wife's dry cleaning, then moving on to basic data tasks, like collating the prices of fruit and vegetables and the movements of ships through the Port of Melbourne.

One editor had me placing bets at the local TAB several times a day. Another duty was restocking the stationery cupboard and—even more importantly—the office beer fridge.

One of the benefits of this early training was that I got to know the printers, secretaries, layout artists, mailroom staff, security guards, canteen workers, and photographers—in fact just about everyone in the building.

I saw first-hand all aspects of how a newspaper is put together. You really can't beat that training in the newspaper trade.

Every day brought a new experience. That building in Flinders Street thumped with the sound of the presses and the walls had veins that throbbed with printer's ink.

Journalists with copy boy and copy girl backgrounds were regarded highly by the editors compared to the university-educated students with journalism honours degrees who would never learn who Steve in the printing department was, or what he contributed to the process of getting the paper out.

After a year as a copy boy, I moved up to begin my three-year cadetship, which included a lengthy stint arranging horseracing details and working alongside fellow cadet Lachlan McDonald, who taught me another important lesson—that it is not the loudest voice that is the most effective. Short and lightly-built, Lachlan had none of the ego or even arrogance that a lot of our colleagues bore but he was always worth listening to. He would later become a senior and highly influential adviser to several Victorian Labor governments.

One of my tasks gave Mum and my sisters a big laugh. The paper had an in-house doctor who provided a weekly medical column by sending in a cassette recording of himself talking about his latest subject which the copy person then had to type up.

The tape I had to type out was on severe dysmenorrhea (period pain). He could have been talking Swahili for all I knew and the Stewart women thought it was the funniest thing ever.

A cadetship back then involved working on all the different rounds of the paper to gain experience. An early stint saw me take over the Star Watch column where the goal was to interview up-and-coming film and stage actors.

One of my first jobs was to go to Victoria Park, then the home ground of the Collingwood AFL team, where they were making the

1980 movie *The Club*. I was told to interview 27-year-old actor John Howard, who was making his first movie.

He and one of Collingwood's star players Renee 'The Incredible Hulk' Kink, were feeling mischievous and decided to have a little fun with me. I was interviewing Howard on the boundary line when Kink came charging straight at me while doing his training laps. I dived to the ground just as Kink swerved to avoid cleaning me up, leaving them laughing and me shaking.

The Club went on to become an iconic Australian movie.

Another early assignment was to interview the then little-known American actress Jamie Lee Curtis (less than two years older than me) at Melbourne nightclub The Underground. I spent the whole interview stammering and darting my eyes around the room as she had a very tight low-cut top and huge breasts, and she seemed to enjoy my discomfort. Later she would go on to become a big name thanks to movies like *A Fish Called Wanda*, *Halloween* and *True Lies*.

A more successful outing was when I managed to get some face time with Hollywood star Nicholas Cage. He was in Melbourne in 2008 making *The Knowing*, a multimillion-dollar movie about the end of the world and everyone wanted to talk to him.

The problem was the movie's makers didn't want their star disturbed by any media.

The day he filmed a scene outside Victoria's Parliament House, the set was in tight lockdown with an army of security men on hand to keep fans and nosey journalists away. My editor sent me down with the near impossible task of getting some words from Cage. When I arrived at the top of Collins Street the most remarkable thing happened: I became invisible. I mean, I must have. How else could I saunter right pass the scores of police and security men who ringed the set?

I walked straight up to Cage and blurted out, 'Did you know in 1959 Ava Gardner also made a movie about the end of the world in Melbourne, called *On The Beach*?'

'No, I didn't,' replied the rather startled star.

'Gregory Peck, Anthony Perkins and Fred Astaire were also in it,' I went on. 'Actually, Ava said Melbourne was the ideal place to make a movie about the end of the world.'

Cage laughed and said, 'I'll have to track it down.'

Just then one of the security guys approached me and said 'Sorry, who are you?'

When I said I was from the local paper I was escorted away by two burly security men. It didn't matter as I had my angle: Nicholas Cage to watch *On The Beach* for research purposes.

Some of the veteran journalists when I started in the trade were real hard cases. A lot of these seasoned newspaper men and women would sit at their typewriters drinking longneck beers and chain smoking.

Miraculously, the journalists almost always somehow managed to deliver copy that was fair, meticulous and accurate.

I can remember *The Sun*'s editor Rod Donnelly calling me into his office and saying he was going to teach me the No.1 Rule of Australian journalism.

'Get a pen and a paper, son—now write this. When you go to the pub to get the editor's beer … make sure it is cold. And underline cold.'

Years later when I told people that I needed a liver transplant most assumed it was because I had spent a lifetime in hard-living rock 'n' roll bands.

Wrong. The biggest drinkers and drug takers I came across were definitely the journalists and photographers.

I got my big career break when Donnelly asked his daughters over breakfast one morning why they never read his paper.

'There's nothing in it for us,' they said. 'What about some more rock music, Dad?'

The editor marched into the newsroom the next Monday and scanned the room. Who could he rope in for such a task?

He looked my way and his eyes lit up. Hey, what about that freak cadet with pink hair and one shaved eyebrow?

Yours truly.

I became the editor's pet project and he gave me my own prominent column, All the Rage, a rare privilege for such a junior reporter. The name was a play on an expression of the time for something fashionable, and it played neatly on the use of 'raging' to mean partying.

Many still recall the day the editor was walking through the newsroom and stopped suddenly at my desk to stare at my nail polish, which for some reason was red on the left hand and black on the right. There were strict dress standards and reporters would be sent home for minor infringements, let alone a man wearing make-up.

'Okay Paulie, that's it, enough's enough!' he said.

The room hushed.

'From now on, the nail polish on your left hand has to match the nail polish on your right hand.'

The newsroom was gobsmacked. After this I was kind of given a licence to be as cheeky as possible ... well I thought so anyway.

Being outlandish became my thing.

One Monday morning I was summoned before a senior and very conservative executive named Bill Hoey, who said, 'We have had a report of a man dressed as a woman who assaulted a cab driver at Tullamarine airport this morning after being thrown out of the international bar. Your name was mentioned. Tell me it wasn't you?'

I thought long and hard.

'Well he started it,' was all I could meekly answer.

If life could end at any moment I felt obliged to push it as far as I could.

Lawrence Money, a celebrated Melbourne newspaper columnist, still recalls one competition I ran in my music column that management never picked up on.

I urged contestants to write in and complete the name of an Elton John song.

'For a great prize just finish this Elton John title: "Don't Let the Sun ..."'

Yes, without the editors having any idea, the nation's biggest family newspaper received several thousand entries from readers who came up with the correct answer:

'To Paul Stewart: Go Down On Me. Becky Jones, Morwell'

'Dear Paul Stewart: Go Down On Me. Brad Smith, Carnegie'

It was childish but I loved messing with the rules. After Tony died, I mocked any kind of seriousness with absurdity. I can remember thinking that people can die at any moment so there was no need to take life too seriously.

There was no chance I would ever treat journalism as a sombre craft after sitting in the reporters room between Wendy Harmer and Mark 'Bob Downe' Trevorrow, who would go on to become two of Australia's funniest comedians.

I have to give credit to Mark for urging me to go and check out a new musical that he said would change my life, *The Rocky Horror Show*. It was staged at the old HSV7 studio just off Brunswick Street in Fitzroy, and he was right. I adored the over-the-top cabaret which starred the best Frank-N-Furter I ever saw, veteran Australian actor Max Phelps.

Mark also showed me you could work as a journalist while being in your own band.

During his early years at *The Sun*, he formed a cabaret band called The Globos with friends including comic Gina Riley of *Kath and Kim* fame and Georgie Malon, a gorgeous and ferociously smart young woman who was the third copy person assigned to the paper with Peter Wilson and myself in 1979.

I can still remember the fantastic show they put on for Georgie's twenty-first birthday party. Mark and Gina were clearly destined for stardom, while Georgie quickly became a respected journalist.

Wendy Harmer had a huge interest in live comedy and would become part of the early Melbourne cabaret scene that flowered at the Last Laugh in Collingwood and smaller venues like The Flying Trapeze in Brunswick Street. She later hosted ground-breaking ABC TV program *The Big Gig* and became an acclaimed ABC Radio DJ and comic.

As a young cadet I got to work in areas I would never have dreamed of. One novel stint I had was working in the paper's racing department, which was one of the most important sections of the paper.

Now cadet journalists, Peter and I performed the weekly task of meticulously recording the horse race results. Heaven help you if you got them wrong.

We never missed the Saturday race meeting at Flemington or Moonee Valley because you were guaranteed a feed of soup, a roast lunch and dessert. This was a godsend for two young chaps who barely found time in their budding social life to eat.

Another young cadet, who shall remain nameless, was a mad punter. Where I might have fifty cents on a race at Caulfield or Moonee Valley, he would spend $1000 backing a long shot at a race meeting in outback South Australia. More than once we had to go straight from work to his home and pawn his stereo, leather jacket or TV to repay the murderous-looking Turkish chaps he gambled with.

Part of the racing job was working on one of the most prestigious days on the Australian social calendar, the Melbourne Cup.

One year, one of the senior guys had to leave early so he left me his VIP pass into the member's enclosure. It was a ticket into an elite fun park I had only ever read about and I managed to sneak in just after the last race.

I had never really seen the wealthy at play. Crikey.

There was a couple having sex in the back seat of a stretch limousine, others doing lines of cocaine off the bonnets of their cars, people passed out, women half-naked urinating near the rose beds and raucous little parties all over the carpark.

To me, it had all the trappings of a Roman orgy. Indeed, at one point I was passed a golden goblet that promptly had some Moët champagne splashed into it.

It was much less fun doing a stint as a court reporter. In fact, it was heartbreaking as I covered a number of cases in the Coroners Court. Four decades later, I still remember one about a father who dropped a bit of ham on the floor, only to slip on it later and bang his baby's head on a kitchen counter, killing the infant.

Then there were the two 'dopers' from Phillip Island who had stabbed an old homeless man to death with a screwdriver. The main thing they wanted to know in court was whether they would be able to share the same cell.

So many tears, so much pain, so much unfairness. No, I didn't like the Coroners Court.

Police rounds, where all major news outlets had an office at the Victoria Police headquarters in Russell Street, was the only part of the paper that refused to give me a stint of work experience.

By that time, the Painters & Dockers had started doing our wild first shows and, apparently, I had an unsavoury reputation that they didn't think would sit well with the police. This wasn't helped by one of my early media interviews about The Dockers, in which I was asked if I had any hobbies. 'Taking amphetamines' was not a wise answer.

My fascination with outsiders only increased when I moved into a house that happened to be over the back fence from the Hare Krishna temple in Albert Park.

Along with housemates Paulie Greene and Francis Duke, I was often found in the Temple—not because we were new believers but because you could always get a free feed. My father used to laugh himself silly, saying I was the cheapest man in town when, after inviting girls out for dinner, I would take them to the Krishnas for a free meal.

Members of the sect, quite often from well-to-do suburbs, took to dropping into our house when they wanted a break from temple life.

The Krishnas certainly attracted an odd group of people, including one chap they dubbed 'Neil the Eel', who spent six months living in his Morris Minor out the front of our house. He would eat with the Krishnas and then sit in his car. That was his whole existence.

I can remember one of the devotees in our kitchen telling us one breakfast time how odd he thought Neil was.

'The guy is unbalanced. He is a weirdo,' said the Krishna.

I looked at him with his shaved bald head, beads and yellow saffron pants thinking, 'Yeah right mate, you say that guy is unbalanced.'

But who was I to judge?

We moved out of the house after we threw a party and 300 people turned up, promptly followed by the police riot squad, who refused to accept that such a large and loud gathering could possibly be a private party.

The house was seriously damaged, as was the neighbour's roof. The house was so crowded that people were dancing up on its tin roof, which was fine until they spilled onto the tiled roof next door.

The next day I cowardly bolted to a shared household on Beaconsfield Parade. It was in one of the upstairs apartments where I met a new arrival from Perth, Ross Greene—Renaissance man, first cousin of my dear pal Paulie Greene and a music enthusiast.

Ross and I became regulars at the New Romantics nights at the Inflation nightclub, which were a chance to party big-time, even on Mondays and Tuesdays, and we went to any gigs by The Birthday Party when they played Melbourne.

Ross held a couple of backyard barbeques where we locals could meet musicians visiting from his home state, Western Australia.

I was introduced to Le Hoodoo Gurus (later to morph into chart-topping outfit The Hoodoo Gurus) and a bunch of long-haired, moody and shy chaps who called themselves The Scientists, later widely acknowledged as the godfathers of grunge; a genre label that began in Australia and was popularised in Seattle.

The thing I started to realise about myself at this stage was that I was attracted to the quirky characters of life—outsiders like the members of American punk band the Dead Kennedys. We went to see them one night, met them after the show and they ended up coming back and spending the night at our house.

My growing interest in music was fuelled when I moved into a house in East Melbourne where a new housemate Peter Lindley played saxophone with a number of local bands.

4

YOU DON'T BELONG HERE, MISTER
(1980)

Part of the deal with being a cadet at *The Sun* was that you had to do a part-time journalism course at the Royal Melbourne Institute of Technology (RMIT) in Swanston Street, Melbourne.

Young cadets attended the course from the metropolitan and suburban papers, along with a handful of hopefuls looking for work in the industry. Ridiculously I was later listed as an illustrious alumnus, despite the fact I failed the journalism course … twice.

I spent far too much time in the Oxford Hotel across the road and that proved my undoing. I ended up standing out the front of the RMIT building in Swanston Street in tears as it looked like I was going to fail for a third time, which would mean instant dismissal from *The Sun*.

'Please, you can't fail me,' I pleaded to the head of the course, Lyle Tucker.

This guy just hated me as I did not fit his idea of what a journalist was and the smile on his face showed he took great satisfaction in thinking he would finally be rid of me.

As I have admitted, I was certainly no scholar. My only defence is we were being taught about newspapers based on the old printing system. There just seemed to be no point to it all, especially as the industry was rocketing into the computer age. Learning about the defunct hot and cold metal printing system seemed a big waste of my time.

However, this lecturer would not budge in his old-fashioned ways. I thank the God of Unconventional Journalists that another RMIT lecturer, Les Carlyon, stepped in and saved me.

I had to do one final assignment and Les gave me one last chance. I had to come up with a feature article and Les told me to write about a topic that actually interested me so I chose to do an interview with an obscure American singer-songwriter named Jesus Rodriquez who was about to tour Australia.

He had a cult following in Australia but was virtually unknown in his homeland. Thirty years later his remarkable life story was made into the award-winning movie *Searching For Sugarman*.

A promoter friend who was bringing Rodriguez Down Under said he could get me an interview. He gave me a number to ring in Los Angeles, which turned out to be a high school.

I rang and asked the switchboard operator if I could speak to Mr Rodriquez and she said there was no such person. I persisted. My journalism career now hinged on this interview and I told the operator I had been assured Mr Rodriquez was definitely there.

She said, 'Let me check with the other operator.'

After a few minutes she came back and said, 'Apparently the janitor is called Rodriquez.'

'Can I speak to him then please?' I asked in desperation.

A quietly-spoken guy came on the line and sure enough, it was the musician. We discussed his upcoming visit and that phone call became a turning point in my career.

I really enjoyed combining my course work with my growing passion for music. Les read my story and thankfully he liked it and passed me.

'Stick to the entertainment stuff and you will be right, Paulie,' were his parting words.

Les Carlyon stood out from the other lecturers because he could actually 'do' not just 'teach'. As well as being a revered former editor of Melbourne's broadsheet, *The Age*, he was an elegant feature writer and would later produce classic books on Gallipoli and The Great War.

He was easily the best writer I ever met.

Years later, it was with great satisfaction that I returned to RMIT's Storey Hall as a guest speaker during the Melbourne Writers Festival and recalled for the assembled students that moment when I had stood in front of the building crying with dismissal hanging over me.

I said I had a message for Lyle Tucker: 'I am still here, mate. So up yours!'

A mighty cheer went up.

My life changed dramatically in 1983 when the annual intake of new cadets included Jacinta Le Plastrier, a good-looking seventeen-year-old copy girl from Benalla, in country Victoria.

Right from the get-go her intelligence was obvious and I was smitten. I knew we would end up together and I also knew it wouldn't last because we were so young when we hooked up: I was twenty-two and she was just eighteen.

Jacinta was actually staying with a group of nuns when she first arrived in Melbourne so for our first date I had to drop into the convent in East Melbourne and assure the Mother Superior that I was taking her out for a light supper and would bring her straight back.

I had no such notion and took her to the Seaview Ballroom in St Kilda for a night of punk music.

We were a couple for seven years and in 1988 our relationship produced my first daughter Frances.

Jacinta is committed to writing and loves the English language. After a successful career as a journalist, she ended up at Melbourne's prestigious Wheeler Centre as head of the poetry department.

I am very proud of the fact that despite our almost inevitable break-up we have remained friends all our lives. She is a great mum and a poet of note. And Frances was the best thing that happened to me.

When I told a rock 'n' roll acquaintance that Jacinta was pregnant he mocked me saying, 'Well that's it for you, then. You have just lost all credibility.'

He couldn't have been more wrong. In fact, I may never have been able to keep "Docking" for 2000-plus gigs and nine albums if Frances had not kept me from totally wiping myself out.

With a young child to look after, I had to work harder and put the brakes on. Children need to be fed, entertained and listened to, whether you are hungover or not, and Frances remained a constant in my life arriving most weekends and school holidays.

'I did get sick of seeing you perform so many times,' she now laughs.

I will always feel guilty that she had to complete Year 12 while I was in hospital battling liver disease. All support and sympathy was diverted to me. One of the things I am most proud about in my life though is that Frances is such a kind and happy person.

5

MUSICAL PORNOGRAPHY
(1983)

My punk rock career began at the banana stand at the old South Melbourne Market one Saturday morning in April 1983.

That is where I ran into Phil Nelson, who belonged to a student club at Melbourne University known as The Emus whose members I regularly drank with at the Oxford Hotel opposite RMIT.

One of their favourite activities was following new wave/punk band Models from venue to venue, fanatically drinking and dancing.

Future bandmate Chris O'Connor was another of these crazy Emus, as was Mark Burchett, the first manager of the Painters & Dockers and now a much-loved member of the Melbourne entertainment industry.

An early girlfriend and lifelong pal, Jenny Draper, who had bright blue hair at the time, was also an Emu and thanks to her I was introduced to punk rock and the mysterious world of the Seaview Ballroom in St Kilda. It was exciting stuff hanging out with her and her pals. I wasn't particularly into music and at this point had not seen many bands live but I was fascinated by the rise of the Sex Pistols in the late 1970s.

The first time I ever saw the infamous Pistols was on *Countdown*. In fact, it is the only time in my life that I can ever remember Mum turning off the TV saying, 'You are not watching this rubbish.'

The next day at school, the headmaster ended his weekly assembly speech by saying, 'Punk rock is musical pornography' and forbidding us from listening to it. Even established musicians called it an abomination.

Of course, I immediately needed to know more about this punk rock thing so I snuck out of school with a mate one lunchtime to go to a nearby record shop in Malvern.

I asked the hippy who ran the shop to put on the debut Sex Pistols album *Never Mind The Bollocks*. He looked at me with distaste and said, 'I'll put it on but it is rubbish.'

Oh, I so needed to hear this.

I waited excitedly as he lined up the vinyl disc and dropped the needle. On came the record and then bang, the song 'Bodies' snarled its way out of the speakers.

> She was a girl from Birmingham.
> She just had an abortion, she was a case of insanity.
> Her name was Pauline, she lived in a tree.
> She was a no-one who killed her baby.
> She sent her letter from the country.
> She was an animal.
> She was a bloody disgrace.

Wow. Wee.

I loved it. It was angry and hard. The perfect antidote and musical soundtrack for the anguish I still felt over Tony's murder.

The members of the Sex Pistols looked totally inexperienced and made The Rolling Stones seem like self-indulgent old farts who were a million miles away from their audience. It seemed anyone could be in a punk band and the oldies and critics hated it.

All the better.

So there I was at the South Melbourne Market chatting with Phil Nelson, who I had met at my first Models concert.

He said he was putting together a band and had started jamming with a couple of mates, Chris O'Connor and Vladimir Juric.

'Hey, didn't you say you played trumpet at school?' he asked.

'Yeah, but I was pretty hopeless,' I admitted.

'That doesn't matter—it's punk,' he said encouragingly. 'Billy Walsh [a good pal and later drummer with the Cosmic Psychos] has got a whole heap of parking fines and his band is playing a benefit in a couple of weeks and they need a support act. I said I could come up with something.'

'Alright, count me in,' I said.

This was an era when music groups were admired for raising funds for good causes. I'll admit that paying off Billy's parking fines was not exactly battling famine in Africa but hey, it seemed like a good excuse for a fun night.

I think our original line-up had about nine members including one who just banged an empty beer keg.

So why did we call ourselves the Painters & Dockers?

Simple. We were playing the benefit at a small Port Melbourne pub and Chris O'Connor's girlfriend had suggested the name because hardcore members of the waterside union hung out there.

And besides, we were only supposed to do one gig. Little did we know this would lead to a lifelong involvement with music and more than 1500 shows in Australia and around the world with different Dockers combos.

The pub was the Rising Sun and in hindsight we were somewhere between brave and foolhardy to name ourselves after the most notorious trade union in Australian history.

The Federated Ship Painters and Dockers Union had a long history of being seen as public enemies in Australia. During the war years 1939 to 1945, the Communist Party had a huge influence in the union and the union's leaders later became recognised exponents of organised crime. The union was forever in the media headlines over alleged murders. State secretary Jack 'Putty Nose' Nicholls had won his job after the previous union secretary Pat Shannon was shot dead, and Nicholls raised eyebrows after another violent incident when he dismissed the need to call in the police, saying, 'We catch and kill our own.'

Mum actually rang in several times over the years when newspaper banners read 'Painter and Docker shot' just to check on my wellbeing.

The union was feared on the waterside and inside the infamous Pentridge Prison, where a large number of its members could always be found. The union became even more controversial when an inquiry into its operations was launched in 1980. This found evidence of tax evasion and drug trafficking that spread throughout Australia.

The Royal Commission was overseen by Frank Costigan and I was later to become friends with two of his children: Tim who played in local act The Shower Scene from Psycho and his sister Genevieve, a DJ on radio station Triple R.

The Federal Government deregistered the renegade union in 1993.

Pressed to come up with a band name to shock and outrage for our one and only gig, the Painters & Dockers seemed just perfect. We never expected that decision to cause such an uproar. In fact, we got great mileage from it all.

Anyway, we did a few rehearsals and when the benefit for Billy Walsh's parking fines went ahead in May 1983, we got up and played a set with Billy himself playing drums.

The first song I ever performed was our version of The Hunters & Collectors tune 'Talking to a Stranger'. For some reason I didn't follow the script and changed the lyric to 'talking to an Italian'. (God knows why I picked an Italian; it could have been any nationality.)

Anyhow, the lyrics I made up on the spot went along the lines of, 'Would you mind if I took you from behind? It's like talking to an Italian.' The crowd started laughing their heads off and dancing like crazy.

Well, it was like giving an alcoholic his first drink. A heroin addict his first blast. I loved the crowd's spontaneous reaction. I fell, hook, line and sinker. And I have been hooked now for forty-plus years.

Then Billy Walsh's band Spring Plains played a set.

Suddenly a man with an axe appeared. Yes, you've read right, a man with an axe.

Apparently, he was a neighbour who lived next door to the pub with his sick mother. He hated our music so much that he ended up jumping the fence with his axe and proceeded to chop up the sound-mixing desk. In a way he was just delivering the first of many bad reviews we would receive over the years but the effect was pandemonium.

The pub went from packed to empty in about three minutes flat and the police were called. Now one thing the real Painters and Dockers never allowed was the long arm of the law entering their watering hole.

A stand-off ensued between police and wharfies, then blows were thrown. Suddenly you had angry trade unionists fighting cops, with young music fans running screaming into the night. It was chaos and I was even more firmly hooked by the drama and adrenaline rush of it all.

Years later, one of the most frightening shows we ever performed was when the head of the union, Bob Dix, who was in Pentridge Prison at the time, sent his wife along to watch us to give us the thumbs up or down.

Dix had replaced Putty Nose Nicholls as state secretary in 1981 when the job became vacant in the traditional way for the union. Nicholls was found dead in his car with a bullet wound to the head on the day he was due to give evidence to the Royal Commission.

At the Prince of Wales pub in St Kilda, Mrs Dix approached us before the show and said, 'If I like it you can use the union's name but if I don't, you will stop using it immediately.'

She stood right in front of the stage with a couple of mean-looking blokes.

The thing in our favour, however, was that some young members of the union were keen on punk music and were actually chuffed that there was a band named after them. These young guys had pleaded with the union's leadership to let us keep using their name.

After the gig Mrs Dix came into the band room, sat down and asked for a drink, which we were happy to get for her. Luckily, she liked the set and gave us the thumbs up.

But back to the riot at our first show. News of the night spread when Damien Murphy of *The Age* wrote of this new punk band the Painters & Dockers who caused riots.

Well, the next shows organised by Phil were cancelled by venue owners scared of having riots on their hands. But it wasn't long before we got another gig and managed to fill the place with people wanting to check out this wild new band.

Billy the drummer went off to concentrate on his other musical pursuits so my old school buddy Andy Marron was roped in to play drums.

Shows in the first years of The Dockers were off-the-wall affairs that would often feature twenty people on stage dancing and singing to a thirty-minute rendition of 'Stepping Stone' by The Monkees.

Who knows, maybe it would have helped if we had learned to play the instruments properly, or if I had been able to read sheet music.

Still, we would go on to release nine albums, tour Canada, New Zealand and the United States and be inducted in 2009 into *The Age*'s rock 'n' roll Hall of Fame as part of the annual awards ceremony now run by Music Victoria.

6

KILL, KILL, KILL
(1985)

It's only in hindsight that I realise just how appropriate our band name was. Like the infamous trade union, we stood on our own, outside both the mainstream and the left alternative scene. Rugged individuals, you betcha.

Dave Graney, whose commercial pandering saw him crowned King of Pop or Best Male Artist at the 1996 ARIA (Australian Recording Industry Association) Music Awards, went on the record saying he existed as an artist to 'counter acts like the Painters & Dockers.'

We came along when Goth bad boy Nick Cave ruled the Melbourne music scene. Now don't get me wrong, Nick is a fantastic artist. At one of the very first punk shows I attended he was passed around the room at the infamous Seaview Ballroom on the raised hands of his fans. It was wild.

But what annoyed me were all the copycat bands and the dour scene that surrounded them. Thousands of nice middle-class teenagers took to wearing black, acting gloomy and dropping their parents' antidepressant drugs.

The Dockers considered ourselves a direct reaction against this glum affectation. Rather than drone on about suicide and teen angst, we would take to the stage with nothing but dead fish strapped to our bodies, drink far too much and sing songs like 'Die Yuppie Die' and 'The Boy Who Lost His Jocks On Flinders Street Station'.

We actually ended up supporting Nick Cave one night and he came backstage to get ready, only to sit on one of our stage props: a huge fresh fish.

'Hey what's with the snapper?' he asked.

We soon found ourselves part of a small niche of acts that wanted to put the absurdity, and most importantly, the fun back into rock 'n' roll. Having a laugh was the number one priority. That was never understood or appreciated by the Sydney music press, who all seemed obsessed with the band Radio Birdman with their humourless quasi-fascist stage persona.

In the early 1980s, Melbourne developed a whacky underbelly, with bands like I Spit On Your Gravy, Shower Scene From Psycho, Huxton Creepers, This Is Serious Mum, Olympic Sideburns, Corpse Grinders, The Cosmic Psychos, Tombstone Hands, King Jerklews, Teddy Turner and The Bunsen Burners, Alloy Head and the Victor Motors, Large Number 12's and Gas Babies.

The name of the game was rock 'n' roll, high energy, absurdity and a drunken good time.

The Dockers were determined to perform as much of our own material as possible and I was never going to let the fact that I couldn't play or read a note of music stop me writing a lot of those songs.

I wanted songs that were funny or angry, silly or political, timely and naughty and sometimes all of those things at once. I certainly didn't want to write 'boy meets girl' pop-flavoured ditties. It is telling that the first song I ever wrote was 'Pull Me Off (My Silly Pedestal)', which was designed both to offend and to get a cheap laugh.

Once I had a catchy phrase I would sit with bandmates from The Dockers—and later the Dili Allstars—and hum imaginary lines or even clap out a tune while a guitarist or bass player would translate my ramblings into actual chords and notes. The funny thing is that the simpler the song, the catchier it was, and I loved being able to base a song on anything I wanted.

My anger at American imperialism produced 'New World Order'. Support for both gay rights and an Australian republic translated into 'I Know Better Queens Than That', and an old Palmolive ad was the inspiration for 'You Know You're Soaking In It'.

'Holiday on Ice' was about the crystal meth epidemic, 'I'm Selling Out' was based on the ethics of the Murdoch news empire, and 'All Men Are Bastards (Except Me)' was the cynical anthem of a chancer using his pseudo-feminism to try to get into a woman's pants. No idea where I got the idea for that one. Ahem.

Our only Christmas song, 'Merry Xmas, Carrol', was a typical piss-take and totally upended the stereotype of a cheery seasonal tune. With a melancholic harmonica making it sound like the theme tune of a spaghetti Western, it told the gloomy tale of a condemned man who had killed his girlfriend (yes, that would be Carrol) for planning to leave him.

I loved the way Skyhooks crammed their songs with references to Melbourne, burying the days when Australian bands like Axiom felt the need to appeal to a foreign audience with songs like 'Laying on Arkansas Grass', which was set in the American Civil War.

One of our most popular tunes, 'You're Going Home in the Back of a Divi Van', is instantly familiar to anyone who has heard that chant from a sunburnt crowd at the Melbourne Cricket Ground as an over-lubricated fan is being led off by the police. I added one verse about Indonesian military atrocities in East Timor, and another about Australian police brutality against blackfellas but the song's birthplace is definitely the Outer at the MCG.

Phil Nelson took me aside after one song-writing session and said 'Let's have less foreign correspondent commentary and more songs about girls, cars and Saturday night, Paulie,' but the band was generally happy to indulge me.

Chris O'Connor wrote our first recorded song, 'Mohawk Baby', which was included in *Asleep at the Wheel*, a 1984 compilation released by radio station Triple R featuring a dozen bands from Melbourne's underground scene.

Many of those bands found their feet playing at the infamous Gong Show at St Kilda's Esplanade Hotel hosted by Paul Elliot, a loveable local ratbag.

The Gong Show was based on the madcap US television show of the same name where performers could do anything they liked as long as it wasn't boring. Many of Melbourne's young bands and comics got their first breaks there.

Anything could happen at The Gong Show, perhaps because many acts were paid in LSD. Some of The Dockers' first gigs were part of this truly crazy scene.

We cut our teeth in front of these crowds and I learned a lot. For example, never ever tell the crowd to throw things at the stage. I encouraged them to do that one night and was promptly hit by three chairs and a table, ending up in the Alfred Hospital with a big gash to the head.

Lying next to me in the hospital corridor was a guy who had broken his arm at the same gig. 'You guys were grouse,' he grinned.

Yes, The Gong Show was pure anarchy. So were the afterparties. I once ended up with four naked members of I Spit On Your Gravy in an overflowing bath in a St Kilda flat.

Apart from the bands you had 'performance artists' like Rod Walloper (who was billed as The Man With The Giant Shlong), Kim The Crazy Clown, The Butcher From Brighton, Pooh Pooh And The Bed Wetters, Viola And Her Singing Chinchilla Dog, The Super Cream Caramels, The Wiggly Bits and comic Anthony Morgan whose first shows involved literally hanging himself by the neck from the lighting rig bringing members of the audience running to help him as he passed out.

Funniest performer of all was infamous punk, noted cartoonist and good friend Fred Negro. I know mainstream newspaper editors in Melbourne, like Alan Howe at the *Sunday Herald Sun*, who never missed Fred's weekly strip.

Howe even wanted to hire Fred but his material is pretty risqué and all the exploding vaginas and erupting penises were not quite right for a family publication. To make it into Fred's 'Pub' comic strip was to really make it in the Melbourne music scene.

Negro's wild visions came to life at The Gong Show and he would perform acts like The Human Vacuum Cleaner, which involved someone holding him by his legs as he gobbled up cheese Twisties off the floor. Many of his bands such as I Spit On Your Gravy, The Brady Bunch Lawn Mower Massacre, and The Band Who Shot Liberty Valance also appeared there. But his Gong Show highlight was the act where he would simulate having sex with a chicken, leaving crowds open-mouthed.

One of my most memorable rock experiences was standing backstage at The Club in Collingwood with the crowd going berserk waiting for The Dockers while Fred and a few of us from The Dockers frantically used cigarette lighters to try to thaw a frozen chook carcass so he could have his wicked ways with the bird.

Negro eventually took to the stage, performed his act and then took it one step further by having sex with a pig's head while singing 'If You Could See Her Through My Eyes'.

Disgusting, juvenile and over the top? Sure, but also surreal and unforgettable.

Interestingly, despite—or maybe because of—our riotous reputation we kept our strong trade union links and used to appear at building sites for workers, who instead of the usual barrel and stripper on a Friday afternoon got The Dockers and a barrel. It's a tough audience when you are the act depriving them of a stripper.

A young union organiser would often join us on stage to play trumpet. This was the ratbag Martin Kingham, who went on to become state secretary of the powerful Construction, Forestry, Mining and Energy Union (CFMEU).

When we first met Martin he just loved getting up to have a blow of his trumpet and join in the mayhem that is The Dockers live.

We performed many shows for the striking wharfies during the 1998 waterfront dispute and the impromptu performances we did standing around the picket lines on those long, cold nights were some of our most enjoyable ever.

At these demos we also got to meet Father Bob Maguire, the inspiring 'people's priest' of Melbourne, who became a staunch supporter of our band. He performed more than one funeral for slain members of the Painters and Dockers Union.

During the waterfront dispute there was the unforgettable night we played before one hundred striking wharfies and one hundred cops in the pouring rain. When we burst into 'You're Going Home In The Back Of A Divi Van' both sides started singing along and laughing. It was an icebreaker that released some dangerous tension. The song was later used in *Bastard Boys*, the ABC television drama about the dispute.

7

BOYS IN THE BAND
(1986)

After performing for a few years in Melbourne's inner-city suburbs, The Dockers got a big break when we hooked up with Australian guitar legend and rock icon Lobby Loyde.

He had seen the crowds we were attracting, the fun we generated and our unashamed love of dirty, filthy rock 'n' roll, and he told us that he would be interested in being our manager, sound guy and record producer.

Lobby was well known as a 1960s guitar pioneer, record producer, band mentor and musical visionary. He was also the unofficial King of the Sharpies.

Sharpies, or Sharps, were young gang members from the late 1960s through to the 1970s who had their own youth subculture of fashion, music and tribalism. The style spread to Sydney and Perth but was mainly a Melbourne thing.

Being a Sharpie was more about the tight clothes and 'tough' mullet haircuts than serious organised gang stuff—the name comes from their focus on looking and dressing 'sharp'—but they could still be pretty menacing.

As a teenager, I was scared witless of Sharpies after a few run-ins with the likes of the Jordy Boys, Chelsea Skins, and the East Bentleigh Sharpies. Their musical soundtrack was always Lobby Loyde and The Coloured Balls.

Lobby said he hated the violence associated with his music and that it got so bad he stopped playing and shifted to London in the mid-1970s.

There he mixed with musicians from the burgeoning UK punk scene, including one young guy he said he taught to play bass guitar … Sid Vicious, who went on to join the Sex Pistols.

Lobby had returned to Australia and taken the Sydney band Sunnyboys under his wing, turning them into one of the country's biggest rock acts.

We were flattered that he wanted to work with us. When we hooked up with Lobby we decided for the first time on a permanent line-up, which included Phil Nelson on bass, Chris O'Connor on guitar and vocals and Colin Buckler on drums. Lead guitar was the mild-mannered Vlad Juric, whose explosive style blew even Lobby away.

Brisbane music critic Andrew Stafford always said that it was Juric who was the real signature player in The Dockers.

Rounding out the line-up were the Brassholes: Dave Pace on trumpet, Mick Morris on saxophone and me on vocals and very bad trumpet.

Music historian Ian McFarlane described the Brassholes sound as 'adding an earthy R&B edge to the band's raucous, punk-infused power pop'.

Let's make no mistake here: the Painters & Dockers were Phil Nelson's baby. It was his band. He was the one who stayed sober to drive the rest of us ratbags home from country and interstate shows. He was the one who ran the gauntlet of collecting the money from shady pub owners. All this from a chap who was a shy, qualified geologist bitten badly by the rock 'n' roll bug.

One of my major life regrets is that Phil fell out with most of the band and stopped playing with us. We assumed that this was because he was just tired of it all. In fact, Phil was terribly sick and had been for a number of years.

I can't believe we spent so many hours in the van together without him saying anything or the rest of us noticing that something was seriously wrong. It shows how self-obsessed I was that I did not know Phil had the debilitating bowel condition known as Crohn's disease.

The trigger for our bust-up was being offered big money to do a show at Torquay, the surfing mecca about 100 kilometres south-west of Melbourne. Phil knocked it back and I was furious because I had a young child and wanted the money.

Phil didn't explain that the real reason he had rejected the show was that he wasn't physically up to it. We did the show with a fill-in bassist and Phil quit the band.

About eighteen months later, in April 2000, I was in Auckland for the *Sunday Herald Sun* covering Macy Gray's upcoming Australian visit. I hadn't thought about Phil for months but that night I dreamed I went to his funeral and placed a brand new window washer on his coffin.

Phil was always obsessed with cleaning the windows of our vans on our long drives. I woke up thinking, *what a crazy dream*. I got home to Melbourne and saw a message on my phone from a long-time fan of the band asking, 'Did you hear the news about Phil?'

I rang and said, 'What do you mean, the news about Phil?'

'He's dead!'

Phil was only forty-two. I took him for granted, assuming that every band had such a self-sacrificing character. It's a shame that those last months when we all fell out with him outweighed our many years of adventures and laughs.

Chris O'Connor, easily the best singer in the band, unfortunately had to deal with the rampant ego of the other singer: me. Chris sang but I screamed.

He was also our best songwriter and author of crowd favourites like 'Mohawk Baby', 'Nude School', 'Jack's Car', 'Gun For Fun' and

'Basia'. Basia Bonkowski was the first music host on public broadcaster SBS and Chris realised that a lot of young Australians were fascinated by her.

Sadly, Chris did not share the philosophy of most of the band that having fun and entertaining people was more important than musical purity. He drifted away, not wanting to play or rehearse.

Colin Buckler was a classic wild-man drummer. At first, he didn't even want to join The Dockers, preferring to concentrate on his more serious band, the mod-influenced Fifth Column. But after seeing The Dockers play one hectic sweaty night at the Prince of Wales in St Kilda and the chaos and fun we generated, he wanted in.

Buckler was adamant that he always had to have a good sound from his drum kit and heaven help any roadies or sound crew who didn't give it to him. At one show at an army base in Townsville, he was so angry about the sound quality that he punched the sound man on stage and then smashed up a lot of the musical equipment. The show was over just six songs into the set, much to the anger of promoters, who refused to pay us.

Colin was later caught up in the terrible Ash Wednesday bushfires. His house at Kinglake in the bush north-east of Melbourne was destroyed and he only survived by hiding in a creek with his wife, fellow band member Sonja, and infant son. Many of his neighbours burned to death and Colin's drumming days were over.

He was replaced by Dahl Murphy of the Geelong-based Glitter Gang, a top bloke who was a fantastic drummer and easy to get along with. Later, Dahl was replaced by Michael Barclay, a long-term friend of ours whom we first met when he played with Paul Kelly.

Dave Pace, our trumpet player and backing vocalist, saw the band perform an early show in a small St Kilda pub one Easter where band members were dressed as Roman soldiers and I was Jesus Christ (modest fellow that I am) handing out bread to the audience.

He loved it and turned up to our next gig with his trumpet. He drifted into the line-up and has been there now for almost forty years.

Dave brought a sense of absurdity to the song list, stage show and line-up and was always dressed immaculately.

Dave was also an Australian wildlife expert, working as a teacher at the Melbourne Zoo. Quite often at gigs in Queensland and Western Australia the band would start late, not because of heavy drinking or drug use but because Dave was out the back of the venue with a bucket collecting frogs.

I stole an ice cream container from him in the van one day and almost puked when I saw it was full of maggots he was using as bait to catch frogs. It was Dave who wrote the song 'You are Killing Us', which recites the names of dozens of extinct Australian animal species.

Mick Morris is a loveable bear of a guy who always makes you feel safe being beside him on stage no matter how wild the audience might get. A builder by trade, he had only recently taken up playing the saxophone when he asked if he could come along for a blow at one of our earliest rehearsals in 1983.

In a band full of drama queens he has always been a steadying influence with a dry sense of humour and a deep musical knowledge.

Vlad Juric was a shy guy, nicknamed 'Steig' by Chris and Phil because of his supposed resemblance to US actor Rod Steiger.

There were a million guitarists around, most of whom looked more rock 'n' roll than our Vlad but he was one out of the box and could floor you with his innovative guitar playing.

As Dave puts it, 'Vlad produced a mosaic of syncopated notes that effortlessly entwined themselves around the band's deafening power chords and punk rhythms. This was interspersed with long guttural notes, enriched with feedback, that added an atmospheric tension and left the listener begging for more.'

Lobby Loyde was super impressed and called Vlad a genius.

Vlad was never one for the rigours of the road, and he was particularly upset by the bad food at truck stops. He would floor the staff dishing out greasy burgers by asking for things like 'fresh sprouts' and 'real chicken not pressed chicken'. While the rest of us could roll out of bed and into the van in a few minutes Vlad would spend another hour on personal grooming and breakfast.

Other long-time Dockers included guitarist Darren Garth, who toured outback Australia and North America with us, and then his replacement, Colin Badger.

Like Ronnie Wood of the Stones, Badge was cursed as 'The New Guy' for the next twenty-five years. For his introduction to life as a Docker he joined us without a rehearsal at Johno's Blues Bar in Cairns where he carefully laid out sheet music to our songs on the floor in front of where he stood.

At the start of the night I drunkenly stumbled up on the stage and trashed the laid-out charts explaining, 'Listen mate, this is The Dockers, I don't give a fuck what you play, it is how you look when you play it.'

He gave me a surprised smile and we have been playing music together ever since, with Badge becoming one of my main collaborators in not only the Dockers but my other bands The Dili Allstars and then The Transplants.

It says a lot about The Dockers that we put Lobby in charge of our sound system without giving any thought to the fact that he was deaf in one ear.

One of the first things Lobby did was to get us to release an EP in 1986 featuring one of our favourite live songs, 'Kill, Kill, Kill', which was lifted from the TV comedy *Get Smart*.

Unbelievably, it got picked up by a commercial radio station and distributed by EMI Records. Now, name yourself after a notorious trade union, release a song called 'Kill, Kill, Kill', add slam-dancing fans to your live show and you are bound to get some over-the-top media coverage.

I was only too happy to be flown to Brisbane by Channel 9's *A Current Affair* program to debate the Reverend John Pastor Kemp, who wanted to get the evil Painters & Dockers banned from Australian stages and airwaves.

We were, after all, "Satanists", he declared.

The Reverend told the Gold Coast Bulletin, 'I know a teenager who, after listening to this type of music, said he was very close to grabbing a gun and killing his family.'

'Many members of various rock groups are deeply involved with drugs and alcohol and they are influencing our children. The Painters & Dockers song "Kill, Kill, Kill" particularly angers me. I mean listen to the lyrics, "Get a gun, kill your mum, don't you know love is out, hate is what it's about, just kill, kill, kill".'

Funnily enough, the Reverend was a really nice guy off-air. Once the studio lights were on and the cameras rolling, he played the part of Christian zealot well-doer and I was cast as the evil rock 'n' roll guy.

During our "debate" I pointed out that the song was in fact from the TV comedy "Get Smart" that was aired to children every afternoon. The Reverend's attacks fell flat.

After the televised debate I figured I should live up to the role of hellraiser so I invited some Brisbane punk friends to the expensive hotel I had been booked into. We did not trash the room or turf the TV set out the window but we did order up big, very big, on room service paid for by Channel 9.

'Yes, I will have five roast dinners sent up at 2am please, some cigars, more bath robes and some roses, and yes, more champagne and strawberries as well would be lovely.'

I was offered another TV gig when producer Andy Nehl asked me to take part in a show on the recently-launched Comedy Channel. He said, 'We will fly you to Sydney, put you on this panel that discusses issues and we pay you $500.'

Eager for the cash, I said 'No problems, when do you want me?'

That is how I ended up on a panel where I was told to simulate giving oral sex to the guy sitting next to me. We were watched by another set of panellists who were set to film an episode after us. One of them was a newly elected federal politician who shook his head in amazement at my antics. He would later emerge as Australia's leading conservative spokesman and then prime minister, Tony Abbott.

Not long after that, The Dockers had another interesting run-in with a conservative Christian. We were playing in the mining town of Broken Hill in outback NSW so we decided to visit the workshop of one of the nation's most celebrated artists, Pro Hart. We wanted to give him a copy of our latest album, *Kiss My Art*, which had a fold-out painting of the band at the Last Supper sharing beer and pizza with Jesus.

We found Pro in a big studio behind his house, painting the front covers of thousands of Bibles, which were to be distributed in Papua New Guinea.

'They don't throw them away if they have a nice cover,' he explained.

When we showed him our Last Supper he fell into a stony silence that had us quickly out the door.

Also unimpressed by our provocative songs and reputation was the conservative politician from the Western Australian Government, who wanted us banned from the annual Bindoon Biker's Festival run by the Coffin Cheaters.

We were met at Perth Airport by tattooed bikers and some of their mates with vintage cars. They escorted us to the state parliament where, under the glare of TV news cameras, we dropped off free tickets for the disgruntled minister.

More religious interaction came when we played at a pub in remote Albany, Western Australia. We were sitting around in the band room upstairs waiting to go on when there was a peculiar sound.

We looked out the window to see the local born again Christian chapter shaking tambourines and waving placards, urging punters to avoid the evil band from Melbourne.

What great promotion! The gig was packed.

Whatever else we were, we were hardworking and played in literally hundreds of venues all over the country. After one wild night in Wollongong I was left behind by the band—supposedly by accident—in a seedy hotel and had to hitchhike to Sydney in just underpants, a fur jacket and boots, carrying a trumpet.

Thank God for the truck driver who saw the funny side of it all and gave me a lift.

8

WE WILL NEVER EMPLOY THAT BAND AGAIN
(1987)

I loved the fact that The Dockers had an unsavoury reputation. When people spoke of the band, it wasn't about chord progression or our song structure but the chaos we caused. For a bunch of soft ex-Catholic schoolboys, we were suddenly Public Enemy No 1.

You Am I frontman Tim Rogers remembers getting his nose broken at one of our shows and TV funnyman Alan Brough of Spicks and Specks fame recalls losing his pants in the wild crowd throng at a show in New Zealand.

When a group called the Art Terrorists stole the rare and expensive Picasso *Weeping Woman* from the National Gallery of Victoria, the police thought they would find it in our offices at Richmond Recorders.

I suppose it didn't help that we used the ransom note for the return of the painting on the cover of our single 'Die Yuppie Die', which also pictured the band in a bed with the missing painting as our doona cover.

I had lifted a copy of the ransom note off a desk at *The Sun* thinking it would make a great cover. I didn't realise that it contained information the police hadn't released to the public.

After marching upstairs at Richmond Recorders, a burly police sergeant simply said 'Right, where have you got the painting?'

The painting was returned sixteen days after its theft but the culprits have never been caught and the case remains cold. We plead total innocence—I suppose there is always a chance that we knew the people who did it, but I will leave it at that.

I liked the anarchy we brought to many a suburban pub and I liked shit-stirring. The thought of being a normal, mainstream popstar appalled me. With a murdered brother forever lurking on my mind, I couldn't tolerate normal and relaxed. If life was short, I wanted to make my mark and scream into the night. We liked to push crowds over the top. The wilder the show, the better.

It's not surprising then that The Dockers were blamed for instigating the riot when we played at the Year 12 social for prestigious Melbourne school Scotch College at the St Kilda Town Hall.

The crowd was rowdy well before we even hit the stage and our presence only seemed to make them angrier. It wasn't long before they started chanting 'faggots, faggots, faggots' and hurling rubbish at us. It didn't help that I was wearing make-up and women's clothing.

The students did not like it one bit when I suggested that maybe they were the ones with homosexual tendencies, after all, they were the ones jumping up and down and rubbing up against each together with no shirts on.

I suppose I did camp it up, taunt them, and strut around the stage kissing other members of the band and flashing my arse. One chap responded by jumping up on stage and biting me on the stomach. I had not expected this.

The show was called off after about five songs and we were barricaded in a room at the back of the Town Hall with a ring of security men protecting us from a mob that wanted our blood. We were eventually escorted out of the building by police.

I later learned that one-time Victorian Liberal Party leader and later Lord Mayor of Melbourne, Robert Doyle—then a teacher at Scotch College—had been at the show.

One day he was talking to my editor Alan Howe in the office of the *Sunday Herald Sun* when he spotted me and asked, 'Hey that guy over there, he's not from that band the Painters & Dockers is he?'

Alan nodded, 'Yes, that's Paulie.'

'And you employ him?'

The school was furious about the show, my behaviour in particular. The headmaster wrote to our booking agents, Premier Artists, saying that under no circumstances would they ever hire us again because of the 'crude vulgarity of the lyrics and more particularly the overt and deliberate obscenity of the lead singer'.

Our manager Lobby loved it. He had the letter blown up into a poster, added all our forthcoming live shows and used it as a press advertisement. We had great crowds at the next lot of shows, including some students from Scotch who said they had 'never had so much fun' as at their disastrous school social. Later, a doctor at the Austin Hospital told me he had also been there and pleaded for a copy of the headmaster's letter. He had it framed and displayed in his office.

Being considered 'over the top' did not always work to our advantage, like the time we had a lucrative approach from the AFL football club the Fremantle Dockers.

The year before entering the national competition, the club contacted us and said that perhaps there could be a relationship between the two sets of Dockers. It seemed a grand idea. They were so keen that club officials dropped into the band room at one Perth show and gave us seven brand new Fremantle Dockers jumpers to wear.

'You beauty,' said the band members and we found ourselves daydreaming of MCG half-time Grand Final appearances.

We were all up for sponsorships and free footy merchandise and tickets. After the show, the club's representatives rushed into the band room and said, 'Give us back our jumpers.'

'But what about our relationship?' I asked the club official.

'Mate, we are a family club, we can't be involved with you guys,' he said.

'Why on earth not?'

'Mate, there were naked men and women on stage, a guy breathing fire and a crowd going bloody berserk. And what about the songs "Pull Me Off", "All Men Are Bastards" and "Eat, Shit and Die"? How can we be associated with you?'

Our beautiful AFL partnership was over before it started.

9

WE CAN ALL MAKE MONEY FROM THIS
(1987)

A real coup came when Lobby hooked us up with Australia's leading music powerbroker Michael Gudinski, who signed us to his Mushroom Records label and then to his booking agency, Premier Artists.

A lot of people have varying opinions of this fella, but I will always maintain that you have to admire him because, like Lobby and Molly Meldrum, he was first and foremost a fan of the music and a big supporter of Australian talent.

Gudinski didn't particularly like our music, but when Lobby invited him to a show at Chasers nightclub in South Yarra, he saw the frantic crowd reaction and he wanted in.

I can still remember the day just after we signed to Mushroom Records, he put his arm around my shoulder as we walked to meet Lobby at The Great Britain Hotel in Richmond.

'Paul,' he said. 'you have to understand. We can all make money from this.'

Gudinski passed away in 2021 and I'm still waiting to 'make money from this'.

Gudinski always respected Lobby's opinion. After all, the two of them had helped put Australian rock 'n' roll on the map going as far back as the early 1970s when they both worked at the Sunbury music festivals outside Melbourne.

Gudinski was impossible to get on the phone, yet he always took Lobby's calls. They had a mixture of rivalry and respect for each other—Lobby envied Gudinski's industry clout and independence, while Gudinski coveted Lobby's ear for talent.

It was because of their relationship that acts like Sunnyboys, X, The Olympic Sideburns, Machinations and the Painters & Dockers were signed by Mushroom.

Lobby convinced The Dockers, and some investors he roped in, to start our own record label, Doc Records; buy our own recording studio, Richmond Recorders; rent a retail outlet, The Dock Shop; invest in our own live sound system and buy a record pressing plant.

I swear I actually remember him talking about buying a few old planes and opening Dock Air.

Lobby's grand vision was fantastic. The only problem was that we had no money apart from the door takings at live shows. The band was sceptical but it did mean the workers involved had ultimate control.

'No worries, we'll borrow it,' said Lobby, whose favourite businessman at the time was high-flyer Alan Bond. 'The trick is, as Bondy has shown us, you borrow so much money that the banks can't afford to let you go bust.'

It's a great theory really and it all chugged along nicely for a few months before the worldwide finance industry collapsed, bringing Lobby's grand plans of a business empire tumbling down. Our advantage over Alan Bond was that unlike him we didn't really have any assets or buckets of cash that creditors could come and take.

Lobby: great guy, great musician, utterly useless businessman.

At one point he drove me crazy by having a lengthy dispute with Gudinski over our record deal. Lobby refused to sign it unless Gudinski agreed that if life were found on other planets, Lobby would have the right to negotiate a separate deal with the aliens.

Seriously.

Jacinta and I had just had Frances and I couldn't afford milk, bread and nappies. Just sign the bloody thing Lobby!

Mysterious business deals seemed to happen all the time, straining our patience and occasionally putting us at serious risk. Like the time Victoria Police busted Lobby after learning that our record pressing plant was manufacturing the latest copies of Prince's new album. We had no desire to become the artists formally known as convicted criminals and we were sick of holding more business meetings than rehearsals.

The Dockers decided to cut everything back to the bone, so we said goodbye to Lobby in an amicable split in 1988. He left without a fuss and became a house husband in the outer Melbourne suburb of Belgrave, caring for his five children with wife Debbie Nankervis, who had found fame in one of the Alvin Purple movies.

10

PIGS
(1988)

Without a doubt the highest profile thing the Painters & Dockers ever did was make the now infamous video for our song 'Nude School' at a pig farm just outside Melbourne.

Why the pigs? Mainly because everyone, particularly our record company, expected us to make this clip surrounded by glamorous models, and we wanted to send up the whole pop star thing. Undermining the system fitted in with my philosophy.

How did we find the pigs?

Easy. I opened up the Yellow Pages and looked up 'pigs' and there was the address of a farm outside Melbourne. The pig farmer had no problem with us making a video, although I doubt he knew what a storm it would create. A deal was made and so on a freezing winter's day we found ourselves naked and frolicking in pig shit.

I think we knew we were coming up with something pretty different and that people would sit up and take notice. When I got home that night my housemates took one sniff of me and made me hose myself down with cold water before letting me anywhere near the back door.

We got a big break when the pig shit really hit the fan.

At the same time that we were editing our first big-budget video, a new television program *MTV*, hosted by Richard Wilkins, was trying to build its profile in Australia and needed something that would grab attention.

They took one look at our Nude School video and a switch went on. Some unknown *MTV* executive chose it as the opening video clip for about four weeks on Australia's newest and most hyped music program.

Before we learned of *MTV*'s decision, we chose Melbourne's infamous porn cinema The Barrel at the top end of Swanston Street to launch the clip, complete with enormous amounts of cold beer and a line-up of poets, male and female strippers and about fifty friends and music industry types.

We did not know what to expect when we finally screened our video. Well, the crowd just went crazy and we were forced to play it over and over again., each time provoking howls of laughter. Something special was clearly happening. Rock 'n' roll and pigs seemed to be a winning combination. Little did we know that this mix would have its downside.

At our next show, at the University of Tasmania in Hobart, a couple of pigs' heads and a few pounds of raw bacon were thrown on stage, much to our amazement. It showed that our fans were as mad as us—who takes that sort of stuff to a music gig?

A Tasmanian music lover contacted us thirty years later to say that one of his and his best friend's life regrets was that they missed that show because they were underage. That friend was now terminally ill, he said, and his dying wish was to finally see the Dockers up close.

So off we went to Hobart.

We did a show for the fan in question and 200 of his best friends. It was a hell of a night, topped off when the former Premier and frustrated drummer, David Bartlett, joined us on stage, resplendent in a pig outfit.

'Nude School', our highest-charting song, set us up for three decades of onstage nudity. Members of the audience—mostly blokes, but sometimes women—would regularly end up dancing naked on stage with us. We became quite blasé about this and embraced it as an easy way to get a laugh.

Four years after the first Dockers gig, we received the great honour of playing our song on Australian TV's music institution *Countdown*.

Like the rest of our generation, we had grown up watching the Sunday night show for the big overseas names and scores of local acts who got their first big break on the show. Nowadays, TV rock shows look like one big Coke advertisement and you hardly ever get to see Australian emerging talent, unless they have the right look. The rise of the *Australian Idol* era means you must have a bland image and risk-free songs. True individualism is not exactly encouraged.

The real charm of *Countdown* was its star and host Ian 'Molly' Meldrum. He was one of the first openly gay personalities in Australian entertainment and he would stumble and bumble his way through each episode, but make no mistake, he is a very intelligent guy.

His other great attribute is that he genuinely loves the music. I can't believe we ended up good friends (he had a lovely boyfriend from Timor-Leste for a while), and that I also got to work with other *Countdown* legends like Ross Wilson, Skyhooks, Split Enz and Russell Morris. It amazes me still.

A family friend, Mark Harvey, went to legend status in my mind when he appeared on the show playing drums for the Teenage Radio Stars in my final year of high school.

On our *Countdown* performance we got the program's crew into the act when cameramen, soundmen, lighting riggers and even the director donned fake pig noses. They were only too happy to help out.

Amid all the hype of 'Nude School' we did one of my favourite recording projects. The B-side of the single was called 'Dung Di (Don't Go)'. We invited three Vietnamese singers into the studio and co-wrote a tune with them that was arguably Australia's first such collaboration.

The studio was in Richmond, home to many Vietnamese people, and I thought it would be great to bring a minority group like that into a mainstream project.

Bizarrely, we so-called Satanists later performed the song on Channel 7's annual Good Friday Appeal for the Royal Children's Hospital with our new Vietnamese mates. The studio crew looked at us bewildered.

'Nude School' put the wind in our sails. Now for the follow-up.

We filmed our second expensive video the following year outside the Melbourne stock exchange on Friday 13 October, when the markets happened to have a worldwide collapse.

The song was 'Die Yuppie Die', an angry shout-out against consumerism and greed.

Time Magazine later joked that the global financial collapse had been triggered by infamous Melbourne punk band the Painters & Dockers shooting the clip in front of the stock exchange. You couldn't buy such publicity but the video got only minor airplay.

'Give us something like Nude School with the pigs again,' pleaded the *MTV* executives.

11

YOU GUYS ARE WEIRD

One of the great benefits of playing in a band is when you get chosen as the support act for a big-name band. You get a glimpse of what success really looks like, you usually play a much shorter set and you get to enjoy all the comforts that go with being in a major band: recognition, respect and lots of alcohol. Awesome.

Yes, not only do you get to play in front of big new crowds but you can also watch and learn from the major acts up close.

As we were signed to Michael Gudinski's Mushroom Records who also ran the Frontier Touring Company and the Premier Artists booking agency, we were offered some great support spots over the years.

The artists we shared the stage with included punk godfather Iggy Pop, who always gave 110 per cent. At Festival Hall we were exhausted after an hour but he went on for more than two. Then there were reunited Australian 1960s pioneers The Easybeats and fellow veterans The Loved Ones. Performing alongside US pop stars The Monkees was a highlight because we had all grown up in Melbourne watching them on television.

An unusual act we supported was Mexican rockers Los Lobos, then there was the American band Wall Of Voodoo, best known for the song 'Mexican Radio'. We also performed alongside Los Angeles band The Gun Club, fronted by the moody Jeffrey Lee Pierce, who was said to have started a whole new musical style, 'psychobilly'. With his peroxide blonde crop and snarl, Pierce had a brooding presence. We added The Gun Club's song 'House on Highland Avenue' to our set for many years.

When we played with English punk poet John Cooper Clarke, I decided to write a small beat poem to mark the occasion, mimicking his eccentric raps on working-class English life. It was just a muck-around thing we planned to do on that one occasion but the track we created, 'The Boy Who Lost his Jocks on Flinders Street Station', became a Dockers staple. We ended up performing it more than 1000 times and crowds would often refuse to let us leave the stage until we had done it.

It is a rambling ditty about nudity at Melbourne's most famous transport hub, set to a driving bass line that builds to a rampaging crescendo, and amazingly, it is now often cited on lists of the top songs ever written about Melbourne.

But appearing with famous acts could have its drawbacks as well. One came at Frances' first day of kindergarten when all the parents had to sit in a circle on the floor and get to know one another.

Small talk was exchanged and the progress of children discussed. Suddenly one mum pointed at me and said, 'I remember you. You were rolling around on broken glass on stage supporting The Cramps at Festival Hall two nights ago.'

Oddly enough, after that there were not too many invitations to look after the other children on play dates.

One of the most interesting acts we appeared with was Japanese lesbian duo The Frank Chickens with whom we toured New Zealand. What a double act we made. The girls would end each show in wedding dresses performing a tongue-in-cheek number called 'Sacred Marriage'.

Our first international support gigs were in the mid-1980s with a little-known three piece from Milwaukee called The Violent Femmes, with whom we played in Sydney, Canberra and Melbourne. Fronted by Gordon Gano, the Femmes were here to promote their debut self-titled album which had attracted a huge buzz on Australian community and university radio.

In those days, union laws meant there had to be a minimum number of Australians performing alongside any overseas visiting act.

Some of the venues the visiting Americans were due to play at couldn't afford, or did not want the full Dockers line-up and that is how Dave, Mick and myself, and Charlie Todd from Melbourne act The Wreckery, found ourselves on stage for several shows as the Femmes' official brass section.

This was bizarre really because I was a very average trumpet player. I mean I could play a few notes but playing sheet music or staying in time with other players was a different thing altogether. It certainly made for an interesting couple of shows and thankfully the musical skills of my fellow brass players got us through.

The biggest artist we supported on a national tour was fabricated English punk rocker Billy Idol and his band on their first Australian visit. This was a major coup engineered by Lobby as Billy was massive in Australia at the time with hit singles like 'Rebel Yell', 'White Wedding' and 'Mona'.

We soon learned that Billy and his band seemed to have a problem getting through each show unless a guy with a briefcase arrived before the performance and spent a bit of time out of sight with the singer and his band. The band would all then emerge from their "business meetings" as high as kites.

One night the guy didn't turn up and Billy lost the plot. First up, he totally alienated the Melbourne Festival Hall crowd by saying, 'Good evening, Sydney.'

He then really blew it after a fan touched his boot on stage. Billy started ranting at the punter and only calmed down when he realised what a massive dickhead he was being.

The tour showed us first-hand what major rock stardom and excess were all about and looking back from today's #MeToo era, some of it is hard to believe.

Each night after his performance, Billy's roadies would go into the crowd and hand out cards to female fans with numbers written on them and then invite the girls backstage. They were ushered into a room and told to wait where we were gathered as the support act, hanging around a free bar.

The head roadie arrived and said, 'Okay girls, numbers in the air please.'

Billy walked in, scanned the crowd, and told the roadie, 'Number seven, number fourteen, and send in number nineteen for fifteen minutes at the end.'

His whole band then took their turn and repeated the procedure. Amazingly to us, the girls happily trotted off if their numbers were called with grins from ear to ear. We were startled and found ourselves left in the room with the rejected girls.

'Hi, we are The Dockers,' we volunteered sheepishly.

'Piss off, you're just the support band,' was the general response.

Each night we went through the same routine.

At the time, we fancied ourselves as outrageous punks and my particular look was complete with a thick toothbrush moustache, a half-shaved head, one shaved eyebrow, a fur coat and lipstick.

I will never forget Billy's celebrated guitarist Steve Stevens checking me out from the side of the stage one night as he stood there in pink jumpsuit, pink boots and a massive teased crop of hair.

'You guys are weird,' he said to me as we walked off stage.

'Yeah, right mate.'

We were invited to the official end of tour party complete with strippers and working ladies of the night. I actually managed a few words with big Billy himself, when the spiky blonde singer said, 'I love you guys, the Painters and Doctors.'

I am not sure he heard my reply: 'Dockers not Doctors, Billy. Dockers.'

It was after one of Billy's shows in Sydney that we met two dancing madmen who leaped out of the crowd to join us on stage. They later told us they were on this new drug called ecstasy. It was supposed to be a magic drug that caused no side effects and made you feel wonderful. I would later meet many sad cases who had become addicted to the stuff. But this night we were so up from the Billy show we would have dropped anything and I readily accepted half a pill when offered.

After popping our tabs, Colin Buckler and I headed out on the night with our new friends and visited a blur of Sydney bars and nightspots. We ended up at the huge cliffs of the Heads in Sydney Harbour at sunrise.

Around dawn, one of the guys said to the other, 'Shit, look at the time, we have to start work.'

'So where do you guys work?' I asked.

'At Sydney airport—we are air traffic controllers,' one replied.

Sure mate, pull the other one.

I woke up late afternoon in the hotel room I was sharing with Colin and laughed as I roused him. 'Those guys last night reckoned they were air traffic controllers. What a joke, hey?'

I lay there thinking for a while, then grabbed the bedside phone and rang the control tower at Sydney airport. I asked for either of these two guys and was put on hold. Lo and behold, one of them came on the line. They were looking forward to seeing us again that night.

I think about them every time I fly into Sydney just hoping they are not rostered on.

The most full-on rock 'n' roll personality we ever met was Shane McGowan from UK folk-punk act The Pogues, who we played with at a venue in Byron Bay called The Piggery. To say this guy and his bandmates liked a drink is putting it mildly.

Our own band would go through quite a bit of alcohol over the course of a night, but The Pogues drank that amount before they went on, the same amount while they played and even more after the show.

We had just finished our support spot when McGowan entered our band room with blood streaming from both nostrils.

'Okay guys, first we will start with "A Pair of Brown Eyes", then "Fairytale Of New York" then we'll do "Dirty Old Town".'

There was an awkward silence.

'Ah Shane, we are actually the support band. Your band is in the next room,' somebody piped up.

He looked at us and said, 'Well you can fuck off, then,' and shuffled off.

I went out in the crowd to watch The Pogues play and Shane lasted about three songs before collapsing and being carried offstage. The crowd loved it and cheered wildly. I turned to a big skinhead standing next to me and said, 'Shit, if we did that you guys would throw beer bottles at us.'

'Yeah, but they are from Ireland,' was his reply.

Aussie artists we backed included Sunnyboys, The Birthday Party, Hoodoo Gurus, Models, Crowded House (just as their single 'Don't Dream It's Over' raced up the US charts) and The Angels.

Supporting the mighty Midnight Oil at two shows in Portarlington and Phillip Island in the late 1980s was an opportunity that changed our career. It was no easy task—far from it.

Oils fans are absolutely fanatical and our first songs were met with stony silence and then followed by chants of 'Oils, Oils, Oils'.

Soon there were missiles flying, including chicken carcasses, old thongs, a bong and empty stubbies. Thank God singer Peter Garrett walked on stage and told the assembled throng to, 'Give the Dockers a go.'

They did give us a chance and The Dockers rose to the occasion by delivering a blistering set that won the crowd over. It was a turning point for the band as our audiences suddenly tripled after those two Oils gigs.

We were amazed at the way Midnight Oil conducted themselves. Having seen big acts like The Pogues and The Billy Idol Band consume vast amounts of drugs and alcohol, we were surprised to find that The Oils were fuelled by cups of tea and a devotion to their music.

There was a different crowd vibe when we played with Australian music icon Slim Dusty at the Darwin Casino in 1998 at a huge benefit for flood victims in Katherine in the Northern Territory.

Slim had the laid-back audience in the palm of his hand even though it was a mixed mob who had turned up to see the rock bands from down south and the top local Indigenous acts in action.

Singer Rebecca Barnard and guitarist Shane O'Mara also appeared as Rebecca's Empire and Bec later told me they were given a lift after the show by some police who drove away singing 'You're Going Home in The Back Of A Divi Van'.

Actor Damian Walshe-Howling joined us on stage to play didjeridu. He went on to do several more shows with us in Melbourne and recorded on our *Advance Australia Where?* CD. He later starred in the TV series *Underbelly*, among other productions.

Another character we worked with was legendary English piano player Nicky Hopkins, who played on John Lennon's *Imagine* album, including on the track 'Jealous Guy', and on many of the biggest hits of The Rolling Stones, The Kinks, The Beatles, Donovan and The Who.

Sadly, by the time we met Nicky in the late 1980s he had seen better days.

A rather dodgy American named Jeffrey James had hired him to come to Melbourne to work on a number of recordings but, as so often happens in rock 'n' roll, it had all fallen through at the last minute. Lobby Loyde found Hopkins in a cheap Carlton hotel, a blithering mess being bossed around by James, his loudmouth, overweight manager.

Hopkins needed some cash and was happy to work with us on our third Mushroom Records single, 'Love On Your Breath', a catchy pop song with provocative lyrics written by Chris O'Connor, singer in the band.

Unfortunately, James took over and hired backing musicians, including John Farnham's backing singer to come up with what he assured Lobby would be a hit.

My entire contribution was when the Yank turned to me in the studio and said, 'Paul, isn't it?'

'Yes,' I replied.

'Would you run up the street and get me one of those sausage roll things?'

Poor old drug-wrecked Nicky actually dribbled on himself and was lost in confusion. But as soon as the song started coming through the studio speakers his piano would somehow come alive with great sounds and inspired riffs.

Despite our impressive guest, the single got little airplay. The radio stations wanted another song like 'Nude School' and we made the basic error of setting the accompanying video in a dentist's surgery—nobody likes the inside of a dentist's surgery, we were later told by TV tastemakers.

The excesses of rock 'n' roll were further on display when we supported New York drag queen Divine, who had his own 'wig roadie', whose sole duty was to maintain the lush creations his boss wore on stage.

At least Divine was a happy chap, unlike English new wave band Killing Joke who we supported at a Melbourne University show. Their foul moods were rumoured to be caused by them suffering from sexually transmitted infections picked up on a recent Japanese tour.

At another Melbourne University show, American singer-songwriter Jonathan 'Roadrunner' Richman shocked all by insisting that no one in the audience smoke during his show. It is now a common demand, but at the time it was an outrageous request. Richman also insisted on playing second spot of the night's three acts as he didn't want to be up too late.

We never copied that trick but some of the other acts we supported did have a huge effect on us.

Despite being twice our age, Iggy Pop simply amazed us with his energy at a summer daytime show at Melbourne's Festival Hall. It was stiflingly hot but he performed like his life depended on it.

As well as supporting Iggy in concert in 1989, I got to interview him for the *Sunday Herald Sun* where I had been appointed staff rock 'n' roll reporter. Regardless of his wild image, the rocker said he shunned drugs and alcohol.

'I'm hooked on live performance. I love it now more than when I first started out in the late 1960s,' he confided. 'I saw music as a way not to go into the office every day, not having to use Listerine and not having to use deodorant.'

Despite our many TV appearances, great support spots and our own huge concerts it amazes me that what many people seem to remember about The Dockers is our appearance in the TV series *Wilfred* about a dog that thinks it's human, written by my old pal and journalist colleague Adam Zwar.

The Dockers were asked to perform when Wilfred's owner, played by Zwar, gets married at the show's conclusion. As the credits rolled, we played as 'the wedding reception band'.

To this day, people stop and tell me, 'Wow, Paulie, I saw you in *Wilfred*.'

12

THERE'S NO MONEY OR FAME IN CHILDREN'S ENTERTAINMENT
(late 1980s)

If ever there was a line that came back to bite me, it was a flippant comment I made to Sydney rock band The Cockroaches. Anthony Fields from the band had told me they were planning a radical career change and had decided to leave rock 'n' roll and take up entertaining young children.

My smartarse reply: 'There's no money or fame in children's entertainment.'

I gave Anthony the benefit of my astute judgement after our two bands had pulled into a cheap hotel in Surfers Paradise at about 2.30am one Saturday morning at the end of the 1980s.

Both bands had played that evening to half-empty crowds at nearby pubs. Tired and disappointed, we unloaded our stage gear in the car park and mused about the future.

Several members of The Cockroaches had trained as pre-school teachers and told us they planned to set up an act that perform for young Australians. Anthony's brother and Cockroaches lead singer Paul Fields, a genuinely lovely guy, would later become their manager. Their proposed children's act sounded interesting but I was massively unconvinced.

I tried to break it to them gently but really, what future could there possibly be in performing for five-year-olds?

The one-time Cockroaches are now superstars. With a rejigged line-up and a new name—The Wiggles—they enjoy a level of success that most Australian acts could only dream about. Year after year, they are listed as the nation's highest-earning entertainers, with total revenues measured in the hundreds of millions of dollars.

After rejigging their tunes—the Cockroaches song 'Hot Tamale' became The Wiggles' biggest hit, 'Hot Potato'—they have had numerous line-up changes but remain an entertainment juggernaut. They perform live to an average of one million people a year and have been viewed on YouTube a staggering two billion times.

In 2002, when they were starting to make an impression in the US, the guys invited me to join them on an American tour to witness first-hand their growing popularity. I reported on the tour for *Rolling Stone*, as well as News Corporation newspapers.

Every young Australian performer could take a leaf from The Wiggles' handbook in terms of their work ethic and relentless focus on entertaining their audiences. On that US tour they did two or three strenuous shows a day and by night-time they were well and truly spent.

You had to love the fact that even though they were buggered, the boys always had time for their young fans and would spend hours after each show being photographed or signing autographs.

Everyone knew about The Wiggles, including the tough-as-nails detectives from a New York police unit who invited us down to their precinct station when the tour hit Manhattan.

These guys, who are used to dealing with the hard cases of New York, surprised us all by breaking into an impromptu performance of 'Hot Potato'.

When I asked one if he had ever had to use his gun, he nodded and said, 'I have shot bad people,' before quickly changing the subject and telling the assembled Wiggles, 'My son adores you guys.'

The Wiggles became so big on that tour that people started complaining about their lack of merchandise and parents spent hours lining up to get tickets to Australia's Fab Four. By the time the tour reached the famous Beacon Theatre in New York, I had seen the show half a dozen times so I decided to wait for them in their dressing room. This is where it got freaky.

There was a knock on the door and in walked actor Robert De Niro and his young son, desperate to meet The Wiggles.

I like to tell people that I said, 'Are you looking at me?' in the same menacing tone he used in the movie *Taxi Driver*. The truth is that I realised my mouth was moving and no words were coming out. Not a peep.

Then there was another knock on the door and in walked funny man Jerry Seinfeld and his wife and two-year-old daughter, also anxious to meet the act. When The Wiggles finished their show and came backstage, I swear the two VIPs jostled to see who could get in first to meet Murray, Anthony, Greg and Jeff Wiggle.

I knew no one in Australia would believe it. Nowadays, The Wiggles are *the* celebrities to name-drop in the US. Many American musicians are major fans, including John Fogarty from Creedence Clearwater Revival and Duff McKagan from Guns N' Roses.

I swear McKagan once started an interview with me on the eve of an Australian tour by saying, 'Before we get onto the smack and the pussy, tell me, do you know The Wiggles? My kid loves them.'

Jeff Tweedy from top US alternative country act Wilco also confessed to being a fan.

'I had Lou Reed, I mean Lou Reed, come over for dinner one night and my young son couldn't have cared less about the old grumpy guy in the lounge room,' he told me. 'Later while doing the dishes I told my son that I saw Murray from The Wiggles in the audience at one of our Australian shows. He dropped the dish he was drying and stood there speechless.'

On the US tour, The Wiggles became interested in my Timor-Leste story and sympathised with me about Tony's death there. I had supported the fledgling East Timor independence movement and then worked to raise funds for charities there. This caught The Wiggles' attention, which ended up paying huge dividends for the people of the newly-formed country.

Working behind the scenes as they often do, The Wiggles organised a massive concert in Sydney that helped build water and sewage facilities in six isolated villages. They followed this up by donating close to 180 big boxes of their merchandise to poor children in the former Portuguese colony, which I distributed in 2017, and they paid for another shipment of goods in 2019.

I love The Wiggles and their work for social justice.

A surreal moment came when I walked with the guys alongside their pirate ship as it sailed down the main streets of New York as part of the famous Macy's Thanksgiving Day Parade—surely the only way to see Manhattan.

The stardust and scale of that trip made the one show The Dockers ever did in New York, in 1990, look even shoddier in retrospect.

It had been great when we first arrived to be able to stay at the small flat of Karen Lee Khan, a typical New Yorker who had become The Dockers' number one fan in America after hearing us on college radio.

Standing in front of the scruffy and tired Dockers in the airport arrivals line had been the blonde Aryan twins from British boy band Bros who had recently had a huge international hit with their song 'When Will I Be Famous'. With their perfect black leather outfits, perfect teeth and perfect hair they looked at us with utter disdain.

We had no major record company support at that stage so we promoted Karen from Number One Fan to be our official North American representative, a job she threw herself into with glee.

It was a rocky arrival in the Big Apple, with the band standing on a busy New York street corner freaking out and surrounding our gear like cowboys circling their wagons to fend off Indians.

Trumpet player Dave Pace was elected to go into a huge high-rise block and find Karen's apartment. He still shakes at the memory of knocking at one door that was opened by a huge black guy who told him, 'Get the fuck out of here, white boy.'

Eventually we found Karen's apartment. It was a tight fit with six band members on her lounge room floor, but we had little money and bad jet lag, so we were comfortable enough.

We were to perform in New York at a music festival, the first date of a two-month North American tour. The venue was an Irish bar in the shadows of the Twin Towers of the World Trade Centre.

'I hate this punk rock shit,' grunted the red-haired Irish bouncer as we carried in our gear.

This made us a tad nervous as we were then a very loud six-piece band and our first song was the raucous 'Eat Shit Die'.

As luck would have it, half the audience turned out to be radio DJs from places like Ohio and Nebraska in town for a music conference. What a break. We started our first New York set and this was it, we had finally made it to the Big Apple.

Both guitar amps instantly blew up. There was nothing we could do so we had to perform most of our show with just two trumpets, a bass guitar and drums as the guitarists frantically tried to find out what was wrong.

It sounded so bad we were soon wetting ourselves with laughter. After years of playing every rat-hole in Australia here was our first shot at New York, and it was all going horribly wrong. You just had to laugh. In the great tradition of rock 'n' roll it was a mix of despair, glory and defeat all rolled into one drunken hour. We even had the Irish bouncer laughing.

Half the crowd left as soon as they heard this racket while the dozens of DJs sat in stunned silence. They seemed to be mesmerised and several came up afterwards to praise this new avant-garde musical comedy style we had come up with.

We later sent a press release to Perth, where we were touring next in Australia, declaring that 'members of Blondie and The Ramones attended the show'.

This was reported word for word in *The West Australian* newspaper and our next gigs there were sold out. In fact, I remember seeing a headline saying, 'Dockers Take New York By Storm', and I reflected once again on the power of a punchy press release.

The Wiggles actually did take the whole of America by storm. I can remember the huge arena gig they played in Memphis and thinking how other Australian acts like Skyhooks, Cold Chisel and so many others had spent fortunes trying to crack the market.

It took countless tours by INXS, Little River Band and AC/DC to finally do so. And none was as big as The Wiggles.

13

DON'T ASK ME WHY, I HAVE NO IDEA
(1989)

When laid-back Canadian rocker Bryan Adams, a master of the soft-rock ballad, decided to set up his own international record label and sign bands from around the world, one of the first acts he chose was the Painters & Dockers.

Given all the bands in all the world, why us? I have no idea.

His record company had heard the big production sounds on our first album for Mushroom, *Kiss My Art,* and thought we could be a commercially viable mainstream product.

The only problem was that we were actually a nasty-arsed left-leaning anarchist punk band more interested in putting on fun-filled, sweaty gigs than in-chart positions and units shifted. Someone in Canada obviously didn't do their homework.

When the six of us arrived at Vancouver airport in late 1989, three record company guys welcomed us and told us to go ahead because they were going to wait 'for the band to arrive'.

They looked horrified when we told them we were in fact the band, not the road crew.

The confused conversation went a bit like this:

'But where is your lighting guy?'

'Well, that would be the drummer.'

'Who is looking after sound?'

'That would be the guitarist.'

'What about merchandise?'

'The drummer has that covered as well.'

'Transport?'

'Ah, that is the bass player.'

'Publicist?'

'The singer.'

Their thoughts were transparent: 'Oh my God, what have we got here?'

That night we played our first gig at a huge promotional event organised by the record company at legendary Vancouver venue The Town Pump. When we got up and started playing you could hear jaws hitting the ground over the thrashing guitars as the Canadians saw their latest signing in action.

After our rowdy show, they did not want a lot to do with us and were happy to bundle us into a van and send us out into the wilds of Canada. We played a gut-busting twenty-eight shows in thirty-two days.

In fact, we played in every major Canadian city except Banff and Quebec City. It didn't hurt us that the legendary Rolling Stones were touring Canada at the same time.

The Vancouver Sun carried the memorable headline (I kid you not), 'Painters & Dockers Cheaper and More Fun than the Stones'. Arguably the best press review we ever received.

To help with our tour costs and because we had a song called 'Safe Sex' that promoted careful sex in the era of AIDS, we had lined up a sponsorship deal with a company called King Kong Condoms.

The deal involved us throwing condoms into the crowd at each show. That is why at every hotel we checked into there would be 500 condoms waiting at reception for 'the Australian band'.

'You guys like to party then,' said one bemused receptionist.

The tour was up and down—great when we were playing because the venues gave us top quality meals, but on our days off we often had to scrape our coins together to eat.

In Toronto one day the six of us lived off a jar of Vegemite someone had brought with them. And I hate Vegemite.

Things perked up though when we played at a huge festival in Montreal and met a number of new fans, who were all gorgeous French-speaking girls of Jamaican descent.

The most memorable show was in a place called Saskatoon in the province of Saskatchewan, south-west Canada. We were booked to play at a Mexican restaurant on both Friday and Saturday night and when we arrived, the owner asked if we would like a drink.

Loving the idea of a weekend of free drinks we lined up tequila shots, jugs of beer, jugs of bourbon and coke, and bottles of red wine for ourselves and the many new friends we made that weekend.

Ever heard that saying, drinking like there is no tomorrow?

The shows went really well, but it turned out there was a tomorrow. When we went to check out on the Sunday morning the owner said, 'Great, just wait a minute while I tally up your bill.'

Oops, did he say bill? We had no money.

'I owe you $2,000 for the two shows and the bar bill is $2,400. So give me the $400 and we'll call it quits.'

'Um, sorry mate, we haven't got any money.'

There was an angry and embarrassing silence until the ever-resourceful Phil worked out a new deal. We would stay and play for free on the Sunday night to square the ledger.

That weekend, the local football side had made it into the Canadian Football League grand final against the mighty Toronto Jayhawks. It was David versus Goliath, and nobody expected the lowly Saskatchewan Roughriders to have any chance.

In a gripping fairytale game, the small-town side won with the final kick of the day and the whole place went nuts. Cars were overturned and set on fire, bottle shops did a roaring trade, and spontaneous parties broke out everywhere. Luckily for us, this eruption of joy coincided with showtime.

We ended up playing for four hours to a very drunken full house. I took the occasion to pay tribute to the local First Nations and mention the fact that they had suffered the same fate as Indigenous Australians in having many of their children taken away by white authorities. The local mob were so moved that several gave us gifts and it did not help the quality of our performance that those gifts included some wicked magic mushrooms.

Even the club owner gave us a huge drink rider and a wink as he took wads of cash over the bar thanks to the unplanned live entertainment.

When we dragged our hangovers and sound equipment out onto the street early the next morning to head off to the next town, the place resembled a war zone with burned-out cars and vandalised buildings.

After three great shows, rock 'n' roll showed what a trickster it is. Our next crowd numbered five people, three of them sitting quietly reading newspapers. That is the nature of life on the road with its extreme highs add lows.

We were supposed to play in Edmonton and then fly onto Vancouver the next day. This wasn't as easy as it sounded.

Travelling with us was an Australian fan who had decided to follow us for part of the tour. We were going through security at Edmonton airport when this guy walked through an X-ray machine and the alarm went off. A security guy asked him what was in his pocket.

'Oh, just this big block of hash,' he said pulling the offending item from his trouser pocket to the amazement of both the security guard and the band. The security guy was so shocked he just motioned us through the checkpoint.

'Do you think I should toss this?' our friend asked.

'Ah, yeah, that would be a good idea,' I said.

Landing in Vancouver we were met by a line of police, taken

straight into a private room and vigorously strip-searched. Amazingly, Phil Nelson walked straight through the security cordon as if he were invisible. When we got back to our hotel he was in bed with a rum and coke and a toasted ham sandwich, oblivious to all the fuss.

Checking into my Vancouver hotel room—which was above a strip joint called Champagne Charlies—I found a Bible in one of the bedside drawers. Inside the bible was a blood-streaked syringe.

It was great to be back in a place where some locals actually liked us. We got a full house first night back at The Town Pump and a guy who ran a local Aussie-themed restaurant called Diggers saw the cash flowing over the bar and hired us for two nights.

The small crowd at Diggers hated us with a passion from the word 'go'. The biggest complaint seemed to be that we were disturbing their weekly darts competition. The dartboard was near where we were playing and we soon had these sharp projectiles heading at us. The next night was one of the rare times when The Dockers were paid *not* to play.

There would be a memorable ending to what was already a tour we would never forget.

Our last show in Canada was back at The Town Pump, where the Scottish-born chef had a special request. No worries, we said, as he had looked after us really well at meal times.

He said he wanted to marry his girlfriend, a waitress at the pub, during our show interval that night.

'Sure mate, um, no worries.'

We weren't expecting the ginger-haired chef and his twin brothers dressed in Highland kilts to take to the stage complete with a preacher. The bride appeared dressed in black suspenders and a tight black bra. For their wedding song, they requested 'Your Turn on Top Tonight'—one of our raunchier numbers.

The next time I went to Canada was to organise press coverage for a tour featuring Australian Indigenous performers Archie Roach, Ruby Hunter, Kev Carmody and Tiddas.

We hooked up with the local First Nations mob who considered the Indigenous Australians as first cousins, given their shared experiences at the hands of British invaders. Both had children taken away from their "savage" parents, leading in some cases to generations of drug abuse, alcoholism and suicide.

We later performed traditional ceremonies with the locals. One night they were preparing for a North American healing ceremony involving chanting and the burning of leaves when I noticed one of the young Canadians excusing himself and saying he would return later.

'Where are you off to mate?' I asked.

'The ice hockey is on and our side is playing tonight,' he said.

'Any chance I could come?'

'Sure, no problems.'

He passed me a helmet and, without telling the Australian tour manager, we got on his motorbike and headed off into the night.

At the game we had to sit on a side of the rink that was reserved for his team and community. The entry stamp on my arm was just one word: Indian.

I told the young guy I couldn't wait to tell my friends back home I had been officially labelled an Indian.

After our team won a tight game, I was invited by my new friend back to one of the players' houses in the back blocks of Vancouver for an after-party. I had no idea where we were going.

I walked into a room filled with First Nations mob dressed in black leather jackets, chains, studs and red bandanas. I must admit I was a tad nervous.

After a stony silence, one of them piped up. 'Do you like Australian Rules footy? We watch it on cable every Tuesday night. Who is this guy called "God"?' he asked.

With our new shared passion, we launched into a discussion about the legendary Geelong footballer Gary Ablett Sr and these chaps soon became my pals. Funnily enough, years earlier I had been in Jerusalem watching television from Jordan during the Gulf War when the local sports program showed its Top 10 moments in sport. At the time, Australia was at war with Jordan's ally Iraq so this was almost 'enemy television'. Making the final cut was footage of Ablett taking a screamer at the MCG.

I thought to myself, if only your average Australian could see that Saddam Hussein's allies were Australian football fans there might be less conflict with them.

Ablett is considered by many to be the greatest Australian Rules footballer ever and years later I got to meet him under very unusual circumstances.

Mum had always been a real worrier and towards the end of her life, her fears and anxieties grew even worse because of the unresolved questions about Tony's murder. Things got worse in 2002 when Dad died of a heart attack lying next to her at home in Mentone. Not long after that she started having panic attacks.

The years of bottled-up grief overwhelmed her and we booked her into the Albert Road Clinic, a facility dedicated to mental health. During one visit she told me she had met a very nice man who said he had played 'a bit of footy'.

'Here he is now,' she said as her fellow patient dropped in to say hi.

Imagine my surprise when in walked Gary Ablett.

14

WE DON'T HAVE MUCH CALL FOR THAT KIND OF THING UP THIS WAY

The Painters & Dockers were one of the last bands to extensively tour small towns in far-flung Australia—not just going to Melbourne and Sydney but through countless rural towns the length and breadth of the nation.

Nowadays most bands stick to playing the capital cities on weekends but in our prime, thanks to Lobby, we would go to any place that would have us. His mantra for rock 'n' roll success was to play, play and play.

Places like Drouin and Sale in Victoria, Burnie and Devonport in Tasmania, Albany and Kununurra in Western Australia, Victor Harbour and Mount Gambier in South Australia, Toowoomba and Cairns in Queensland, Katherine and Nhulunbuy in the Northern Territory, Canberra and out of the way places like Bathurst and Broken Hill in New South Wales. In beach towns and the snow fields, universities and pokie venues. At strip joints and church halls. In Horsham we played at one pub that had a classic blackboard message out front: No Thongs, No Singlets, No Farmers.

We certainly racked up the kilometres. If you want to test yourself, try life on the road driving from Perth to Darwin. It's five days straight of ten-hour hauls in rough-as-guts old Tarago vans, with no air conditioning, seven other smelly blokes and bad, yep really bad road food. It can make or break you.

One town we played on that run in the early 1990s was Port Hedland at the infamous Pier Hotel. It had the claim to fame that more beer glasses were smashed there than at any other pub in the world.

The temperature is so freaking hot that the patrons, ninety-nine per cent horny male miners, only drink small glasses or else the beer gets too warm. They then usually smash the glasses. Playing there was real Daniel in the lion's den stuff. It was put on an entertaining show or you were in trouble. Our performances there were just crazy.

At our soundcheck, a huge spider appeared from nowhere and bit my forehead, which then blew up to the size of a huge red balloon much to the amusement of my bandmates.

What else could go wrong?

I soon found out our gig was to follow a performance by The Raunchy Girls, a group of strippers who would slide down poles and perform other gymnastics, and I use the word gymnastics very loosely. They had the horny miners howling for more.

It was at this moment, shaking with nerves in the band room, that you realised it really was a case of entertain or die. That gig, we felt like troops on the battlefield in World War I. 'You are about to enter no man's land, so give it all you've got.'

Trying to ingratiate ourselves with the crowd, we swore endlessly, sang quickly, played loud and fast and invited the strippers back onto the stage to dance. Luckily the miners liked us and we drank long into the night with some of them. But try a hangover in thirty-five degree heat sitting in a van for ten hours.

I can remember dry retching when I woke up in the Tarago beside a roadie who proceeded to have a breakfast of a cold pie, a warm chocolate milk, a stale can of beer and a huge joint.

'Want a puff?' he grinned.

'Spare me, dear Jesus,' I whimpered.

Such is the life of a road warrior.

On one of our trips from Perth to Darwin, we were accompanied by an unusual character called Burton C Bell, who was a friend of the Western Australian concert promoter Ken 'Squasher' Knight.

Burton at the time was a little-known American rocker who stayed on in Australia for a holiday after his band had toured here. The only work he could get was road-managing us through the Outback. He was a glamorous-looking chap who lived in Hollywood complete with his tribal tattoos and long blonde hair. The locals in the Top End loved such an exotic character.

Burton actually ended up with a new "friend" most nights and was certainly more popular than anyone in the band. He kept telling us about his band called Fear Factory and how huge they were going to be. 'Enormous,' he said.

'Sure mate, pull the other one.'

Years later, there he was at the Big Day Out festival in Melbourne with 20,000 fans going right off and singing along with him. The bugger had proved good to his word.

Touring the Outback is an amazing cultural experience. You see a side of the country unknown to most Australians. One pub we stopped at in Tennant Creek, for example, had white people drinking in one bar and blackfellas drinking in the other. The drinkers in both bars were disdainful of a group of colourfully dressed punks from Melbourne with unusual haircuts.

On one tour it was written into the contract that any pub that hired us had to provide a meal. In the dusty old Western Australian township of Derby we sat down for our nightly feed and the barman delivered seven huge steaks that covered each dinner plate.

One of the boys asked innocently, 'Any chance of a salad with that, mate?'

You could have heard a pin drop.

'Mate, we don't have much call for that kind of thing up this way,' replied the disbelieving barman.

We had been told that the gig would be packed with nubile young nurses from the nearby hospital. Instead, a guy named Pedro took all his clothes off and stood right in front of the band, while the rest of the small bemused crowd stood 200 metres back, at the outside bar.

It was funny for three songs, then tragic for the next ten.

15

MISS BINDOON
(1995)

When you write a song called 'Nude School', it is probably no surprise that shows become marked by public displays of nudity.

At Adelaide University we once said that anyone turning up naked would get in free. That cost us twenty-three entry fees.

In Perth, one well-built lass turned herself into a much-acclaimed performance artist by regularly appearing on stage with us and taking off her clothes. The Dockers merely provided the soundtrack. She loved showing off, which qualified her as a Docker really. She became a great friend and came with us several times to the huge annual rock concert at Bindoon in WA run by bikie gang the Coffin Cheaters.

For two years running she won the title of Miss Bindoon by displaying her well-endowed physique. One year after the gig, we were downing ice-cold beers while driving back to Perth in the boiling heat. On the highway we passed a dry-as-a-bone paddock where a farmer in a cloud of dust was on his tractor going about his energy-sapping task.

'Stop the van,' said Miss Bindoon. 'Wait here a minute.'

She whisked off her top, got a cold can from the Esky and leapt out. She jumped the paddock fence and ran towards the farmer on his tractor. He took one look and slammed on the brakes. He leaned down, took the can and stood on his tractor seat, downed it in one gulp and flung his old hat in the air. Our friend ran back to the van, jumped in and we moved on to Perth. We laughed ourselves silly thinking of him at his local pub that night trying to convince his mates of what had happened that day in the paddock.

Miss Bindoon was not the only 'character' we met on tour. When it came to downright loons, it was hard to match Kim the Crazy Clown, who we had first met at the infamous Gong Show in St Kilda in the early 1980s.

Like Miss Bindoon, he also liked to strip naked, but would often do so wielding a chainsaw. His other acts included magic tricks and breathing fire while blind drunk. One night he lay in the dressing room covered in petrol looking for a match for a cigarette.

He caused a riot another time at the Shenton Park Hotel in Perth, a cramped venue that usually held about 400 people, but on this occasion was jammed with 600 mad punters.

During the last song, Kim appeared naked on stage and threw an emergency boat flare into the crowd. The room filled with toxic orange smoke and the crowd ran screaming. Some left via the pub's windows, so the owners were far from impressed.

Much to the disappointment of some band members, Phil banned Kim the Clown from ever appearing with us again after his behaviour one night at a fine Indian restaurant in Perth.

All was going smoothly until Kim removed his clothes, put them on a plate and ordered the waiter to give them to the chef because they were not yet fully cooked. The owners lost it.

Kim would regularly perform his clown act with a chicken named George as his sidekick and they would both come and stay at my house when they were in Melbourne. It was confronting to hit the breakfast table and find a clown and a chook both munching away on bowls of cornflakes. Several of The Dockers' girlfriends insisted we have nothing more to do with Kim after a trick went horribly wrong one night when George was burned to death at a show at St Patrick's College Ballarat.

I have to also mention Docker, a pint-sized dancer and Aussie Rules footballer, who often joined the band on stage in a pig suit to sing or have a dance. She even got a small pig tattooed on one breast after our Nude School video release and moved from being a devoted fan to a friend.

Once, on the way from Cairns to Townsville we stopped for a pub meal. The place was full of cane cutters and you could have heard a pin drop when these "fags" from Melbourne walked in.

There was a pregnant pause as a midget worker approached us. 'Hey boys,' he said. 'Get a load of this.' He dropped his pants to reveal the largest penis I have ever seen. Talk about the Loch Ness Monster.

We all took one look at the thing and ran out of the pub squealing, much to the delight of the assembled throng who jeered and wolf-whistled us on our way.

16

GIRLS ON TOP

I have explained the band's main line-up but let's not forget the female musicians with long service records in The Dockers. Trombonist Sonja Parkinson was a shy girl who worked at the Melbourne Zoo with our trumpet player Dave. He invited her along one night for a blow with The Dockers at the legendary Esplanade Hotel in St Kilda. Her previous musical experience had been with the Salvation Army youth band. It was a raucous audience at the Espy and Sonja admits that she was scared witless. But like the rest of us, she had had a taste of the rock 'n' roll mayhem and was instantly addicted.

Coincidentally, The Dockers had a long association with the Salvation Army and did many benefit gigs for underprivileged children with their brass band joining us on stage. The funny thing is, they were the ones who really wanted to play songs like 'Die Yuppie Die' and 'Kill, Kill, Kill'. I suppose it was of a change from 'Onward Christian Soldiers'.

We ended up playing with the Salvos on top-rating TV show *Hey Hey It's Saturday*. However, we were banned from doing 'Nude School' because the show's producers considered it too risqué. Strange, given that the show was full of Benny Hill nudge-nudge wink-wink jokes and it was fronted by a wide-eyed ostrich with a bloke's arm up its arse.

Another long-time female band member was the one-in-a-million, saxophone-playing tornado Jenny Pineapple.

I have often said that if you ever want to get rid of the Taliban just parachute Jenny Pineapple into the Middle East with a baseball bat and tell her the chaps there don't treat their women too nicely. She would have them sorted out quick smart.

We first met her one night during a Docker's gig at The Esplanade when she jumped on stage and sang the old Saints hit 'Know Your Product', which brought the house down. I really wanted her involved in the band, so backstage I asked her what her name was and she said, 'Jenny Monterello'.

I said, 'That will never do, where do you come from?'

'Queensland,' she said.

'Okay, we will call you Jenny Pineapple.'

The name stuck and she became a regular with the band over the years. I have always loved playing with Jenny Pineapple. She was fearless, and she would not hesitate to tell the heaviest male punters to 'fuck off' and humourless lesbians to 'lighten up'. If I took my shirt off, so would she. The fact that she often had a blue, green or red Mohawk haircut made it even better.

Politically active, she got the band heavily involved with the anti-uranium movement and lined up a gig playing at the picket line on the proposed uranium mine site in Kakadu National Park. After hours of driving, we played the picket line and watched with amazement as fellow protesting rockers Midnight Oil flew in and out by helicopter to play.

Sonja and Pineapple both ended up doing stints in The Dili Allstars and toured Timor-Leste with me.

I'll never forget the look on Timorese singer Fatima Almeida's face when Pineapple waltzed off stage after playing before thousands of Australian peacekeeping troops and whipped off her top to cool down.

The East Timorese just loved Sonja and her trombone, with many of the local women amazed that she had a role front and centre stage with the boys in the band. By the end of our trip up there, crowds were chanting her name.

The Dockers' later line-up was rounded out with the addition of Colin Badger's son Michael, an innovative guitarist and music producer who grew up listening to our songs, and Richard Bradbeer, a bass player and genuine sweetheart who plays in half the bands in Melbourne.

Others with long time service records in the band included bass player Dali Platt; Alex 'Trombone', the tuba player from the Tasmanian Symphony Orchestra; violinist Karen D'Nardi who toured Australia with Bruce Springsteen; Indigenous didjeridu player Russell Smith; guitarist Darren Garth; drummers Dahl Murphy and Michael Barclay; and bagpipe player Doug Scott.

The number of people who have jumped up on stage to sing with us literally ranges in the hundreds.

17

UNITS SHIFTED

The Painters & Dockers only ever had one No. 1 single, and that was in the late 1980s when 'Die Yuppie Die' topped the charts on Brisbane's alternative music station 4ZZZ.

I first listened to 4ZZZ while holidaying in Mullumbimby in the 1970s. It was the first time I had ever heard artists like The Dead Kennedys, Elvis Costello and The Attractions, Talking Heads, The Clash, The Saints, Radio Birdman and other cutting-edge punk and new wave acts. This was the voice of the revolution.

The station was indeed the voice of the underground in Queensland during the last years of the ultra-conservative rule by the authoritarian Joh Bjelke-Petersen and his National Party. It was radical, it gave a voice to new sounds and new ideas and it was fiercely independent. Airplay on 4ZZZ helped us to tour Queensland for the first time.

It was an unusual place in those days. I landed in Brisbane once to see a newspaper reporting that Father Christmas had been arrested for marching through the city's main mall, an act deemed illegal under Joh's oppressive regime.

Many of our new fans were stopped on their way to our shows in The Valley and searched by police. Even the band came under the watchful eye of law enforcement. Our shows there were wild. The crowds were irrepressible and we acted-up accordingly.

To this day, 4ZZZ remains one of our biggest supporters and we regularly visit Brisbane to play at Punkfest, run by the station's Chris Converse.

It was airplay on community stations like Triple M in Adelaide, Top End FM in Darwin, 6NUR in Perth, and the mighty Triple R and 3PBS in Melbourne that enabled us to play.

We were proud to perform many benefits to help PBS when the station was first set up in Fitzroy Street, St Kilda. Triple R has been another major supporter, and we have played at many of its events, including barbecue days, Radiothon gigs and station benefits.

When the ABC's youth network Triple J expanded from Sydney to Melbourne, they hired the Painters & Dockers to help launch the station. We agreed even though it pissed off our friends at Triple R and 3PBS. The station launch was a big show at The Palace in St Kilda, then Triple J proceeded to give us almost no airplay.

The rationale for publicly-funded alternative radio stations is to provide a vehicle for Australian artists who might not get commercial airtime. Unfortunately, by championing some bands, they neglect others and narrow the marketplace.

During our career we were released on all manner of record labels. Our first two albums, *Love Planet* (1985) and *Bucket* (1986) came out on US label Big Time Records. The follow-up studio album, *Kiss My Art* (1988) was on Mushroom Records, but they dropped us because it sold "only" 28,000 copies (a gold record was 32,000).

Undaunted, we released our next album, *Touch One, Touch All* through another company, Musicland Releases in 1989, and then used our own Doc Records label for our subsequent releases, *The Nervous 90s* (1992), *The Things that Matter* (1994), *Advance Australia Where?* (1988), *Overt and Deliberate* (2009), and *You Know You Want To* (2020).

Funnily enough, we never really made any money from these releases.

The giant Warner Music Group took control of *Kiss My Art* when it bought Mushroom in 2005. It continued to sell the album, but somehow could never tell us how many copies were sold. It also used songs from the album on several compilations without ever feeling a need to compensate us.

In the end, 'Nude School' was our only tune ever to crack it for commercial airplay and to this day it still pops up on the playlist of digital radio station Triple M Classic Rock.

Luckily, units shifted and chart positions never really interested us. Having a full crowd in a hot sweaty pub or club singing our songs back to us was the greatest achievement of all.

18

SUNDAY SUN
(1990)

I quit *The Sun News-Pictorial* after a decade to risk being a full-time performer, but a year later when we ended our lucrative Mushroom Records deal I was desperate to find another gig because I had a young daughter to support.

Thank God for veteran journalist Rex Lopez, a colleague from my cadet days, who rang me out of the blue in early 1990. He had a senior position on a new newspaper, *The Sunday Sun*, (later amalgamated with the *Sunday Herald* to form *The Sunday Herald Sun*) and asked if I was interested in writing a regular music column.

'You betcha,' was my immediate response, and so began my stint with a publication I would work at for two decades.

After a number of editors, I was blessed when Alan Howe took charge as he loved his music, particularly home-grown Australian stock. I was given free rein to write about any band I liked as long as every now and then I talked to the latest pop sensation or visiting overseas chart-topper.

Those were fun days where drinking vast amounts of alcohol was encouraged and there was always someone in the office up for a glass.

We basically made the River Bar at Southbank an annex of the paper's nearby office.

Regular drinkers and my fellow newshounds included Gordan Dann and Bill McAuley, a photographer with a repertoire of stories that never failed to amuse. He was quite the character and a true eccentric. Most Friday nights he would have me in hysterics retelling his favourite story about gay Melbourne actor Frank Thring. This story grew and grew in the telling and went something like this:

One Monday morning, a photographer and a reporter from the paper were sent to Frank's house in Fitzroy. They planned to do a colour piece on the actor who had found fame in Hollywood epics like *Ben-Hur* and *The Vikings*. At the agreed time of 9am, the newsmen knocked on the door only to be greeted by stony silence.

They tried again but still no luck. They found a phone box (this was before mobile phones) and rang the office to say, 'There is no sign of Frank.'

The chief of staff replied, 'Keep trying, we need this story as not a lot is happening today.'

So the pair returned to Frank's to try again, once more with no success. Eventually Frank's manager was summoned, then the police. Two officers arrived at noon and broke open the front door. Accompanied by the photographer, manager and reporter they made their way in, fearing the worst.

In the main lounge they found the actor stark naked hanging from the ceiling, his skin pinched painfully by clothes pegs and a billiard ball stuck in his mouth.

'Frank, Frank are you okay?' cried the manager as the police lowered him to the ground and ripped off the masking tape that held the billiard ball in his mouth.

Thring took a gasp of air and looked up at the five of them before saying with his characteristic drawl, 'What a fabulous weekend!'

I must have heard that story a hundred times, and I laughed a hundred times. It was almost too much fun working on the Sunday paper.

19

TIMOR TIME

While the Painters & Dockers were busy causing strife and I did my journalism cadetship at *The Sun News-Pictorial* in the 1980s, the situation in Timor-Leste and my brother's death there were never too far away.

My first trip to East Timor was an eventful one with the incident where I had to sing 'Cotton Fields'.

I had earlier begun attending small rallies in Melbourne calling for justice for my brother and the Balibo Five. The most notable of these was in Melbourne's City Square in the early 1980s where a Channel 7 employee, a mate of Tony's, punched out a drunken heckler who gatecrashed the event. It was an early indication of how emotional people still felt about the murders.

My interest changed dramatically in the mid-1980s after I met a Melbourne bus driver from Timor-Leste, Abel Guterres, who would later become that country's first ambassador to Australia when the seeming pipe dream of independence was finally achieved twenty-five years after the Indonesian invasion and Tony's death.

Getting to know a member of the Timorese community and hearing first-hand about the growing independence movement motivated me. Learning about the continuing oppression of the local population under the brutal grip of the Indonesian military regime made me want to help.

The first thing bus driver Abel and I decided to do was to hold a benefit concert to raise awareness about East Timor and to buy buffalos for impoverished farmers there. To organise our benefit I had to regularly catch his bus on his Port Melbourne route as it was the only time we could meet and talk.

We held that first fundraising concert at Fitzroy Town Hall, featuring The Dockers and a number of local acts, with good mate Peter Wilson as master of ceremonies. I didn't imagine my involvement lasting beyond that one event, but my interest just grew and grew.

My first visit to East Timor came in 1993 when Dockers drummer Colin Buckler suggested that he and I should go there after the band was scheduled to do some shows in Darwin. To be honest, I had mixed feelings: part grief, part anger and part reluctance to visit the place my brother was murdered.

We both realised at Darwin Airport that we were in for an unsettling experience when we met members of East Timor's national soccer team who were flying out after a tournament in Darwin. These young men were all about our own age and they were in tears at the thought of having to go home.

We arrived in Kupang, the capital of West Timor, which had been a Dutch colony before being incorporated into Indonesia after World War II. The only way to East Timor in those days was by catching a small overnight bus from Kupang across the border to the capital Dili.

We shared the bus with a dozen freshly shaved Indonesian soldiers being sent to their first posting and looked totally out of place in our paisley shirts and punk haircuts among the sharply dressed eager young recruits.

We arrived at dawn in a bleak Dili. Indonesian troops, including red-bereted members of the infamous Kopassus special forces, patrolled the streets and manned roadblocks and machinegun nests all over town.

They stared at us menacingly before we had even left the bus. After checking into the Hotel Turismo, where Tony and his colleagues had stayed before making their way to Balibo, we went for a walk around the city for several hours.

Even though they were putting themselves at risk, locals approached us and handed us bits of paper saying, 'Please contact my uncle/brother/sister/aunty/cousin and tell them we need help.'

They filled us with dread as they told us about horrifying visits by the 'Ninjas' (Indonesian special security police), who took people away in the middle of the night never to be heard from again. They explained how they were forbidden to hold meetings and were constantly watched by Indonesian security forces. Their fear was palpable.

One young guy told me the only way the resistance could ever get together was in the church choir and it was while singing hymns that they would plan ambushes and raids.

When we got back to the Turismo we had an interesting conversation with two very drunk white guys at the bar. They told us they were in a special military attachment working for the Australian Department of Foreign Affairs.

They assumed we were just a couple of eccentric musicians taking time out to visit an exotic destination that received almost no tourists. They said they loved their regular 'East Timor junket' where they would be flown in by the Australian Embassy, get on the drink, and after several days report back that the situation on the ground was 'quiet'.

One asked me why I had decided to visit and I told him my brother was one of the Balibo Five. You have never seen two guys sober up so quickly.

I don't know for a fact, but I suspect that they passed the information on to the Indonesians because after meeting them we suddenly began being photographed by mysterious strangers who kept us under constant surveillance.

One obvious plainclothes officer stood in the garden beneath our second-floor room and pretended to take photos of two small children, but actually pointed his camera at us on our balcony, taking a series of shots, much to our amusement.

On our one and only Saturday night in Dili we met some locals who invited us to attend a wedding. Returning to the hotel we showered, shaved and dressed up, very excited to be going to a party but when we went to the front of the hotel to meet our new friends, two jeep-loads of Indonesian soldiers were waiting for us.

'Where are you two going?' asked the officer in charge.

'To a wedding,' we said.

He thought long and hard before replying. 'Put it this way,' he said grinning, 'if you go to the wedding we will go as well, and there will be no party. If you want it to go ahead you should stay here.'

We reluctantly agreed not to leave the hotel.

Our last encounter on that visit was on the trip back to Kupang when we got off the bus in the mountains near the border and spent a night in the small town of Atambua. We met some starving refugees in a mosquito-infested town with no mosquito nets. If you owned a grass skirt or a shack with a roof you were doing well, but they still offered us all they had, opening their hearts and hospitality.

A few hours after we left East Timor Colin and I were back in Darwin, guests at a BBQ in a friend's backyard where what seemed like a whole cow was cooked and gallons of beer drunk. I was in a daze. The contrast between the affluence of Australia and the poverty just one hour's flight away was both offensive and disorienting.

Coming back to Melbourne, I was determined to get further involved with the East Timorese independence struggle. Nobody thought East Timor and its population then of just 807,000 had any chance of defying the military might of Indonesia, which was rapidly approaching 200 million people, but I soon learned that the independence fighters were never going to give up.

20

GIL SANTOS COMRADE NO. 1

As the busiest years of The Dockers wound down in the mid-1990s, it was either luck, my desire to keep performing, or my growing interest and need to support the emerging independence struggle in East Timor that led to the birth of The Dili Allstars.

When I say need, it became increasingly important to me, and almost therapeutic, to channel my anger, grief and sense of injustice into something positive by supporting the brave underdogs who were fighting the same army that had killed Tony.

I lost one brother in Timor-Leste, but picked up a hell of a lot of new ones from there.

I lost Tony but found Gil Santos. He changed my life. I first met him in a battered old caravan parked at a protest rally outside the Indonesian consulate in St Kilda Road, Melbourne.

It was an emotional day, as East Timorese resistance leader Xanana Gusmão had recently been captured by the Indonesians. Gusmão, a former corporal in the Portuguese army, had got his Xanana nickname from the US rockabilly band Sha Na Na, but by this stage he was a famed freedom fighter who was treated like a messiah by his followers.

I invited Gil along to a Dockers gig and our friendship just grew. Australian journalist Garry Linnell later wrote about Gil and me in the popular The Two of Us section of *The Good Weekend* magazine in *The Age* and *The Sydney Morning Herald*.

In the story, Gil told Linnell that his first impression of me was that I seemed very quiet, very shy.

'And then I saw him on stage, he was like an animal,' he said. 'His personality changed. I thought, "this is great". Our friendship goes beyond the things we do for Timor, even the music. We're like brothers. Our families are also close.

'Paulie's very passionate. He has a lot of heart for Timor and it was something that really captured me. Whenever I've asked him to do something for Timor, he's never asked why. He's really trusted me. I think because I've told him everything.

'We shared the same grief. We still don't know where my father was buried. He was killed in 1975, and most of my uncles also. That's the ultimate price you pay for freedom. I was five years old at the time and there were eight children. The youngest was only a few weeks old and the eldest was twelve.

'Paul's personality goes from one extreme to another. With good news, he gets very excited, over the moon. When it's bad news, or something doesn't go right, he gets really angry and sad. I try to settle him down whenever that happens. But I wouldn't want to see him change. If he changed, he probably wouldn't have the energy to do other things.

'I'd never had a friend like him before, in fact, I don't think any Timorese person has ever met someone like him before. He's larger than life. He makes me laugh all the time. He is a music journalist and he has lots of stories about the music industry that I love listening to. He is very good with words, whether telling a story or as a lyricist. Life would be very dull without him.

'I've never had a fight with him. When we went back for the concert [for Dili peacekeepers in 1999], I sneaked out of the compound because I wanted to see the family, people I hadn't seen for twenty years. I missed the rehearsal and sound check, so when I came back everything was done. Paul was very upset with me but he never said anything. I felt bad but on the other hand, I hadn't seen my family for so long, and nothing could have stopped me that day. These were the people who nurtured me.'

Gil taught me about his homeland, its history and political machinations. Even though he's nine years my junior, I always feel like I'm with an elder. He has a wise old soul and he is a patriot who would do anything for his country.

On our second visit there together in 2000, Gil insisted that we visit his hometown Liquiçá, on the coast thirty-two kilometres west of Dili. Small, but filled with colonial architecture, it was spared from the Allied air raids that devastated the rest of East Timor during World War II because it was the home of the Portuguese colonial administration during the Japanese occupation.

On 6 April 1999, in the campaign of intimidation and violence that preceded the independence referendum, about 200 people were killed in the Liquiçá Church massacre, when pro-Indonesia militia backed by regular Indonesian troops and police attacked the parish church. (Indonesia disputes the death toll.) Many of the dead were Gil's extended family.

It was a sombre place when we visited. Gil said for me to truly understand him we had to visit his grandmother's grave. On the way he pointed to an infamous clifftop in the mountains where scores of independence supporters were taken by the militia and given a brutal choice: 'Join Greater Indonesia, or jump.'

Many jumped.

I was amazed when I learned more about Gil's life. After growing up in rural East Timor he shifted to urban Portugal before finally relocating to the Melbourne outer suburb of Endeavour Hills.

In World War II his mother lost her mum and other relatives when they assisted Australian soldiers in defending the tiny island against the Japanese. His family sheltered ill-equipped Australian troops in the mountains, but always wondered why the soldiers left them to fend for themselves after the battle.

Only 800 Australian soldiers were posted to East Timor during World War II, and yet more than 40,000 Timorese were killed. When the Indonesians invaded in 1975, Gil's father was a nurse and he raced to the Dili hospital to assist. He was never heard of again.

For ten years as a child Gil didn't know what had happened to his father. When he disappeared, Gil's terrified mother Berta decided to hide her eight children in a cave in the mountains near their family home.

Aida, the oldest, was only twelve, but helped look after the five boys—Joaquim, ten; Aderito, nine; Nelson, seven; Gil, five; and Lewis, three—as they trekked into the mountains. Berta carried the two youngest, twelve-month-old Teresa and baby Maria Assunção, just two weeks old.

The family hid in the mountains for a year before Berta concluded it was no life for her children as she wanted them to be educated, well-fed and safe. She decided to head to Dili and take her chances.

As the little troupe walked down from the hills into the nearest coastal village, Maubara, nervous Indonesian soldiers started shooting at them, but Berta kept walking until the soldiers realised it was a woman and her children. All their belongings were confiscated and they had to rely on relatives for food and clothing. Gil remembers it was mostly aunties who minded him in those early days for the simple reason that all the men in the family had been killed during the invasion.

His mum got a job cooking for Indonesian soldiers and Gil remembers she would bring leftovers home to her children. She also had work in the hospital.

Berta was clever as well as brave and a born entrepreneur. With eight mouths to feed, she set about making and selling palm wine and cakes. After earning a little money she was determined to try to find out what had happened to her husband. She also arranged tickets for herself and the baby to leave East Timor, planning to fly the others out when she could afford it.

Gil and the other children stayed with their grandmother until Berta sent the Red Cross to fetch them one by one. It took her four years to organise tickets for all her family to leave the country but finally the Santos clan was reunited in Portugal. They spent three years there and Gil learnt to speak Portuguese. He also took up playing his father's guitar.

Berta bought other instruments for her children and music became a central part of Gil's life. The two oldest boys studied music at school and would show their eager young brother what they had learned.

A big break for the family was when Gil's mum met Australian journalist Jill Jolliffe in Portugal. Jill was a fearless veteran journalist who had been in Dili during the invasion and spent some time with Tony and his colleagues before they left for Balibo.

She knew East Timor's story well and wanted to help Berta and her children. With her encouragement, Berta decided that Melbourne would be a better place to educate her children and so once again she gathered them up and moved to the other side of the world.

The Santos family arrived in Melbourne in 1985 and went to live in Dandenong. The children were sent to a specialist school to learn English and then fifteen-year-old Gil went to Cleeland Secondary College. It was only then that he started to learn more about East Timorese culture.

His childhood had been so governed by survival that it seemed a tremendous freedom to be able to head to the Dandenong Library to read about his homeland, and Gil spent hours there.

When the United Nations eventually took over administering East Timor, Berta and other members of the family began making regular trips there. On one of my first trips to Dili she was working at a restaurant across the road from a huge crocodile enclosure. When the Indonesians had withdrawn from the country their soldiers opened the zoo gates so the beasts could terrify the locals.

Gil remains one of the few Timorese I have met who returned to his homeland on numerous occasions to help set up aid projects in the newly independent country. On each visit we would find up to twenty locals waiting for him at the airport anxious for his advice on a range of issues.

The only time I ever really pissed him off was when we were leaving a Dili bar early one morning. There were a bunch of children out the front pleading for money and I put my hand in my pocket and gave them a few dollars.

'Don't ever do that again,' said a fuming Gil. 'These kids have parents who should be watching them. We don't want our young people to grow up living off handouts from foreigners.'

Fair call.

Gil would become firm friends with Australian musicians Paul Kelly and Peter Garrett, enlisting them to help the Timorese cause through benefit concerts and albums.

Garrett helped The Dili Allstars on a number of occasions when we needed to bring in a heavy hitter, whether it was writing references for government funding, or talking up the band to the music media.

Gil is no doubt one of the best-known Timorese musicians in the world. Over the years I have seen so many people seek his help. He never says no. In rock 'n' roll, there are so many other people who make promises and then you never hear back from them.

People think popular music these days is all about chart positions and marketing your T-shirts. But Gil showed me there is still a part of it that remains revolutionary and life-changing.

We formed The Dili Allstars in the mid-1990s during the campaign for independence to lift morale and provide a soundtrack for the stubborn resistance movement. Our greatest impact came from us becoming the musical opposition to the Indonesian Governor of East Timor, José Abílio Osório Soares, who fancied himself as a pop star.

Soares wrote songs leading up to the independence referendum in 1999 saying things like, 'Let's stay part of Indonesia', which were played on government loudspeakers at Dili airport and on local radio stations.

To counter this, Gil and I came up with the pro-independence song 'Liberdade', the Portuguese word for freedom. Working with Melbourne-based Scotsman Billy Abbott we reworked one of Billy's tunes and in just a few minutes we had written what many people have since called the unofficial anthem of Timor-Leste.

One verse was sung in the local language Tetum by The Dili Allstars vocalist Paulo Almeida, while I sang the others in English.

Earning all the gold records in the world would never match the feeling of having joyful ten-year-old Timorese children dancing around me in the streets singing that song, which they knew by heart.

The tune was recorded with several other songs in English and Tetum on a bright green six-track cassette, and about 500 copies were snuck into Dili by activists from Melbourne University.

Cassettes were handed out free to local students, owners of bars and shops, and taxi and bus drivers. Some of the Melbourne Uni students took them up into the hills where the guerrillas had a big sound system that played it non-stop. One activist, Sam Maresh, complained later that he had heard the song so often he was sick to death of it.

'I rank it with "Achy Breaky Heart" by Billy Ray Cyrus—I just never want to hear it again,' he told me later.

At one of the first Dili Allstars shows in Fitzroy I was staggered when a Timorese member of the crowd walked up to the stage and spat at me.

'What the hell is happening, Gil?' I asked my bandmate.

He explained it was probably the large Fretilin flag that we usually used as a stage backdrop. Fretilin was a left-leaning political party that fell into a brutal civil war with the conservative UDT party in 1975 when Portugal was preparing to end its neglectful 273-year colonial reign.

'That guy who spat at you was UDT.'

As usual, it was Gil who taught me the machinations of East Timorese politics.

He and I laugh now that one of the first pro-independence demonstrations we staged featured fifteen lonely people marching through the streets of Fitzroy. Hoons threw eggs at us from their cars.

Several years, and a lot of work later, we stood in a crowd of 80,000 in Melbourne's Bourke Street Mall calling for Australian peacekeepers to be sent to East Timor.

Old pal and long-time independence supporter Tracee Hutchison later included Gil and me in a celebrity rock 'n' roll cookbook to raise funds for the Mirabel Foundation to support the children of drug addicts.

Tracee, here is my confession: we did not actually cook the mouth-watering Timorese fish dish in the photo we sent you. It was the work of Gil's lovely wife Linda. We just appeared in the photo standing next to it.

I thought the best two recipes in the book were offerings by Sydney band Mental As Anything, and the late Ian Rilen of X that each captured the reality of rock 'n' roll life on the road.

The Mentals' Savory Jug dish used one of the electric jugs that are found in most Australian motel rooms plus one egg, a slice of salami and two pieces of bread. Inspired.

Rilen, who wrote the Rose Tattoo song Bad Boy for Love and made Keith Richards seem like one of the Young Talent Team, offered his favourite breakfast recipe … a bottle of Tia Maria and a packet of Coco Pops.

Gil and I had decided early in the piece that music would be a great tool for our needs so The Dili Allstars were born from a combination of The Dockers and his reggae outfit The Natural Mystics, which included Zeca Mesquita, Paulo Almeida and Nelito Riberio.

Also in the Allstars' floating roster were the Araujo family, who were once dubbed 'the Von Trapps of East Timor', as they resembled the singing siblings of *The Sound Of Music*.

There were Fatima, Carla, Ines, Amilka, Altino, Carmen, and Conchita. Tragically, we lost Altino early, struck down by cancer.

Walking on stage for a show soon after his death I found a note he had slipped into my pocket which read, 'The Dili Allstars are important, Paulie, do me proud.'

From then on, I gave 110 per cent to every performance.

My new bandmates' passion for East Timorese independence rubbed off on me, even though I honestly thought it was very unlikely ever to happen.

Singer Paulo Almeida had lost his dad on the same day Gil lost his father and I lost my brother. A fantastic singer, he went on to form successful world music act Sol Nation. Bass player Nelito Riberio from Maliana, near the border with West Timor, was easily the best musician in the combo.

A weird thing happened one day when we were touring Timor-Leste. I headed downstairs in the hotel for a mid-morning coffee and there sitting at one table were seven guys. I did a double take because they all looked so much alike. Not similar, but exactly the same.

It was Nelito sitting with cousins, brothers and nephews who had all come in from Maliana to meet him. Nelito had been my friend for years, but I could not for the life of me figure out which one he was, until he spoke up to introduce me to his mob.

Percussionist Zeca Mesquita is part of the chieftain's family from his home village Ramashu and one of the funniest, most loveable guys I've ever met. He plays mean world music percussion and is a leading exponent of Timorese traditional dance. We later performed as a duo at many schools around Victoria from 2017 to 2020, talking about Timor-Leste, and sharing some of its culture through his drumming workshop. The best line up of the Dili Allstars was complete when master drummer, keen surfer and funny fella Mark Grunden joined the outfit.

Bandmate Fatima (who married Paulo) would later star in the movie, *Answered By Fire*, while her sister Ines played a nun in the Australian stage play *Tour of Duty*, which told the story of Australian World War II commandos in East Timor.

One of the first gigs I did with The Dili Allstars was on the back of a truck driving down Brunswick Street, Fitzroy, as part of the Melbourne Fringe Festival. People stared because we were towing a cage with two children locked inside, to show what was happening in East Timor.

Our first recording project was a cover of Rose Tattoo's song 'We Can't Be Beaten' in Tetum (the most widely-spoken Timorese native language), assisted by Rachel Kerr from Triple J and Melbourne musician and activist David Bridie.

Gil and I went on to compile four benefit albums for East Timor over the next decade, with the help of Louise Byrne, a dental nurse by trade, but the best political activist I have ever met. Louise never allowed a setback to stop a project and didn't tolerate wankers. She got things done.

Our compilation albums featured top-flight Australian and international bands who all agreed to donate songs when they learned that East Timorese charities would benefit. The albums raised money, but more importantly, they raised the profile of the independence struggle and kept it in the news.

The first album was *All in the Family* (1994), which raised money for a trust we set up with Melbourne anthropologist and East Timor activist Patsy Thatcher, the Oan Kiak (Small Child) Scholarship Fund which has now supported almost 2500 orphans.

It featured songs by Midnight Oil, Frente!, Crowded House and others, including Timorese musicians Mariano Abrantes and Agio Pereira. Proceeds were administered by Bishop Carlos Belo of Dili and Bishop Hilton Deakin of Melbourne.

For a media stunt to launch the CD, we had Bishop Deakin arrive by helicopter at a small park behind the Fitzroy swimming pool. He then led Timorese elder, dancer and musician Mariano Abrantes on a Timor pony along Brunswick Street to the Portuguese consulate based above a Portuguese restaurant in the entertainment strip.

The next album, *Love from a Short Distance* (1996) boasted a track donated by Irish super group U2, as well as songs by Silverchair, Billy Bragg, Christine Anu and the Painters & Dockers.

The 16-track CD *Hau Abut (I Am Woman)* in 2008 featured a version of Helen Reddy's feminist anthem in Tetum and songs by other leading Australian female performers including Vika and Linda Bull, Rebecca Barnard, Lizzie Cavanagh, Laura Antoni-Wing, Monique Brumby, Kerrianne Cox, Kerri Simpson, Kavisha Mazzella, Jenny Pineapple's Black Velvet and The Sparnets. Money from this CD went to a clinic in Dili run by popular medic Dr Dan Murphy to support malnourished children, maternal and infant health and the treatment of HIV, tuberculosis and leprosy. We got little if any support from national youth radio network Triple J for this album, but were pleased to get valuable airtime from broadcaster Eddie McGuire on his Triple M radio show.

Lastly there was *Liberdade: Viva East Timor*, a compilation released on Mushroom Records in 2000 featuring Crowded House, Yothu Yindi and others. In a major coup for the project the disbanded Midnight Oil got back together for us to write a song called 'Say Your Prayers'.

A video to promote the album featured The Dili Allstars performing the title track at Victoria's Puckapunyal Army base for newly arrived young Timorese refugees.

The album went on to raise $100,000 for Timor-Leste's newly-formed Government.

Apart from releasing benefit albums, Gil and I devoted a lot of time and energy to doing shows together all over the world promoting the independence cause. We ended up performing for communists (we played in Europe as guests of the Portuguese Communist Party), for capitalists (we performed at a leadership breakfast at the National Australia Bank), for Jesuits (we appeared at the religious order's school in Timor-Leste and many events for Jesuit Social Services) and even for anarchists (we played an event in an old shed under a railway line to raise money for East Timor that was organised by the Sydney Anarchist Collective).

Our activities took us to Brazil, where we performed as an acoustic duo after the screening of the movie *Balibo* at the Sao Paulo International Film Festival.

Gil and I were once even auctioned off at a fundraiser where the winner paid $2000 to have dinner with us and hear our stories.

At one point they were throwing eggs at us. Now people were paying to dine with us.

21

BONO COMES TO THE PARTY
(1995)

The *Love From A Short Distance* CD happened as a direct result of my being deported by armed Indonesian police from Bali airport and a chance meeting with a flamboyant Irishman.

It all started in November 1995, when a bunch of activists, including me, were invited to sneak into Dili to light candles at the Santa Cruz cemetery where an infamous massacre of independence supporters had taken place in 1991.

Video footage of the massacre that was aired around the world had been shot by the late film-maker and great activist Max Stahl. I first met Max at Leo's Spaghetti Bar in St Kilda some time after the massacre when he wanted my advice on what to do with the footage.

The aim of our 1995 subterfuge was to remind the world that Indonesia still occupied the country and its military was still killing people. The plan was to sneak in by the back door, flying to Indonesia's second-biggest city, Surabaya on East Java, and then travelling to Bali before taking a domestic flight into Dili.

It all made sense on paper, but our unconventional travel party stood out a little at Bali airport. You had a Japanese Catholic Bishop and Irish Senator David Norris, one of the world's first openly gay politicians (and an outspoken expert on writer James Joyce), militant Australian Indigenous poet Lionel Fogarty, two female Green politicians from Germany, a couple of black African activists and me.

Not your average Bali holiday crowd.

After hiding out for a time in mainland Indonesia, we flew into Bali and joined the line of passengers heading to Dili. A customs official walked past, did a double take and demanded to know who we were.

Following instructions we had agreed on beforehand, we revealed our identity and were immediately deported to Singapore. As we flew out of Bali, Senator Norris, an impish troublemaker in his campaigns for civil rights; handed me a note and said, 'A friend in Ireland told me to use this if it would help with the struggle.'

I took his letter and thanked him but thought to myself, 'Oh great, another bloody drunken Paddy poet jotting down something on a beer coaster.'

The author in question turned out to be rock megastar Bono from U2.

'Yep, I think we should be able to use it,' I muttered, realising what gold he had just given me.

Bono's poem 'Love From a Short Distance' read:

There is no silence deep enough
No black out dark enough
No corruption thick enough
No business deal big enough
No politicians bent enough
No heart hollow enough
No grave wide enough
To bury your story
And keep it from us.

Love Bono, 12 November 1995.

It was heartfelt and emotional.

Now how could we milk it for all it was worth?

I had a brain wave. Before going our separate ways, I got David Norris to read Bono's poem out loud and I recorded it on a small cassette recorder. Arriving back in Australia I enlisted Daylesford-based electronic music wiz David Thrussell to create a song around my recording. He added some beats and loops to Norris' reading of the poem, and you ripper, we had a song.

I then rather cheekily released a press statement proclaiming Bono had written an exclusive track for East Timor to be issued on the new compilation album *Love From a Short Distance*.

It was easy to get other bands involved when they realised they would be joining Bono on the album. I thought myself very clever indeed, until the night before the album's official launch. While dozing off I heard my fax machine start up and begin printing a mountain of material.

It was a legal warning from a New York law firm threatening to sue me if Bono's name was mentioned in any way on our CD release. These guys were not mucking around. I was in deep shit again because I had already sent preview copies to the media.

There was nothing left to do but contact U2's office in Dublin and plead with the band and their management for the go-ahead. Thank God they relented and gave us permission to release the album with the Bono song included.

I got to meet Bono in February 1998 with Gil's sister Teresa, backstage at Waverley Park in outer Melbourne, during U2's PopMart world tour. He didn't seem too impressed to meet the guy behind the "exclusive" Bono song.

Dressed in casual clothes and accompanied by supermodel Helena Christensen, his opening comment to me was, 'Not bloody East Timor again. I am sick of hearing about the place. Michael Hutchence never stopped talking about it.'

The INXS frontman Hutchence had died in bizarre circumstances just three months earlier and his life story was cast as one of philandering and drugs. I wished the world had known the other side of the man and in 2014 I got it off my chest in a piece for the *Sunday Herald Sun* headlined: 'How Michael fought the good fight for East Timor', which recounted his secret support for the cause.

'I saw a different side of the singer described by Bob Geldof, the former husband of Hutchence's partner, Paula Yates, as a "Neo-junkie philanderer", and have always wanted to tell people about the man I knew,' I wrote.

'Yes, Michael had a hedonistic side, but he was also what I'd call a shy political activist. In 1994 my band, the Painters & Dockers, were set to launch a benefit album for East Timor, *All In The Family*, at a venue in Sydney, but we were stuck in Melbourne. Hutchence paid for us to fly to Sydney to play at the launch but refused any acknowledgment.

'In fact, Michael's concerns for peace in the former Portuguese colony date back even further, to the struggles of the early 1980s. He even used an East Timor protest poster as a prop when he starred in the 1986 cult punk film *Dogs in Space*.

'When interviewed in the 1980s about his political affiliations, Hutchence said, "I vote Labor in Australia. As far as my views go, everyone should support Amnesty International. A little-known fact is that East Timor needs all the help they can get. They've been overrun by the Indonesians".'

The article recounted that Bono had told me Michael met José Ramos-Horta by chance in an airport lounge and they had talked for hours about his country's problems.

The charismatic Ramos-Horta had a similar impact on Norwegian pop star Morten Harket of the band A-Ha, who were famous for their worldwide hit 'Take On Me'. Morten was equally inspired to support East Timor after running into Ramos-Horta in yet another international airport lounge.

Backstage at U2's show, Bono confirmed he had, in turn, been converted to the cause by Hutchence, resulting in the poem he gave to David Norris.

Bono almost gave Teresa Santos a heart attack when he dedicated a song to her during U2's performance that night.

A side note: I couldn't get over Bono's size. He's such a little fellow and he dressed as we Australians would say 'like a dag'.

What is it about short rock stars?

To blatantly drop a few more names, the other tiny stars I've interviewed include Tina Turner, George Harrison, David Bowie, Priscilla Presley and Grace Jones. Giants in the music world but short-arses in real life.

22

PUTTING THE NOBEL LAUREATE INTO *RECOVERY*
(1996)

Becoming further involved in the independence campaign, I got to meet many leaders of the struggle, including activist José Ramos-Horta, who later became President. On his first visits to Melbourne he campaigned tirelessly in his then trademark suit and bow tie.

These were not exactly glory days and he slept rough many nights on a sympathiser's couch in Melbourne with his battered old suitcase nearby. I thought him a bit touched in the head, to be honest. I think the feeling was mutual.

But I will never forget his tears as he told me he had tried to convince my brother and the other journalists not to travel to Balibo in October 1975 because an invasion was imminent.

'They just wouldn't listen,' he said quietly.

Even in the early 1980s when the cause seemed hopeless, Ramos-Horta was convinced East Timor would one day get its independence.

Given the huge Indonesian military presence in the country, where they were supplied with weapons and training by the United States, Britain and Australia, victory seemed highly unlikely. But Ramos-

Horta, a former journalist and law graduate, wouldn't hear of it. In exile after the 1975 invasion, he was Fretilin's Permanent Representative to the UN for a decade. After many years of campaigning he shared the 1996 Nobel Peace Prize with Bishop Belo, who had worked with us on the Oan Kiak scholarship.

The Nobel helped Ramos-Horta spread the word on independence. Weeks after accepting the prize he attended a meeting of hardcore socialist politicians in Mozambique, then came to Melbourne.

The only problem was that no one had organised any publicity for him. I was asked to help but he arrived on a Saturday morning when all the local media were focussed on a big Aussie Rules game.

I hit the phone to call on some favours from media mates, but could not do much on such short notice. Bizarrely, the only place I could get him some coverage was on rock music show *Recovery* hosted by the zany Dylan Lewis with his nose rings and whacky haircut. Thank God the show's producer Bruce Kane agreed to give Ramos-Horta a spot. I was a little worried though because I thought he may be ill-prepared for the light-hearted music show.

I shouldn't have worried. In fact, at the end of his appearance I thought this guy could be president one day.

Ramos-Horta hit the live set with ease and joked with Lewis about everything from football to music and art. The Nobel laureate then talked about his beloved country, the wrongs it had suffered and its wish to be independent.

His relentless campaigning was one of the reasons why the Indonesians started to refer to East Timor as 'the pebble in the boot'—that annoying little thing you could never quite get rid of.

Few Australians had heard of, let alone cared about this little nation to the north, or realised the oppression it had suffered with two centuries of Portuguese exploitation and neglect being followed by Indonesia's brutal 1975 invasion.

Ramos-Horta and I became friends. A noted ladies' man, he always asked after my two sisters. He still does.

His ability to see the bigger picture augured well for East Timor's future. Ramos-Horta was the man who could talk to people from all walks of life.

Despite being founders of the majority Fretilin party, he and colleague Xanana Gusmão left the organisation because they dreaded the thought of a one-party state.

Ramos-Horta's greatest contribution to Timorese liberation was probably in maintaining calm when pro-Indonesian militias attacked independence supporters after the 1999 referendum had backed independence. If Fretilin guerrillas had retaliated, another civil war could have erupted, allowing Jakarta to justify a continued occupation. It was a great example of his diplomatic skills and strategic thinking.

When Timor-Leste was finally recognised internationally as an independent nation in 2002, Ramos-Horta became its first foreign minister and after a stint as prime minister he replaced Xanana as President in 2007. In 2022 he was again voted in as President.

Leading the poorest country in South-East Asia, he and Xanana went out of their way to appease their huge neighbour, Indonesia. Realistically, they had to.

The thing that truly sold me on José's generous spirit was that he took time out of the bustle of forming a new nation to write a note for Dad's funeral in 2002.

Five years later I was downright shocked when the President of Timor-Leste rang me at the Austin Hospital saying he had heard about my liver problem and urging me to stay positive and get back up to his country soon. When an ABC journalist asked him to comment on my surviving a liver transplant, he grinned. 'Heaven didn't want him and Hell wouldn't let him in,' said His Excellency the President.

23

KYLIE: MY TIMOR HELL
(1999)

It was after we recorded the song 'Liberdade' that the Dili Allstars got the call from leading Australian music promoter and band manager Glenn Wheatley about taking part in a truly unique event.

I had known Wheatley, the bass player in pioneering Australian 1960s band The Masters Apprentices, for some time through my journalism as he had managed 1980s act Australian Crawl and set up radio station EON FM.

He once asked me to come and have a coffee with his latest singing star, who he had met through his role as a director of AFL team the Sydney Swans. Apparently this young wannabe had wrapped a cassette of some of her original material in red and white ribbons (the Swans' club colours) and had managed to get it through to him. He spent a lot of time and money preparing his young charge, who I could tell at first meeting was chomping at the bit for her chance at pop stardom.

I asked the young ponytailed lass what her name was.

'Delta Goodrem,' she replied.

She lived up to the potential Wheatley saw in her by becoming one of Australia's biggest acts.

In late 1999, Wheatley invited The Dili Allstars to join a huge troupe of entertainers going to East Timor in the wake of the independence referendum to play a Christmas show for Australian and New Zealand peacekeeping troops. It was to be held soon after the Indonesian forces had withdrawn from a still-smouldering Dili.

The pro-Indonesian militia, sore losers in the independence referendum, had gone out of their way to leave the capital destitute and had taken everything not tied down, including light bulbs and toilet roll holders. They even blocked the drains of Dili and unlocked crocodile viewing pens so these deadly and enormous reptiles could roam the streets. They had a saying for the "ungrateful" Timorese they left behind: 'Let them eat rocks'. This was written in graffiti all over Dili.

The atmosphere in the town was tense and security tight.

Others on the bill included comic duo Roy and HG, country stars James Blundell and Gina Jeffreys, veteran rocker Doc Neeson of The Angels and Australia's No. 1 entertainer John Farnham. The highlight of the bill, however, was singing budgie and international superstar Kylie Minogue

When we arrived in Dili, I noticed an unusual poster everywhere and assumed it was that of an exalted Timorese hero. On closer inspection the poster amazed me. It was in fact a picture of reggae great Bob Marley.

'Of course it is Bob. He is the father of the revolution,' Gil said, explaining that Marley's revolutionary songs had inspired local resistance fighters, many of whom sported the trademark dreadlocks of the reggae scene.

While most of the VIPs involved in the concert stayed in their own comfortable accommodation, The Dili Allstars slept beside the Australian troops on rough army cots. For breakfast, lunch and dinner we would join the soldiers in the line for a feed, and at nights we joined the communal line-up for our stint in the showers.

Organisers were annoyed when members of The Dili Allstars kept breaking out of the compound to visit family. Could you blame them after more than two decades exiled from their homeland?

Finally, it was concert time and The Dili Allstars kicked off the event. A highlight of the concert was the performance by former Army sergeant (the now late) Doc Neeson, who really pulled one out of the bag.

The guy had played a show up near the border area the previous day and was so sunburnt it was unbelievable. You could feel the heat coming off him from metres away.

The bright red Doc needed vitamin shots before going on stage and I seriously doubted he would make it through the show, but the old hand powered his way through some of his classic hits.

Kylie was terrific too, putting on a fine version of 'Santa's Little Helper', dressed in a sexy Santa outfit.

We later found out she had signed an exclusive deal with *New Idea* magazine to cover her involvement in the event. The fact is Kylie flew in, stayed in an air-conditioned room, did the show and flew out. Ridiculously, the cover of the next edition of *New Idea* splashed with, 'Kylie: My Timor Hell'. Hardly, but at least she was there.

Kylie was happy to pose for photos with members of The Dili Allstars and later gave us a glowing reference when we released our 'best of' album on the ABC Music label. On subsequent Australian tours she allowed young fans from Timor-Leste to visit her backstage.

Another great group on the concert bill was Melbourne trio The Living End. The rockabilly punks make it look easy, but they put in long and hard hours rehearsing their act.

During some downtime, The Dili Allstars and The Living End made our way to the big statue of Jesus on a hill overlooking Dili. We bonded and later the trio would let The Dili Allstars perform a Living End song, 'Revolution Regained', in Tetum and included it as the B-side on a Living End single. This was fantastic exposure for East Timor in the mainstream musical community.

The troops simply loved John Farnham, who had been enjoying mega success with his solo album *Whispering Jack*. The great thing about Farnham is that he is the same person offstage as on it. From the heart, funny, and fair dinkum.

After persistent demands from the troops, Farnham delighted them by reluctantly performing his first ever hit single 'Sadie The Cleaning Lady'.

After the concert, all the entertainers were invited to a special barbecue hosted in our honour by General Peter Cosgrove, later to be Australia's Governor-General. He immediately impressed me by coming over to greet The Dili Allstars, particularly our Timorese members.

Other VIPs, including Kylie and Farnham, started hovering about but he did not walk off until he had met each and every one of our band. Over a beer later I asked him whether he had enjoyed the event. He said he loved it, but pointed out that he was sitting next to Bishop Belo during the concert when Neeson sang the Angels' sing-along hit 'Am I Ever Going To See Your Face Again?' with the troops screaming back the famous response, 'No way, get fucked, fuck off'.

General Cosgrove said the Bishop had leaned in and asked, 'What is that they are singing, General?' And Cosgrove said he muttered something about an old Australian saying.

I am no gung-ho nationalist, but I was proud and impressed by the women and men of the Australian armed forces who served in East Timor. I saw no racist put-downs, no taking advantage of the local women, no drug use, and no nonsense shown by them towards the locals.

A common sight was an Australian digger walking down the road holding the hand of a young Timorese child. Many of these serving men and women returned to Timor-Leste after their tour to help with aid projects.

24

SINGING WITH THE PRESIDENT
(1999)

During the long Indonesian occupation, resistance leader Xanana Gusmão took on an almost mythical status with his people.

Born in 1946 and of Portuguese-Timorese heritage, he became involved in the Fretilin liberation movement in the early 1970s, and was its press secretary in late 1975. In the years that followed, the charismatic rebel swapped his typewriter for a gun and led the armed resistance.

Using his experience in media management, he was instrumental in alerting the world to the massacre at Santa Cruz in 1991, giving many interviews to international news networks. Widely seen as the face of the rebellion, he became a prime target of the Indonesian authorities, whose security forces eventually trapped him in a house on the outskirts of Dili in 1993.

Xanana spent six hard years in a maximum-security unit in a Jakarta prison. But his spirit could not be broken, just like the inspirational South African leader Nelson Mandela, with whom he later became firm friends.

It was while he was in prison that he started a relationship with his eventual wife, the Australian former ballet dancer, Kirsty Sword, who visited him as an aid worker. The Indonesian authorities did not know that she was also smuggling in messages from his supporters.

Melbourne activists got a message through, asking Xanana if there was anything we could get him to help cope with his jail time. His answer was a new bed and a punching bag, both of which we delivered.

I knew Kirsty as a fellow activist and cheekily introduced her as one of The Dili Allstars girlfriends to get her a backstage pass to the peacekeepers show we played in Dili in 1999.

Kirsty's account of East Timor's struggle and her relationship with Xanana were highlighted in her book *A Woman of Independence*. She has since set up the much acclaimed Alola Foundation which helps Timorese women in need, and encourages them to enter politics and form their own businesses.

Mounting international pressure led the Indonesian Government to finally release Xanana in 1999. He was overwhelmed with the attention he received when he was released from solitary confinement. Xanana said at the time he would be much happier being a professional soccer goalkeeper or painter and poet, rather than the Father of the Nation.

There was of course a great fanfare when he toured Australia for the first time in October of that year. The Dili Allstars were asked to play at his Melbourne appearance, a huge honour.

The only problem was that I was due to work at the *Sunday Herald Sun* that day. I rang the boss that morning to say I was crook and 'it must have been the fish I had last night.' After so many years campaigning for independence, I just couldn't miss Xanana's long-awaited appearance.

He received a pop-star welcome at the Rod Laver Arena. After he made an impassioned speech about freeing his country, The Dili Allstars were invited on stage and began singing.

Then it got surreal. Carla Araujo, a sister of Dili Allstars Fatima and Ines, suddenly dragged Xanana up to the microphone to sing with the band. She then disappeared, leaving me and the future President to do a duet. A picture of the two of us singing 'Liberade' appeared the next day on the front page of *The Age*. I only found out about the picture when I arrived at work and the chief of staff flung the paper at me.

'Still crook today, Paulie?'

Oops! Luckily, everyone knew what the occasion had meant to me and I got off with a warning.

'Maybe stay off the front of *The Age* when you are pretending to be sick,' the Chief of Staff muttered.

25

TWO PIGS AND NOT THREE
(2000)

I was lucky that my boss Alan Howe, the editor of the *Sunday Herald Sun*, was incredibly supportive of my East Timor endeavours. This was mainly due to the fact that his wife, Carmel Egan, did a stint in East Timor reporting on the aftermath of the Indonesians' bloody withdrawal in 1999. I must say, he was one of the few News Corporation editors I worked with who used the paper's power in a positive way.

In September 2000, when the country was still recovering from the militia violence, we organised an emergency food relief campaign. Howe called on some of his rural manufacturing mates from the Shepparton area in northern Victoria who donated a shipping container full of powdered milk and canned food. A few more of his phone calls ensured it was all quickly shipped to Dili. I was given the job of meeting the container when it arrived and writing a feel-good piece, so all those who had helped would get some credit.

Alan even agreed to send Gil with me as my interpreter. On that trip, however, I lost Gil at the airport because a long line of Timorese were waiting to talk to him about everything from immigrating to Australia, to medical advice for loved ones.

Luckily for me, another Timorese activist and good mate from Melbourne, Etervina Gronen and her Dutch-born husband Leo were in Dili and offered to help me get the shipping container through customs.

The first problem we ran into was that the wharf in Dili was virtually locked down due to an incredible bottleneck of incoming supplies. We were told it could take a month for our goods to be unloaded. A source warned us that we might not be there when it came off the ship and the donated items could end up being sold on the black market. Desperate for help, we managed to get an appeal through to the future president Xanana Gusmão, who used his influence to have port authorities unload our container immediately.

I suddenly had a couple of days to spare before returning to Australia and Etervina offered to take me to the southern coastal town of Suai. Now Suai is actually not that far from Dili and in Australia the distance would take you less than two hours to drive. But with Timor's mountains and poor roads it was a long day's treacherous journey.

We left Dili in tropical heat but it was freezing when we got to the top of the mountains. The roads had massive potholes and hazardous edges as we snaked our way down steep ravines and long bumpy tracks.

Suai itself was a real eye-opener as it had changed little since the pro-Indonesian militia had left parts of the town in ruins a year earlier. There was a sense of sorrow, dread and tension everywhere. Two days after the independence vote, the militia had gone on a murderous spree in Suai, killing up to 200 locals. A year later, the locals and United Nations peacekeepers were still on edge and it made Dili seem sedate in comparison.

There was no sign of farming activity and very little food. The locals were particularly distressed that the angry losers of the referendum had murdered three priests. Etervina, Leo and I were in Suai to attend a huge religious service to mark the anniversary of the killings.

The night before the memorial service we stayed with a kind

Timorese family in the burnt-out remains of their home. I got a spot sleeping in what was left of the kitchen next to two huge pigs. The women of the house were planning to prepare the pigs the next morning for a feast after the memorial service. I surveyed my sleeping arrangements and got Etervina to interpret, 'Don't forget ladies, when you wake up in the morning there are only two pigs to be slaughtered … not three.'

It's strange how people can laugh even in the darkest times.

The service was attended by dozens of priests, nuns and locals in traditional clothing. It was conducted by Bishop Carlos Belo of Dili and my good mate Bishop Hilton Deakin of Melbourne. I was not the only one to cry during the ceremony.

Hilton Deakin really impressed me that day. To calm international relations, a group of Indonesian soldiers were invited to the ceremony and when they arrived they strutted through the crowd. Some local women cowered in fear as these sniggering soldiers decided to stand next to them. Bishop Hilton spotted this and marched up to the Indonesian soldiers in his full attire of pointy hat, staff and long white robe.

'What are you doing?' he demanded. 'You are scaring these women. Piss off out of here … now.'

The soldiers were so shocked, they quickly backed off.

I thought to myself, 'Now this is my kind of priest, speaking out against injustice and telling it like it is. This guy walks the walk.'

Later in the day a strange thing happened as I headed down an old bush track for a stroll in the back blocks of Suai. I ran smack bang into Julian Hill, the mayor of the City of Port Phillip, encompassing St Kilda, who later became a Federal MP for the Labor Party.

He was there working on a recently-signed sister-city relationship with Suai. Another Timor activist who was voted into the Australian parliament was former SAS soldier Luke Gosling, who went on to represent the Darwin seat of Solomon for Labor. The Dili Allstars worked closely with Luke on a number of projects.

My next trip to Suai was more low-key. The Dili Allstars visited the town in 2001 as part of the stage production *Tour of Duty*. We travelled there on a UN helicopter flying just above the tree tops, much to the band's amusement. The pilots were two Russians who seemed to have been on the vodka earlier that day. Riding in the helicopter was like being in an old Combi van, and Gil and I were startled when a few bits came off in our hands.

This time there was no massive crowd in Suai, just an empty town that was still full of despair. Our audience was a handful of peacekeepers but I was happy enough. This little piggie was still alive.

26

THE MORMONS IN TIMOR-LESTE
(2000)

Mention the word Mormons and most people immediately think of those neatly dressed men, usually in pairs, wearing crisp white shirts and black ties, who diligently harangue people on their front doorsteps.

In recent years the musical comedy *The Book of Mormon* has been a big money-maker with its satirical look at the religion. The last thing I ever expected was to come to respect the Mormons as much as I do now.

When you are fighting an independence campaign and rebuilding a country from scratch, you are grateful for any support. That is why I ended up working in Timor-Leste with the church formally known as the Church of Jesus Christ of Latter-day Saints, and accompanying two church elders on a visit there.

Alan Howe knew a leading News Corporation executive from the United States who was a top-ranking Mormon. He had gone to Alan's home one Sunday for a barbecue and got talking to his wife Carmel, who told him how bleak the situation was for the East Timorese, with women lacking soap and hygiene products, let alone clothes and medical supplies. Malnutrition was a major problem due to the shortage of fresh, healthy food.

The conversation obviously affected the guest as the next day he rang Alan to say that he had contacted his church colleagues and they had offered to help. This led to a shipment of nine containers of food worth close to $300,000, mainly from the church's huge rural property in New South Wales.

I ended up doing an inspection of the farm property with Abel Guterres, my old friend the bus driver who would later become Timor-Leste's ambassador to Australia.

We had to take our hats off to the Mormons. Unlike other religious groups, who seemed to be the 'we will feed you if you sign up to believe in us' types, the Mormons gave freely without trying to push their beliefs onto the local population.

They also agreed that the Catholic Church, which had much better local contacts in East Timor, should distribute their massive donation.

I met two senior American members of the church, public affairs director for the Asia-Pacific region Alan Wakeley, and welfare agent William Bush, in Darwin and we flew to Dili in late December to arrange the emergency food drop.

Once again it was caught up in red tape but Xanana came to the rescue again by helping to get our donations through customs.

'This is a great Christmas present for my people,' he said.

The President-in-waiting asked that the food and other goods be sent to the hardest hit of his people who lived in the enclave of Oecusse, which is basically a bubble within Indonesian West Timor.

'I am particularly grateful for the shovels and mattocks, because while it is good to give hungry people food, it is best to give them tools so they can grow their own crops and become self-sufficient,' he said.

Better still, with their contacts in the US Air Force, the Mormons managed to get the material flown into remote destinations. Hercules aircraft dropped off the nine massive containers full of aid.

When the containers were empty, local families moved into them as a cheap form of housing.

Every time I see a Mormon, I make an effort to say hi and thank them for having such big hearts. They always seem surprised when someone congratulates them rather than hurling abuse their way.

After our mission in Dili, Mr Wakeley, Mr Bush and I celebrated the successful delivery of their goods with a glass of mineral water.

Later that day, when the Mormons left town, I thought it was time to celebrate properly. I went for a few beers in the bar of the Hotel Turismo—poignantly, the hotel that Tony and his mates had left to go to Balibo. Lo and behold, I ran into two old journalist pals from my *Sun News-Pictorial* days, Peter Wilson and Eric Ellis, who had just arrived in town.

Bad Paulie had been hiding for some time, but now he came out to play. We laid waste to the bar's beer supply and ended up having not one, but probably ten drinks too many.

That might explain how we ended up in the middle of Dili Harbour on a Thai cargo ship, in the spa in the crew's quarters. We were given the heave-ho quick smart when a group of Thai sailors found us relaxing uninvited in their private tub.

27

TOUR OF DUTY STAGE SHOW
(2001)

The Dili Allstars took up many unusual offers, one of which was to tour East Timor with the stage production *Tour of Duty*, telling one of the forgotten stories of World War II. It dealt with the decision by Australia and its Allies to invade Dutch Timor (now West Timor) and neutral Portuguese East Timor and set them up as advance bases against the Japanese forces, then sweeping south. Japan had not planned to enter East Timor, but the Allied intervention prompted a Japanese invasion that was disastrous for the Timorese.

Sparrow Force, the unit assembled for the task, included hundreds of Australian commandos such as Paddy Kenneally, a Sydney wharfie who signed up the day after the Japanese bombed Pearl Harbor.

He was a short, hardy seventy-year-old with a crop of white hair when I heard him talk about Australia's wartime debt to its northern neighbour at a pro-Timor event in Sydney on Anzac Day 1986. Intrigued, I approached him afterwards and he invited me to a bar to tell me more.

When we had ordered some beers, Paddy recounted that he and his fellow commandos had been hugely outnumbered by the Japanese and after a series of battles were forced to retreat to the mountains. The situation was so bleak that the Australian Government assumed they had all been killed or captured. In fact, some of the commandos had escaped with the help of East Timorese civilians who risked execution to hide and feed them. Many of their Timorese saviours were boys or young men who they called *criados*, the Portuguese word for assistants.

Emboldened, Australian commander Major Alexander Spence conducted one of the briefest negotiation rounds of the entire war when his Japanese counterpart, Colonel Sadashichi Doi, sent him a surrender demand, which pointed out in great detail the overwhelming odds against the Australians.

Colonel Doi warned that anyone who did not surrender would be executed upon capture but the Bundaberg-born Major Spence, who had been a journalist before the war, honed his own negotiating position to just four words.

'Surrender? Surrender be fucked!'

Paddy told me that the beleaguered commandos would not have lasted a week without the help of the *criados* but they fought on and managed to capture enough equipment to build a radio and send word back to Australia that they were alive. A destroyer was eventually sent to rescue his unit but when they reached their pick-up spot on the southern coast, the order was given that 'whites only' were to come onboard.

White Portuguese were accepted for evacuation, but the *criados* were left on the beach. Many to be killed by Japanese troops. It was a betrayal that would haunt Paddy and his colleagues for decades.

Another survivor, Lieutenant Archie Campbell, wrote in his diary that 'it tore your innards out to know that lads (the *criados*) who had been your existence were going to be dropped like hot cakes.'

It is a little-known fact that more East Timorese were killed during World War II than Londoners in the Blitz. Many died in Allied bombing raids and despite being civilians in a supposedly neutral country, the local population suffered terribly at the hands of the Japanese for helping the Allies.

More than 15,000 crack Japanese troops were bogged down in Timor, and Paddy was convinced that if Japan had been able to redeploy them to its New Guinea campaign, the Kokoda battles may have ended in the fall of Port Moresby.

Paddy and other Sparrow Force survivors, such as his mate Jack Levi, were among the most committed supporters of East Timor I ever met, and if I had not heard his story in the bar that afternoon I would probably never have become as heavily involved in the independence campaign as I did.

Over the course of a few hours, this nuggety ex-digger easily outdrank me. But when he spoke about his time in East Timor with Sparrow Force's 2/2nd Independent Company, he openly wept. We were in a pub packed with ex-servicemen so I found it awkward.

He said he would 'never ever' forgive himself for abandoning his nineteen-year-old *criado*, Patricio.

'Before I knew what was happening, we were on the ship pulling off from the shore, and we could see our Timorese mates waiting there on the beach,' Paddy said. 'We owe the East Timorese.'

Exactly nineteen years later, Paddy managed to repay a small part of that debt.

With the Australian Government determined to short-change Timor-Leste, the poorest country in South-East Asia, in their 2005 negotiations over Timor Sea oil, Kenneally and five other veterans appeared in national TV ads on the eve of Anzac Day. Demanding a fair go for Timor-Leste, Paddy had a brilliantly targeted message for John Howard, a Prime Minister who loved to drape himself in the national flag and wartime nostalgia.

'I'd rather that you did not come to my Anzac Day parade,' Paddy said to the camera.

Howard's Government capitulated the next day, offering the Timorese a fifty per cent share of revenues from the contested Greater Sunrise field.

We now know that the Australian Government had been unscrupulous enough to use its intelligence services to spy on the Timorese negotiators to gain an unfair advantage in the talks.

The last time I saw Paddy he was back in Dili, which he continued to visit despite his advancing years in his efforts to remind people about Australia's debt to the Timorese. He and his mates from 2/2nd Independent Company had built a war memorial high in the hills overlooking Dili, and in 2008 he spent his last Anzac Day, at the age of ninety-two, attending a service there.

I have often visited the memorial, a quiet spot with a wading pool and an evocative photo exhibition.

The fate of the *criados* also weighed on the mind of Melbourne playwright Graham Pitt, who wrote the play *Tour of Duty*. It was centred on a *criado* played by Dili Allstars percussionist Zeca Mesquita and a nun played by bandmate Ines Araujo. The production was directed by stage veteran William Gluth and featured another long-time actor Terry Kenwrick. It was the first time most of us in The Dili Allstars had ever performed in a theatrical production.

I was very keen, but my aspirations for an acting career died at the first audition. Director Gluth got us all to stand in a line and he slowly moved along asking each of us to do a brief reading.

To each Timorese cast member he said, 'From you I want more.'

Standing in front of me he didn't pull his punches. 'From you I want less—a lot less.'

My chief role in the production was banging two rocks together for background noise. And my God, those rocks were banged together with style and panache. It was not quite the rock career I had dreamed of but I squeezed my eyes tight with the concentration of a concert violinist and strove for acoustic clarity and crisp syncopation.

One review said the highlight of the entire production was 'the evocative banging together of rocks backstage by a gifted artist who sadly remained unnamed and out of sight'. Well, not really, but I did give my all to my assigned role.

The show had its official opening in Dili in a burnt-out TV studio. The opening-night audience included members of the Australian peacekeeping forces, and many of these tough soldiers were openly in tears by the production's end.

The highlight of the night was when some of the original *criados* rose from their seats in the audience after the final curtain and saluted the cast. The production was staged in Dili several more times, then in Suai before eventually being performed in Melbourne's Gasworks Theatre complex before an audience that included Xanana Gusmão and Victorian Arts Minister, Mary Delahunty.

Lead actor Zeca told me later that his grandfather had been a *criado*, one of these real-life heroes. He said his family had ended up in Australia because a Sparrow Force officer had vouched for them and pressured the Government to accept them as refugees.

The two stars, Zeca and Ines, along with Gil Santos and Ines' sister Fatima Almeida, were later invited to appear in the acclaimed ABC/Canadian movie *Answered by Fire*, starring Australian actor David Wenham. The Dili Allstars contributed songs to the movie's soundtrack. The lead Timorese actor was passionate activist Alex Tilman, now a senior official in the Timor-Leste Government. The most moving performance came from my close friend Fatima, who had to take part in a humiliating rape scene. Shy at first about performing such a task in front of an unknown film crew, she insisted she would do it because she wanted people to know the fate that befell many Timorese women.

Fatima and her family were long-time supporters of a free Timor-Leste. Her father Felisberto Araujo acted in the movie and did a great job. When The Dili Allstars toured Timor-Leste for the first time, he took me aside at the airport and asked me man to man to 'look after my little girl'.

A major turning point for me, which increased my efforts working for Timor-Leste's independence, was meeting a group of Darwin-based political activists led by Vaughan Williams, an outreach worker with homeless First Nations people. This mob didn't muck around.

When the US Navy failed to send its Darwin-based forces to Dili to restore peace when the militia went on the rampage, Vaughan marched along Darwin pier throwing chicken carcasses onto the decks of the US ships. That certainly got the Americans' attention.

On another occasion Vaughan showed me some photos that had been smuggled out of Timor-Leste of Indonesian special forces troops with some local women. These were horrific torture-porn photos. Someone tried to tell me the Timorese had faked the photos for propaganda purposes. This was an obvious lie. No matter how strong their patriotism, the women in these horrific images could never have faked the pain and fear on their faces. The photos actually gave me nightmares and steeled my resolve.

Vaughan talked me into doing my first ever press conference as a brother of one of the Balibo Five when I was twenty-three. On 10 July 1984 I read out the following statement to half a dozen reporters in the office of Labor Senator Ted Robertson in downtown Darwin.

'All five journalists killed at Balibo, Timor-Leste, in October 1975, were murdered with knives after being captured alive. This I have learnt since coming to Darwin, a city close to East Timor, with many Timorese living here. It also harbours the Defence Signals Directorate radio base.

'It is incredible to come here and know that the secrets of my brother's death were available but were withheld from the families. If only the principles of freedom of information were applied. I am told the base monitored the radio messages of the invading Indonesian forces, and the instruction to kill the five journalists was recorded.

'Thus it was immaterial to the soldiers that they identified themselves as Australian journalists. After some bullying, they were cut down like pigs. The last man, a big man, was allegedly used as target practice for the knife-wielding soldiers. (Tony was the tallest of the group).

'I call on Foreign Minister Bill Hayden to make available all knowledge gained through defence, intelligence and diplomatic channels, as to the manner and reason for my brother's death and of his colleagues. I further call on ALP delegates at the national conference not to let my brother to have died in vain.

'Please stand firm for some honesty and justice over East Timor, without which Australia can never hope to establish good relations with Indonesia.'

28

BIRTH OF A NATION INDEPENDENCE CONCERT
(2002)

After years of struggle, Timor-Leste formally gained its independence on 20 May 2002. I found out to my horror, though, that no Australian act would be taking part in the huge celebratory concert planned for Dili. I contacted the Department of Foreign Affairs and Trade, suggesting it would be a good idea if our country was represented.

Thanks to DFAT official Anne Craig, we got the funds to join the show.

The Dili Allstars became Australia's official representatives at the event, where Indonesian President B.J. Habibie officially handed the country over to president-in-waiting Xanana Gusmão.

We flew into Timor-Leste with Fretilin leader Mari Alkatiri, who was to be the new country's Prime Minister. He looked bewildered as we greeted him on the plane with shouts of 'Comrade' and told him who we were.

Dili was full of visitors, so the band stayed with Gil's mum, Berta, sleeping in one-man tents in her front yard.

Our performance that night was just terrific because after years of campaigning for independence, we were finally cutting loose in a free Timor-Leste. The crowd exploded as we launched into 'Liberdade'.

One of the few times I have seen Gil fly off the handle was backstage after our appearance. The Portuguese, former colonial masters, had constructed an exclusive VIP section for their own visiting musicians, full of top-notch drinks and food. Entry was only available for the Portuguese, and they made it clear they would not be sharing. When Gil saw that no locals were allowed in, my always-composed bandmate lost it and confronted security guards, warning them that if the Timorese were not admitted there would be a major incident.

'We have fought for our independence for decades, there is no way we are not coming in,' bristled Gil. The Timorese and their Aussie guests were allowed in and we hit the goodies with gusto.

After the concert there was a massive fireworks display and Dili buzzed with international visitors and people from the rural districts. Beds were scarce. Luckily for me, journalist mate Eric Ellis was in town covering the event and he let me sleep on the floor in his hotel. He even managed to rustle up some sausage rolls for breakfast the next day. Pure heaven.

Former US President Bill Clinton flew in as a special guest and was due to hold a press conference at the airport. I went along with Eric. We stood with the international media waiting for the President when suddenly I looked around and found I had lost my friend.

President Clinton arrived and started his press conference.

'Where the hell did Eric go?'

Then I noticed, standing alongside Clinton on the stage among the US Secret Service agents, was Eric, winking at me. That was bent.

The journalists were ready to give Clinton grief as his reputation had not recovered from revelations of his sexual relationship with White House intern Monica Lewinsky.

What followed from Clinton was one of the most impassioned speeches I had ever heard. The room was transfixed by his every word, advocating international support for Timor-Leste. By the end of the press conference, I was on my chair applauding wildly like most in the room. You could see why this guy had been the most powerful man in the world, and how Monica had been smitten.

29

NOTHING TASTES BETTER THAN THE NEIGHBOUR'S CHICKEN
(2003)

Because of The Dili Allstars' long involvement with the independence struggle, we were invited by the Portuguese Communist Party to tour the country in 2003.

Many Timorese refugees had fled there after Indonesia's invasion. It was straight from the bush in East Timor to urban living in high-rise buildings in Europe for many of them.

The highlight of our tour was playing at the Avante! Festival in Lisbon, which is like a Big Day Out festival for communists, attended by left-leaning organisations from around the world. I was particularly taken by one banner at the festival that read, 'Vote 1 FUCCA'. (Say it out loud!)

Portugal does not have a rock 'n' roll tradition as such because its music scene is dominated by the local fado style, a combination of acoustic guitar and melancholic singing. They did not know what to make of us, nor us of them.

We hit the stage at the Avante! Festival and played the same kind of set we would have delivered at the Esplanade Hotel in St Kilda:

loud and raucous. The locals stood confused for the first few songs but gradually warmed to us. They really have a way with words in Portugal and one journalist blew us away by describing us in his review as 'the stars who fell from heaven'.

The Portuguese communists were impressed by our history of campaigning for an independent Timor-Leste and especially with how we had used music for the cause. I explained to them that the band's efforts owed much to leading Australian sympathiser Harold Mitchell, who had paid for our first CD release. The officials asked us to pass on their fraternal greetings to 'Comrade Harold'.

A multi-millionaire advertising guru, Harold laughed his head off when I told him.

'The only other person to call me comrade was Gough Whitlam,' he chuckled.

We performed a number of other shows in Portugal, including one at a prestigious venue in the coastal city of Sintra and another for the Australian Embassy at an open-air gig in Lisbon. Before we played in Sintra, we somehow adopted a young German punk girl who told us she lived 'on the streets of the cities of Europe'. We were a nice bunch of chaps deep down, so we fed her and let her tag along with us.

After the Sintra show, we were invited to an upmarket reception with the local mayor and other dignitaries. We stood there with the locals enjoying champagne and canapés, but this taste of the high life did not last long because our young German friend freaked out the locals by producing her pink pet rat and letting it run around the room.

We were later invited to the Australian Ambassador's residence in Lisbon for a barbecue and considering the last Australian performer of note to dine there was Dame Joan Sutherland, we felt rather pleased with ourselves. Our Timorese friends couldn't believe that the Ambassador cooked our barbecue himself.

For some reason (probably the strong effects of the local red wine), guitarist Colin Badger decided to take nude photos of himself all through the plush Embassy mansion 'just for a joke'.

We laughed hysterically when the Ambassador mentioned that the Embassy had extensive security facilities, including CCTV, and we realised they would have replayed Badger's antics the next day.

The Timorese community in Portugal treated us like visiting celebrities. Most helpful were three brothers who escorted us around. They were a funny trio, one a former soldier, another an ultra-urban yuppie, and the third a laid-back hippy.

The seven band members and soundman Rodney Bruthin were camped in a tiny two-bedroom apartment in a high-rise complex on the fringe of Lisbon where ninety-nine per cent of residents were African refugees. The neighbours were taken aback to have these white boys from Australia in their midst. The band members actually lived off red meat and red wine. I don't think our kitchen saw a vegetable the whole time we were there. (I just heard my liver say, 'thanks a lot'.)

Each day a band member would be tasked with going into central Lisbon to buy some hash—purely for medicinal reasons, of course. Well, when it was my turn, I ventured into the red-light district and met a gypsy who said buying the stuff would be no problem. I gave him $60 in euros and he took a small piece of foil from his pocket and gave me a smell of my intended purchase before warning me to hide it carefully down my underpants.

To demonstrate, he placed the foil of hash in his own undies then took it out and gave it to me. I put it in my undies as instructed and strode off feeling very worldly and street smart. How was I to know that he had switched foils and I had in fact purchased the world's most expensive cube of chicken stock?

I wasn't too popular with the boys in the band. Funny thing, we smoked it all anyway.

We spent three nights playing at a bar in Lisbon's red-light district where we performed until about 2am. Winding down after the show we would share drinks with other night workers, including a group of Nigerian prostitutes. There were no immoral liaisons, we were all just late-night entertainers sharing a drink.

Inspiration for songs can come from anywhere and we did get one great tune from that tour. Badger and I visited the Lisbon Maritime Museum where they had a huge map of the world, displaying where the Portuguese had visited when they ruled the waves. It was interesting to note the flag near Geelong in Australia, the site where it was rumoured a Portuguese ship had beached in the sand dunes. Colin and I went to the museum café for a few beers.

The old waiter overheard our accents and asked where we came from and what we thought of Portugal.

'We are from Australia and we love Portugal. The men are beautiful, the women beautiful, it is a beautiful place,' I said.

He thought about it, cleared the empties from our table and slowly walked back to the bar. Halfway there he turned around and came back. He bent down and whispered in my ear, 'Yes, but nothing tastes better than the neighbour's chicken.'

As he walked off, I said to my chuckling bandmate, 'Hey Badge, that's our next song.' We wrote and recorded a tune called just that, and released it on the album *Viva la Musica*.

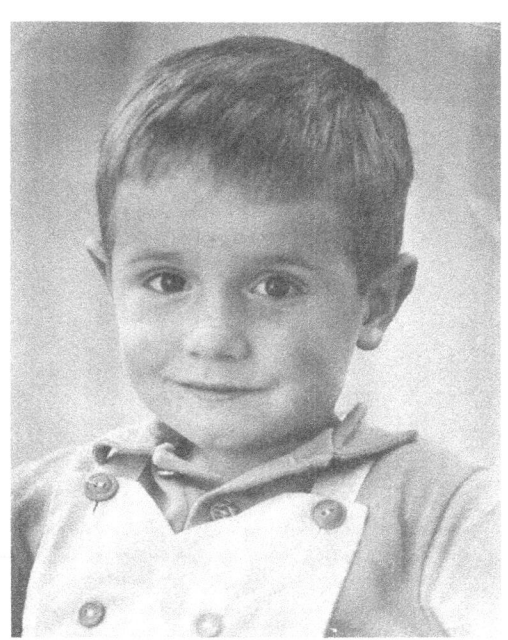

Top: Before I went to the crossroads and sold my soul. *Photo: Lloyd Brown*

Bottom: The Stewarts … 'always had to fight for airtime around this mob.' *Photo: Lloyd Brown*

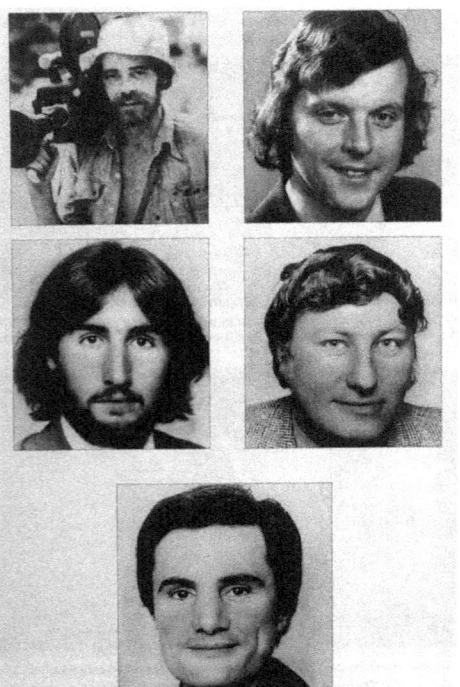

Top: Tony's first weeks on the job loading up gear for HSV 7 film crew.
Photo: Paulie Collection

Bottom: The infamous Balibo Five. (clockwise from top left) Brian Peters, Malcolm Rennie, Gary Cunningham, Greg Shackleton and Tony Stewart.
Photo: news.com.au

Top: Tony enjoys a last meal in Balibo with Greg Shackleton hours before the village was overrun by invading Indonesian forces. *Photo: Gary Cunningham*

Bottom: Half Oscar Wilde/half Barry Humphries. The old journo's took an instant dislike to my appearance. *Photo: Lloyd Brown*

Top: 'Of course I know what chords are … I have a nice green pair at home.' With Vlad at early band rehearsal. *Photo: Paulie Collection*

Bottom: Our main aim was to offend and upset. Predictable was un-acceptable. *Photo: Paulie Collection*

Top: After numerous comings and goings, the first permanent line-up of the Painters & Dockers. *Photo: Mushroom Records*

Bottom: The Painters & Dockers line up of 2017 supporting gay marriage. *Photo: Richard Turton*

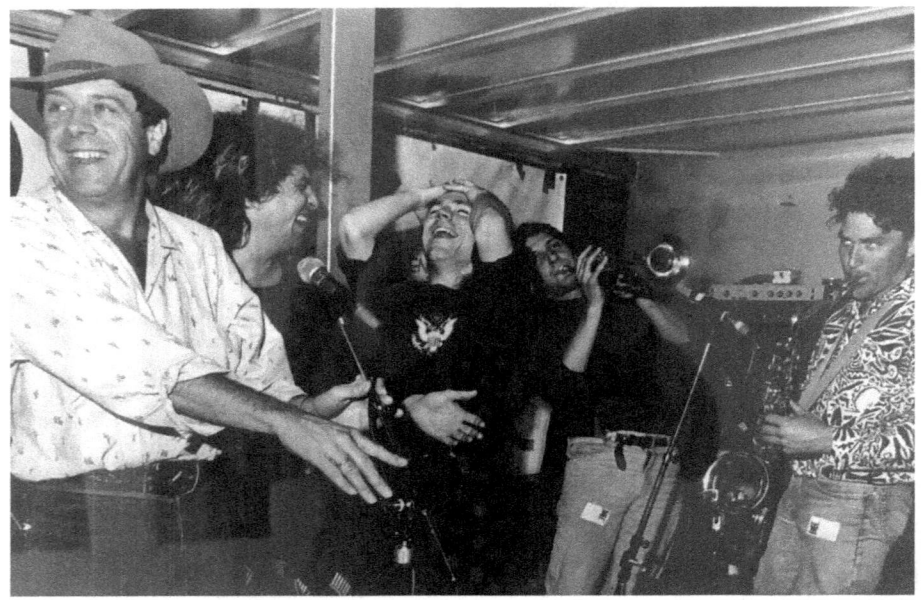

Molly Meldrum joins Rockin' The Rails tour and causes a riot when he launches us into a version of 'I Like It Both Ways'. *Photo: Unknown*

While on tour in Canada with a posse of Indigenous performers Cameron Goold (Propaganda Klann), Amy Saunders from Tiddas and I hit a Vancouver pioneer shop for a bit of cross dressing.
Photo: Vancouver Pioneer Shop

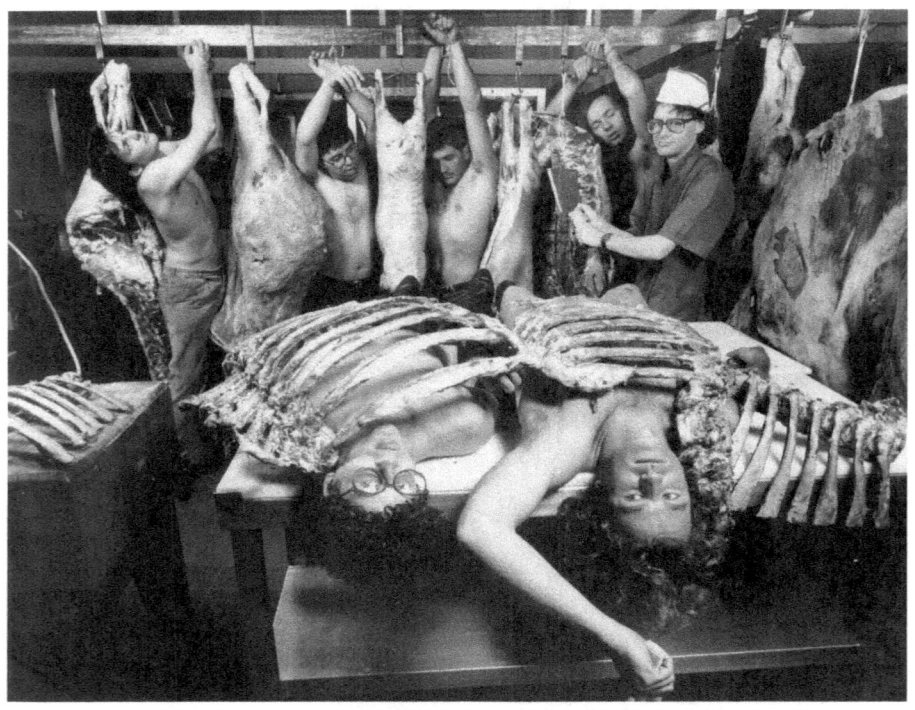

We shot the cover art for our album *Bucket* at an abattoir in West Melbourne. England's NME music paper called it 'the most disgusting album cover of all time'. Job done! *Photo: Neale Duckworth*

Top: The Dockers line up for the 2006 Lobby Lloyd benefit show Nelito Riberio, Michael Barclay, Paulie, Lobby, Sally Morris, Mick Morris, Dave Pace and Vlad Juric. *Photo: Unknown*

Bottom: Have a hit song about nudity and it's no surprise spontaneous things like this have always happened at our shows! *Photo: Richard Turton*

Top: The Dili Allstars hanging out in a newly liberated Timor-Leste. *Photo: Ross Bird*

Bottom: At the Tour Of Duty concert for International Peace Keepers in 1999 in Timor-Leste. The Dili Allstars with General Peter Cosgrove, later Australia's Governor General, at the after show barbeque. *Photo: Paulie Collection*

Top: With Gil Santos in a very unreliable Russian helicopter touring Timor-Leste. *Photo: Paulo Almeida*

Bottom: Burundi rappers Fablice and G Storm of The Flybz getting funky with East Timorese President José Ramos-Horta. *Photo: Richard Turton*

Top: At the shared grave of the Balibo Five at Jakarta Cemetery.
Photo: Donna Brown

Middle: With one of the East Timorese veterans who assisted Australian troops fighting the Japanese during World War II.
Photo: Gil Santos

Bottom: Xanana Gusmao (resistance leader) and Steve Bracks (former Victorian Premier) at a ceremony in Balibo. Bracks was the only Australian politician to show my family empathy and support after Tony's murder.
Photo: Paulie Collection

'Where's Paulie?' *Photo: Gil Santos*

Top: Singing with resistance leader Xanana Gusmao and Carla Araujo at Rod Laver Arena Melbourne following his release from Jakarta Prison. *Photo: Ross Bird*

Middle: Love this woman. East Timor's first female superhero Feto Fantastiku. Love that her male sidekick is called Simple Man. *Photo: Ba Futuru*

Bottom: Irish rock superstar Bono with Gil's little sister Teresa backstage at Waverley Park on U2's Popmart Tour 1998. *Photo: Serge Thomann*

Top: THE PRICS (Performers Releasing Information [About] Clean Syringes). *Photo: Paulie Collection*

Middle: The Dili Allstars who toured Portugal as guests of the local Communist Party. *Photo: Ross Bird*

Bottom: At the Avante Festival in Lisbon, kind of like The Big Day Out for Europe's Communist Parties. *Photo: Ross Bird*

Top: Talking up East Timor independence, Ines Araujo and I corner Hollywood star Willem Dafoe at the Melbourne Festival. *Photo: Unknown*

Middle: Two Australian Entertainment Queens backstage at Tour Of Duty concert in Dili … Kylie Minogue and the inmitable punk Jenny Pineapple. *Photo: Paulie Collection*

Bottom left: My greatest intro ever! 'Mr Brown this is Nicky Winmar. Nicky this is Mr James Brown.' *Photo: Paulie Collection*

Bottom right: Young punk Nick Cave, in his Robe Street St Kilda squat, insisted that he pick the photo of himself to run in the paper with my article. *Photo: Neale Duckworth*

The Painters & Dockers at the RecLink Community Cup sponsored by 3RRR and 3PBS. *Photo: Mary Boukouvalas*

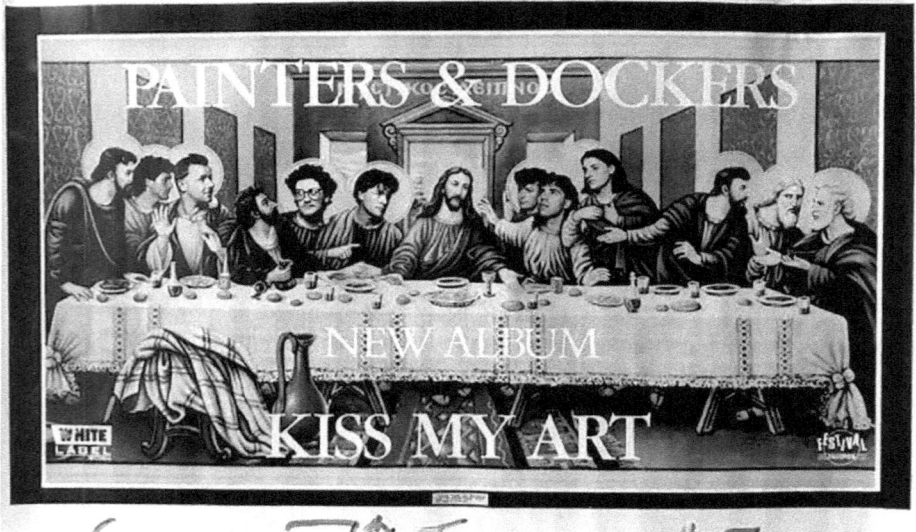

Top left: Single cover for *Nude School*.

Top right: Gig poster, supporting The Saints at the Balloom in St Kilda.

Bottom: The Painters & Dockers 1988 album *Kiss My Art* with the band sharing beer and pizzas with Jesus.

Top: A nod to our association with the Painters and Dockers union.

Bottom: Admission $10 for all you can drink and a punk band. No wonder these gigs were so chaotic.

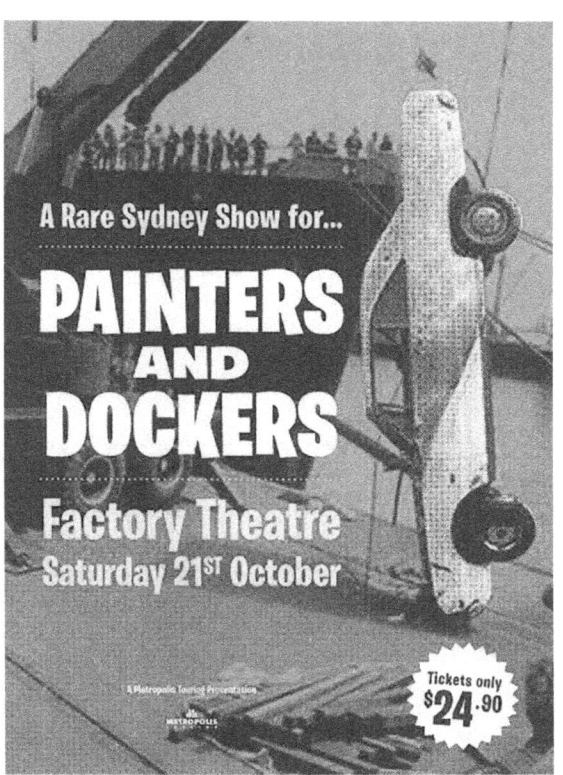

Up on the big screen at Timor-Leste's first Independence Concert.
Photo: Ross Bird

Top: With The Wiggles on the road in the USA. They were huge supporters of East Timor thanks to manager Paul Field. *Photo: Paulie Collection*

Middle: Standing outside the house were the Balibo Five took shelter before being murdered by Indonesian troops. *Photo: Gil Santos*

Bottom: Alma Nun in her Princess costume, with children from the orphanage, all in donated Wiggles gear. *Photo: Maggie Miles*

Top: With 'People's Priest' Father Bob Maguire who always supported us. We stood side by side with him on picket lines during the MUA disputes with Patricks.
Photo: Unknown

Middle: The cheeky Sister Anastasia, one of my best friends. We have done many shows together. She is ALWAYS happy.
Photo: Paulie Collection

Bottom: The real punks The Alma Nuns. Reject material possessions, don't take orders from men, up at 4.30am every morning.
Photo: Paulie Collection

Top: The Transplants with our guest Derryn Hinch who got out of this bed to deliver a very passable version of Joe Cockers' 'You are So Beautiful'. Also pictured young Shaun Miller who was set to perform with us but tragically passed before the show. *Photo: Shaun Miller Foundation*

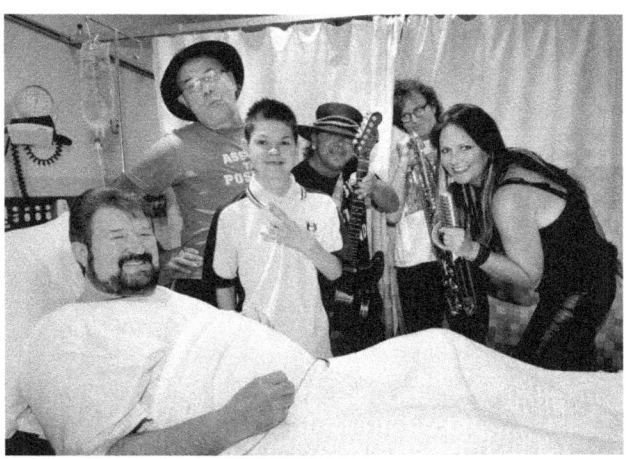

Middle: This is a fading photo but proof that when I woke from my liver transplant I was greeted by Elvis (my pal Paulie Greene) and Donna Brown. *Photo: Unknown*

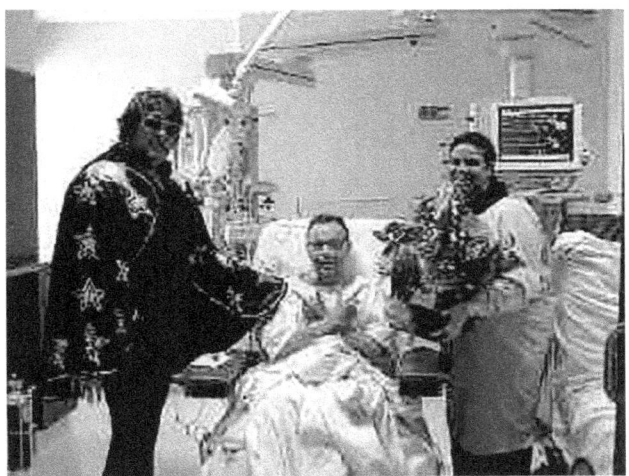

Bottom: With some of the gang from Just Voices. Isiah (Sierra Leone), Raza (Afghanistan), colleague and good pal Danielle Sherry and Jefry (West Papua). We lined up close to 500 school appearances for our speakers. *Photo: Fiona Basile*

Top: Oldest daughter Frances who taught me about parenting and kept me from turning into an egotistical monster. *Photo: Paulie Collection*

Middle: Youngest daughter Aretha Brown at the Invasion Day Rally 2017. Later became the first female Prime Minister in National Indigenous Youth Parliament. *Photo: Darrian Traynor/The Age*

Bottom: Maggie and I in the back blocks of Timor-Leste a long way from where she was born in Broughton Astley UK. *Photo: Eddie De Pina*

30

PORTABLE DUNNIES
(2003)

After Tony's death, our family heard every kind of bullshit imaginable from Australian political leaders of all parties.

I will never forget that it was Gough Whitlam who was responsible for letting Timor-Leste fall into chaos in the first place. He would never talk about what happened there.

Then you had Prime Minister Bob Hawke, who cared more about his stylish haircuts than about anything that had happened in East Timor, and Paul Keating, a great politician who was fatefully flawed when it came to this subject. Talk about being a rent boy for the Indonesians. Keating was actually taught by the same De La Salle order as me and my brothers, but so much for the old school tie.

Liberal Prime Minister John Howard reluctantly sent peacekeepers in to restore stability in East Timor after the 1999 referendum. It was another conservative Member of Parliament, National Party senator Julian McGauran who went on to champion the rights of the Timorese. He tabled a motion calling for an end to small arms sales to the Indonesian military.

One Australian politician forever cursed over his involvement with Indonesia and the plight of the Timorese is former ALP Foreign Minister Gareth Evans. The press photo of him drinking champagne with his Indonesian counterpart Ali Alatas as they flew over the Arafura Sea after dividing up East Timor's oilfields, must now cause him sleepless nights. Gil and I attended a huge rally at Melbourne University where Evans was greeted with the chant, 'Burn in hell, Gareth. Burn.'

Truth be told, Australia's politicians have treated the families of the Balibo Five with absolute contempt. One of the worst was South Australian senator Nick Xenophon, who out of the blue announced he planned to bring back the remains of the murdered newsmen regardless of what their families wanted. It was a cheap media stunt, and I was so happy to see him thrown out of politics when he tried to shift from the Senate to state parliament in 2018 and was rejected by the voters.

Unfortunately, Mum, then eighty-six and living in a Daylesford nursing home, learned about Xenophon's plans to interfere with the remains of the Balibo Five when she picked up a copy of *The Age*. There it was splashed all over the front page.

Towards the end of her life, after decades of putting on a brave face, Mum finally had space to grieve for her murdered son, and she no longer tried to hide that grief. Balibo still rocked her to the core, and it showed.

Mum was shocked by Xenophon's stunt because we had had our memorial service at Balibo to honour Tony and his mates, and now here was this guy threatening to tamper with his remains.

Hats off then to Victorian Premier Steve Bracks, the most honest and commendable of all Australian politicians when it came to Balibo. It was Bracks who negotiated to buy the house where the journalists were killed and then to set it up as a community centre. Lending a hand in its renovation was the Construction, Forestry, Mining and Energy Union (CFMEU), the union that was most regularly vilified by Coalition politicians and the Murdoch media. I will always be grateful for their efforts.

Bracks got all the families together and arranged for them to travel up to Timor-Leste for a special handover ceremony when the community centre was opened. It was the only time the families had worked so closely with each other.

Mum and her four surviving children all went to Balibo. It was an emotional trip and I have to admit I needed a bit of Dutch courage to get through it. I had a bottle of vodka in my pocket for much of the journey.

As visiting Westerners, the families were put in a mansion in Balibo. We were sitting outside the day before the ceremony when there was a commotion. Rushing out to the road, we saw some odd-looking contraptions thundering up the hill.

Two giant portable dunnies on the back of a truck were being transported to our accommodation. The locals were amazed and thinking, 'What do those white people actually do in those things anyway?' It broke some of the tension and we all fell about laughing.

It was a moving experience to finally meet all the families, but the tension rose again when veteran journalist Jill Jolliffe joined us. She had recently released a book which mentioned that Greg Shackleton had left his wife Shirley and found a new partner before he went on the assignment to East Timor. Shirley was seething about this disclosure.

She was accompanied on the visit by her and Greg's son Evan and Evan's wife. Evan seemed relieved to talk to the Stewart siblings and have his own chance to share what he'd gone through. Like everyone else, we had only ever heard his mother's point of view.

We also met the English and Scottish families for the first time. There was Maureen Tolfree, the sister of the Bristol-born Channel 9 cameraman Brian Peters. For years she had felt that she was kept in the dark about the tragedy because she lived in England.

It certainly is a long way from Scotland and East England to the steamy hot Timorese jungle, but that was the journey for the cousins of Channel 9 reporter, Malcolm Rennie.

The Cunninghams, originally from New Zealand, had a unique bond with the Stewarts as cameraman Gary and his siblings Greg and

Anne grew up opposite our grandmother in Moorabbin. Still, we had never really talked to Greg and Anne about the loss of their brother, a firm friend of Tony's.

We also met John Milkins and his wife. John found out long after 1975 that Gary Cunningham was his father so he had never actually known him.

At the ceremony, Premier Bracks handed ownership of the refurbished house to President Xanana and Prime Minister Ramos-Horta, and more importantly, to the people of Balibo. Each family had to volunteer a member for a short speech and so my brother Greg, representing our mob, said the following:

'We lost our brother Tony in this place in 1975. He was twenty-one. The Indonesian military murdered him and the other journalists. Successive Australian governments, starting with the Whitlam and Fraser Governments and continuing with today's Howard Government, have participated in the cover-up of this fact.

'To lose a son at the age of twenty-one, still in the flush of youth, is every parent's worst nightmare. We feel pleased that the refurbishment of the Balibo house has been a positive step in the lives of Timorese people who have also suffered untold atrocities at the hands of the Indonesian military ...

'We are very pleased to come to Balibo as there certainly was no closure at the time of their deaths. We were told the journalists were caught in crossfire and then an inappropriate funeral was held in Jakarta with supposedly some of their remains.

'We hope that this project may give us some closure on the tragedy for our family and for the families of the other journalists.'

An image that will always stay with me was Steve Bracks putting a supportive arm around Mum during the ceremony when there were no cameras in sight.

The Balibo house is now used as a dental clinic, crèche and school for teaching sewing, carpentry and computer skills. It is also a local meeting place and a safe secure environment for local women and children.

31

SONS AND DAUGHTERS OF THE MORNING STAR
(2006)

It was a natural progression from my involvement with Timor-Leste to take an interest in neighbouring West Papua's struggle for independence from Indonesia, as they are both former European colonies that have suffered under Indonesian military occupation. When Indonesia gained its independence from the Netherlands in 1949, the Dutch retained West Papua as a colony. In 1961, after repeated failures to secure West Papua as Indonesian territory through the United Nations, Indonesian President Sukarno threatened to annex it by force.

Amid Cold War jitters, President John F Kennedy feared that if the United States resisted Jakarta's demands, Indonesia might move closer to embracing Communism. He pushed the Dutch into handing West Papua to Indonesia, who took over in 1963 and renamed the country Irian Jaya.

They belatedly held a plebiscite, the so-called Act of Free Choice, in 1969, but it was widely condemned for defrauding West Papuans of a genuine vote on self-rule.

It has been estimated that nearly 200,000 Papuans have died because of Indonesia's occupation, either directly from military conflict or because of long-term neglect.

One of their most notorious acts was allowing prostitutes infected with HIV-AIDS to follow the miners who flocked into the country to work at the biggest goldmine in the world, the Freeport-McMoRan Grasberg mine.

The fact that two of my close mates from the Timor movement, Louise Byrne and David Bridie, got heavily involved in West Papua also drew me to its independence struggle.

Louise played a vital role in Timor-Leste's independence campaign and I was not surprised when she quickly refocussed on West Papua. She became the partner of West Papuan resistance leader Jacob Rumbiak, a diminutive fella who looks more like a fisherman or farmer than a veteran resistance fighter.

He lifted his shirt one day to show me some of the bullet wounds from his struggles with the Indonesians. On one occasion he had to lay in a creek bed for three days without moving as Indonesian troops scoured the area looking for him. He was later captured and spent considerable time with Xanana Gusmão in a Jakarta prison. The two became firm friends.

Jacob was eventually freed and hooked up with Louise to live in the Melbourne suburb of St Kilda, where they campaigned tirelessly for West Papuan liberation.

Louise has done her best to let people know what is going on in the former Dutch territory but unlike Timor-Leste, where the death of six white journalists kept the country in the news, most Australians know little about West Papua.

Louise had famously convinced Bishop Hilton Deakin to jump out of a helicopter to highlight the launch of one our Timor-Leste benefit albums and she could talk anyone into doing anything.

She came to me once saying, 'Paulie, I need a big favour. My mum is a teacher at Bunbury Christian College (in Western Australia) and they are campaigning for Timor-Leste and West Papua. They need someone to talk about the issue at their Year 12 speech night.'

'I figure you, as a Painter and Docker and brother of one of the Balibo Five, could do it. Please?'

'Yeah, sure, but how do I get there?'

Coming to the rescue was WA rock show promoter and good friend Ken 'Squasher' Knight, who lined me up an air ticket. In return, I had to host a lingerie show at the Bunbury Hotel straight after the speech night. It was a tough gig, but somebody had to do it.

The speech night quickly went off the rails. There I was in front of a hall packed with parents, teachers, students and couple of VIP bishops. First I performed a song with the Year 12 band, then it was time for my speech. I quite enjoyed my opening line.

'I've done shows for a couple of old queens in my time but never a bishop,' I said, to resounding silence.

Oops, tone it down Paulie. By the end of the speech, they were happy enough and I rushed out of the hall, jumped into a cab and made my way to the Bunbury pub. I met the half-naked models backstage and got a rundown on what they were wearing, or not wearing, for my commentary. It was a funny night, fuelled by an open tab at the bar.

Towards the end of 2000, Louise came to me with another request about West Papua.

'We have this elder from Papua in town and we're trying to get him some publicity,' she said.

I said, 'Lou, I have to be honest and say no one will be interested. The *Sunday Herald Sun* won't touch this. You need to come up with another angle.'

'Okay, leave it with me,' she replied.

Half an hour later she rang back, saying, 'I've got three brand new canary yellow Ferraris lined up for a press shot.'

'That will do it,' I said.

We ended up racing around Albert Park Lake in the Ferraris, with the elder flying a large West Papuan independence flag out the window. The editor loved it and the picture was seen by hundreds of thousands of readers.

Bridie, a top musician and Melanesian expert, has now put in countless hours of work recording West Papuan artists and organising benefit concerts. He and Byrne were among the campaigners who helped to have residence permits quickly granted to forty-two West Papuan refugees who had escaped to Australia in January 2006. They organised a truly joyous benefit concert to welcome them to Melbourne. The Dili Allstars were proud to play at the event and at several other shows for the West Papuans.

I now work with one of the forty-two West Papuan refugees, Jefry Yikwa, a sharp intellect who is studying drone design at RMIT. Through the Just Voices program at Jesuit Social Services, I have taken him into schools where he shares his remarkable journey.

I learned enough from my dealings with Xanana and Ramos-Horta to recognise that another charismatic young activist Ronny Kareni is destined to be part of any future West Papuan Government when independence is finally achieved.

32

JUST SAY SORRY
(2007)

In December 2007 a coroner's court in Sydney handed down a verdict acknowledging for the first time that the Indonesian military was responsible for the Balibo murders.

I wrote a story addressed to former Prime Minister Gough Whitlam, which was widely distributed in Australia and Indonesia.

It read:

Just say sorry, Gough.

Now is your big chance to finally lay it all to rest once and for all with the finding of the Balibo inquest into the death of five Australian journalists in Timor-Leste in 1975. Ring this paper and ask for my contact details and then ring me, and I will give you my mum's phone number and you can call her.

It won't ever give her back her son, my brother Tony, the 21-year-old youngest of the Melbourne-based Channel 7 television news crew who were killed, and she may even tell you to go jump, but show her some respect, pal. Finally.

Relax, I am not after any financial compensation, just an acknowledgement of the unnecessary pain you caused her. It seems impossible to deny despite your testimony at the inquest that you never knew the journalists had been killed long before you passed the information on to us, his family, especially given two recent revelations.

Firstly, former journalist Geraldine Willesee has come out and told the Australian public that her father, your Foreign Minister in 1975, knew the journalists had been murdered long before your government confirmed the fact.

Her revelation certainly does not paint her father in the most favourable light, so why would she say it if it were not true?

Likewise, Australia's former intelligence chief Gordon Jockel said he personally broke news of the deaths to your then Defence Minister Don Morrison many days before any information was released.

Surely you do not expect us to believe that he never passed on this vital information to you, his boss?

Gough, your apology would be very timely given your call this week with fellow ex-PM Malcolm Fraser, for Australian Government ministers to be more responsible for the mistakes they made in office. It was you after all who was in power at the time of the newsmen's deaths.

The ALP often criticise the Howard Government, rightly in my opinion, for not having the courage, dignity and compassion to apologise to Australia's Indigenous community for past mistakes.

Here is your chance to get in first. Besides, with a new major film on the killings directed by Robert Connolly and featuring Hollywood star Anthony LaPaglia now in the works, it is a chance to come clean before your actions are displayed once and for all on the big screen.

Gough, you might also call Berta Santos, who also lives in Melbourne, who lost her husband on the same day I lost my brother. Say sorry to her that your government never stood by our East Timorese friends who were displaced, raped and murdered in their thousands by the Indonesians after we did nothing to halt their invasion.

Dear ex-PM, please show the families of the murdered newsmen the same kind of respect and compassion displayed by Victorian ex-Premier Steve Bracks. Just be half the man he is.

Bracks' decision to purchase the house where the journalists were killed and turn it into a crèche and community centre for the locals in Balibo is one of the few good things to come from the affair now etched onto Australia's consciousness.

Here is your big chance Gough. I look forward to the call.

The call never came.

But I did receive many emails and messages about the story. One of the more interesting ones was from a guy in Jakarta, who wrote, 'Next time you are up this way we are going to castrate you.'

I wonder if they could cut out a bad liver as well while they are at it?

33

PORT MORESBY IDOL
(2010)

From 1993, I visited East Timor on average almost once a year—at the time of writing I have made twenty-six visits.

On many of these visits I was put up by my pal Maria Gabriela Carrascalão-Heard, who I first met when she worked as a radio journalist for SBS in Melbourne.

A fierce patriot, she worked hard for independence and when the country was freed, she was one of the surprisingly few activists who returned home to work for the new government. She held several top-level jobs.

Born in Liquiçá, Maria was one of thirteen children of Manuel Viegas Carrascalão, a Portuguese exile who married a Timorese woman.

Maria had a plush house and sprawling compound near Dili airport, complete with a lavish tropical garden. She was very proud of the fact she had once housed visiting ABC presenter Jon Faine. It was great going on his Melbourne radio show and startling him with my opening line, 'I've slept in Jon Faine's bed.'

I was intrigued that Maria's schoolmates growing up in East Timor included future leaders José Ramos-Horta, Xanana Gusmão and Mari Alkatiri. It is not a big place and everyone seemed to know everyone else.

Through Maria, I met her husband, an expat Australian named Geoffrey Heard. They were later to divorce and she married again and moved to Portugal, becoming a successful visual artist.

Geoffrey moved to Papua New Guinea where he became involved in that country's fledging media scene. After hearing me give a speech in Timor-Leste, he invited me to Port Moresby to talk at Media Freedom Week 2010 about the importance of press freedom. During my visit I stayed at Geoffrey's house in a hilltop compound for white expats, surrounded by security fences and 24-hour security guards. It's a scary town, Port Moresby.

The talk was held at a business breakfast in front of 300 people at the Crown Plaza Hotel. Geoffrey had told me I would be joined on stage by PNG singer-songwriter George Telek to perform a song together. George and I learned the song 'Freedom' as we walked onstage.

'Just sing, "Free West Papua" when we get to the chorus and I'll do the rest,' George said.

'No worries, let's go.'

Later that night, George and I hit a few clubs and bars in Port Moresby where I didn't leave his side. Most people knew him by sight and I felt protected in his immediate company and very nervous when I found myself alone.

We were at the infamous Paddy's Bar when one woman who had obviously had a few drinks walked up to us and said, 'Okay, white boy, come for a dance.'

Who was I to argue? I took to the dance floor with my new friend and boogied down to some old disco tunes.

After a few songs another lady approached me and said, 'My turn for a dance, white boy.' My original dancing companion was having none of that. She wasn't sharing her prized little white monkey with anyone.

They started to argue and it quickly became a full-on squabble. I was terrified. Luckily George saw what was happening, gave me a wink and we bolted into the night.

Given that I worked in Australia as a music journalist, I was roped in as a 'celebrity judge' at an event called The Media Freedom Music and Dance Competition. Kind of like Port Moresby Idol.

I found myself sitting at a table with two local judges while musical acts from around the country displayed their talents. There were some truly incredible performers, including colourful troupes from the highlands.

34

KEEPING THE FAITH

While losing Tony turned me away from the Catholic Church in disgust, there have been individuals over the years who have gone some way to restore my view of the institution.

Bishop Hilton Deakin was one such man.

No holier-than-thou, Bible-bashing conservative like Cardinal George Pell, Bishop Hilton Deakin championed the rights of Indigenous Australians, the Timorese, West Papuans and average Australian battlers.

I have seen him in Timor-Leste berating Indonesian troops to their faces and standing up for the locals. In Australia the cause of the West Papuans isn't that fashionable, but Hilton supports them none the less.

How many priests would conduct a church service in conjunction with West Papuans wearing traditional penis gourds?

In Timor-Leste he has supported young priests and kindly said mass at a facility for children with disabilities, run by nuns who treated his arrival as if the Pope himself had turned up.

Hilton first made his way into my family's heart when he

accompanied us to Balibo in 2003. Offering respect, comfort and support, he conducted the memorial service for Tony and his colleagues, accompanied by a Timorese priest. It is a mark of the man that Hilton conducted his part of the service in Tetum, while his colleague did so in English.

After the service up in the hills, we returned to Dili and that night he and I laid siege to a bottle of fine malt whisky with the assistance of Timor-Leste's honorary consul to Victoria, Kevin Bailey.

A former member of the Australian Army's SAS, Bailey explained that his interest in the country had been sparked by hearing stories from Sparrow Force veterans about Australia's World War II debt to the Timorese. After the army, he became a successful financial consultant and a trusted investment adviser to the government of Timor-Leste.

Bailey's sister-in-law Mary Ellen, a singer and fluent Tetum speaker, has performed many times with The Dili Allstars, live and in the recording studio.

I will be forever grateful to Hilton for agreeing to conduct my darling mum's funeral in 2014. He announced at the end that he had never held a funeral that featured so much laughing. My irreverent mother would have loved that. I had warned her in her final days that I would play up in my eulogy with inappropriate jokes, and she made me promise that I would.

I was so grateful that Gil, Paulo and Zeca from The Dili Allstars turned up to play some music.

Unbelievably, on the day of Mum's funeral, the Australian Federal Police finally rang to say they wanted to meet us to share their five-year investigation into the Balibo murders. We made them delay it a day so we could lay Mum to rest. We had been waiting almost forty years to hear from them, so they could wait a day for us.

When we finally met them, they said their investigation had come to nothing.

'Hang on, you have just spent five years investigating it. What do you mean there are no further steps you can take?' we asked.

'We didn't interview the Indonesians involved because they fall outside of our jurisdiction. Case closed.'

There would be no prosecutions, no jail time, and no justice. It was the same old slap in the face.

For many years, activists Pat Walsh and John Sinnott were the pilot lights that kept the East Timor cause flickering in Melbourne. I knew little about the history and politics of East Timor and Walsh taught me with patience and kindness. A prominent civil rights activist, he later worked on Timor-Leste's Commission for Reception, Truth and Reconciliation. He is a decent tennis player, too, and enjoyed games in Timor-Leste with my brother Dr Greg, who was often up there assisting at clinics and hospitals.

From his office in an old church in Napier Street, Fitzroy, John Sinnott sent out constant newsletters and provided space for a growing band of supporters. As head of the Australian East Timor Association, he was vigilant when it came to accountability. Nobody got anything for free, he took nothing for himself and maintained a watertight financial set-up.

It was fitting that when Timor-Leste finally got its independence, Walsh and Sinnott were among the first people they insisted be at the celebrations.

Hats off also to my good friend Father Bob McGuire, the people's priest, who lent support and encouragement to Timor-Leste independence supporters.

Another organisation that does an amazing job is the East Timor Hearts Fund, Australia's only aid group dedicated to providing lifesaving heart surgery for our northern neighbours.

I was thrilled when the fund took up my suggestion to enlist as its patron Lin Jong, the only AFL player with an East Timorese heritage, who played as a forward with my beloved Western Bulldogs.

Other noteworthy activists I worked with included Dr Sara Niner, Professor Vannessa Hearman, Rob Wesley-Smith, Ross Bird, Jefferson Lee, Colin Holt, and Sister Susan Connelly.

I am no saint, and the truth is that I have gotten more out of Timor-Leste than I have put in, gaining some lifelong Timorese friends and seeing parts of the country and culture that few whitefellas get to see.

A true highlight for me was meeting the beautiful Appolina.

From a small village near the border with West Timor, she was born with a huge hole in her face where her mouth should have been. She showed me that beauty is indeed only skin deep and what real strength is.

In her late teens she arrived in Melbourne for an intricate and successful reconstruction operation where doctors used skin from her legs to build her a new face.

35

WHITEFELLA, BLACKFELLA

Growing up in an area teeming with World War II refugees, I met people from all over Europe but one group I never came across as a youngster were members of Australia's own First Peoples, its diverse Indigenous population.

At school, the only real mention of Aboriginal peoples was in history lessons where we learned of the annoying "natives" who harassed brave white explorers while they trekked through the "empty and unoccupied" countryside. There was no mention of invasion and the massacres inflicted on the original peoples.

One day my school brought in a Koori elder to throw boomerangs around the footy oval, but that was it.

I never expected the deep links between Indigenous Australia and myself that lay ahead.

The links flowed from meeting Gumbaynggirr artist Donna Brown in Darwin when the Painters & Dockers visited the Top End for a show.

Donna is recognised as a talented artist and after we became a couple, I accompanied her to the US where she was feted for her work at the Australian Embassy in Washington. She was invited to be an artist-in-residence at the University of Virginia in Charlottesville, the city that was later the scene of vicious race riots during the reign of president Donald Trump.

Donna and I bought a house together in Melbourne, and she gave birth to my second daughter, Aretha. I have many beloved Indigenous in-laws, including Donna's mother Jan, who became one of my closest ever friends. She loved two men—Jesus and Elvis—and was a member of the Stolen Generation. She was taken from her mother at thirteen and sent to work at a Sydney North Shore dentist's home as a servant.

'I never got paid and lived off the left-over scraps,' she told me.

Never bitter or twisted, she would raise four children of her own and many nieces, nephews and grandchildren. She would never hear a bad word about Roman Catholic nuns.

'They used to walk miles and miles to drop off food for me,' she remembered. 'Nobody else cared.'

One of my proudest moments came in 2017 when my daughter Aretha Stewart Brown was chosen as one of forty-eight young Indigenous leaders from around the nation to spend a week in Canberra as members of the National Indigenous Youth Parliament.

Aged sixteen to twenty-five, those delegates then elected seventeen-year-old Aretha as the youngest and first female Prime Minister of their Parliament.

I admit to being a shocking 'stage father' and pushing Aretha forward at every chance, telling her that she had to grab any opportunity that came her way, given that her grandmother had none.

I have now spent a lot of time working and living with various mobs in Western Sydney, Nambucca Heads, Victoria and the Northern Territory. While I never had to face the racism and social injustices that they suffered, Tony's death meant I could relate to their pain and lingering, corrosive grief.

Donna eventually got sick of Melbourne and living away from her mob and decided to leave me and move back to Nambucca Heads, a fourteen-hour drive north of Melbourne, taking ten-year-old Aretha with her.

I will forever be grateful to Donna because, after making that decision, she hung around in Melbourne to look after me when I was struck down by chronic liver disease. Rather than leave me in the lurch, she fed and clothed me for an arduous eighteen months, nursing me back to health with all the horrors that entailed.

Twice I fainted in the backyard and she had to pick me up and rush me to the Austin Hospital. You never forget the sacrifices of someone who keeps you alive, confident and on track. I was incredibly hard to handle and Donna often had to stop me going into work when, in my deluded state, I thought everything was normal. Several months after I received my new liver, she finally had the chance to move back to Nambucca Heads.

I remained part of her extended family and had an open invitation to visit Aretha whenever I wanted. Donna later agreed that Aretha's education prospects would be better in Melbourne and so my twelve-year-old daughter came back to live with me and attend Williamstown High School.

She arrived as a very independent girl who took to her new environment like a duck to water. At fifteen, she was chosen by the Victorian Government to be part of a group of students attending the centenary of the Gallipoli landings in Turkey. She went to represent her Indigenous relatives who had fought in both World Wars without receiving any recognition or respect for serving for their country.

Interestingly, it was a white woman, the social activist Jacqui Geia, who had first opened my eyes to the lives, culture, history and aspirations of Australia's First Peoples. I met her when a press release arrived at *The Sun* in the early 1980s, promoting a show by pioneering Aboriginal rock act No Fixed Address.

No one seemed too excited about it, so I volunteered to have a chat with them. I rang the number on the press release and organised an interview for Monday morning with the band in a house just off Brunswick Street in Fitzroy.

When I arrived, I let myself in the open front door and made my way through the debris of what must have been a hell of a party.

Among all the empty bottles, half smoked roaches and snoring band members sat Jacqui. It was an encounter that changed my life.

Jacqui would eventually introduce me to white singer-songwriter Shane Howard of Goanna and leading Indigenous artists, including her husband Joe Geia, Richard Franklin, Archie Roach, Ruby Hunter, Dave Arden, jazz singer Carol Fraser, Dan Sultan, Grant Hansen and the three girls from Tiddas; Amy Saunders, Lou Bennett and Sally Dastey.

When I was sick with my liver problems, Jackie would arrive with food and health advice, even though she was going through her own serious liver problems. The last time I saw her was when I was playing with The Dili Allstars in the rotunda at Williamstown beach. She was shouting encouragement to the end.

When she died of liver cancer at just forty-six, Shane Howard said she had 'seen the injustice in this country and had a beautiful vision of where the country needed to go. She built bridges between Aboriginal and other Australians where there were none before.'

For me, Jacqui will always be a cheeky, capital-R, Rascal. Her son Zac, who also died way too young, told me he had once found rock star Sting from The Police in his kitchen.

'I think he was learning to play didjeridu from Joe,' Zac recalled. 'Sting told Mum that they had been on the road for six months and he missed home and his own domestic duties. He asked Mum if he could do our dishes. So I arrived home to find Sting in the kitchen washing up.'

I am boasting here, but I think Jacqui and I became a great team. She steered me in the right direction to cover stories about not just blackfella music, but also Indigenous politics, health, land rights, history and so much more. She introduced me to leading Indigenous activist Gary Foley, AFL great Nicky Winmar and countless others. I always felt I was working on 'big picture' stories with Jacqui.

Her best introduction of all was to then Prime Minister Bob Hawke at a Songlines music industry function in Port Melbourne. She was so proud of the fact that her infant son Henry, who she was holding, had just pissed on the PM. Priceless.

It took a huge effort to drag myself out of my sick bed to attend her funeral in Williamstown with Gil Santos and I almost fainted in the church.

* * *

I spent a lot of time in the Northern Territory because my sister Annie was a children's librarian in Darwin for four years, and our brother Greg and sister-in-law Beth Quinn worked in Katherine as doctors.

More importantly, Donna was based in Darwin for much of the 1990s. On one occasion, the only way I could get up to visit her was with the Australian Army as an official correspondent during a massive war games exercise in the Top End. I thought I would just rock up to Darwin and file all my stories from there, have a few beers and then have a holiday. Wrong.

The army guy who met me at Darwin airport laughed when I told him of my plans. He bundled me into a truck and drove me down to a remote army base in the desert near Katherine. We were housed in little aluminium huts, which were buzzed about 5am every morning by RAAF jet fighters.

Leading photographer and close friend Ross Bird and I were later taken out to the back of nowhere by the army and dropped off in a dusty creek bed. Suddenly several large transport planes appeared overhead and parachutes emerged carrying Indonesian red beret special forces.

Ross and I stood open-mouthed as they landed all around us. What was amazing was that each carried a photocopied local map to give them their bearings. Australia was basically showing them the lay of the land.

Did this make sense giving our biggest potential threat in the area the keys to the house? I don't think so.

A bigger issue for me was that the guys who killed Tony were suddenly landing all around me in the middle of nowhere. I was speechless and angry.

36

SEXY CAMP DOGS
(1993)

I first met Donna at a Darwin barbecue one night in 1993, introduced by flamboyant Territorian Kenny Minogue, who had adopted my family after sister Annie arrived in the Top End.

We had an interesting courtship, Donna and I. On our first date we ended up at Darwin's Nightcliff Beach for a romantic midnight swim. I hit the cool water and swam out while she waded in the shallows. She must not like swimming, I thought, as I tried to impress her with back flips and fancy dives. I swam back to shore.

'Not one for swimming, eh?' I asked.

'No, I love it. It is just that they have put a fresh donkey leg in the crocodile trap over there,' she said casually.

'They just put what, where?' I shrieked.

We left that beach quick smart.

The Painters & Dockers spent a lot of time in the Top End and met both black and white musicians. One memorable band were called The Sexy Camp Dogs. We didn't really understand the name until we had seen some of the mangy, pink, flea-and pox-riddled animals that hang out around campfires in the Outback, then we got the joke.

On one of our first trips to Darwin in 1986, The Dockers were supported by a great local act, The Swamp Jockeys. We got on really well and Cal Williams and Stuart Kellaway from the band mentioned they had just started playing in a new group with an Indigenous teacher from Arnhem Land.

'We are called Yothu Yindi.'

Years later I arrived in Hanover, Germany, to cover a World Expo and the front page of the local newspaper shrieked 'Yothu Yindi in Town'.

With a floating line-up of Indigenous and non-Indigenous performers, the pioneering band toured more than twenty-seven countries in their thirteen-year career and became huge crowd-pullers in Europe, North America, South America and South Africa.

The band's manager Alan James went out with my sister Annie for a while, and he and my father went into a business selling barramundi shipped down from the Top End to Melbourne restaurants.

I was extremely grateful when Alan and the band invited me to visit Yothu Yindi's inaugural Garma Festival of traditional culture at a site called Gulkula, forty kilometres from Nhulunbuy in northeast Arnhem Land in 1999. It is now an annual and much-praised celebration of the culture of the Yolngu people.

Striving to share this knowledge and culture, the festival is an extravaganza of artists, dancers and musicians from the Top End. At that first festival Yothu Yindi opened a state-of-the-art recording studio with an exclusive performance of its new album *One Blood*.

The crew from Burrundi Pictures, the team who had made the iconic film clip for Yothu Yindi's international hit 'Treaty' were filming the concert. The Yothu Yindi performance at Garma was a magic gig that showed the power of the band on their home turf. The show kicked off with Galarrwuy Yunupingu, brother of Yothu Yindi frontman the late Dr M Yunupingu, pointing to a tree not far from the stage and asking the crowd for a moment of reflection.

'My father's mother is buried under that tree and we would like you all to thank her for letting us be here,' he said.

Yothu Yindi then put on a show that combined cutting-edge technology with some of the oldest musical instruments in the world. One of the support acts was another Top End favourite, Saltwater Band.

The band consisted of eight young Elcho Island musicians with stunning voices, none more impressive than blind vocalist Geoffrey Gurrumul Yunupingu. I thought they were a little rough around the edges but with some finessing here and there, they just might go a long way.

Saltwater Band has a strong Melbourne connection as its debut album, *Gapu Damarrun*, was recorded by Craig Pilkington of The Killjoys. The album was released on Skinnyfish Records, set up by former Killjoys bass player Michael Hohnen, who worked as a musical development officer with the Northern Territory University.

Michael was a dear friend and lined me up several guest lectures for his music students, with the money coming in very handy.

He would often talk about the young blind musician, Gurrumul, saying he had the voice of an angel. Years later I ran into the two of them at Darwin airport and asked what they had been up to.

'Well,' said Michael, 'we have just done a show for the Queen and will play for President Barack Obama next week.'

Gurrumul was now a bona fide superstar. It was a serious loss for the world's music scene when he died in 2017 at the age of just forty-six from liver and kidney damage caused by the hepatitis B he had contracted in his childhood.

A real highlight of that first visit was going to check out two old bark paintings in the art gallery in Yirrkala, about 700 kilometres east of Darwin. They are known as the Yirrkala Bark Petitions and go a long way to explaining the motives of Yothu Yindi. Created in 1963 by elders of the Yolngu people in relation to a court case around a mining lease, the paintings represented the first formal assertion of native title in Australia and were meant to show *balanda* (non-Indigenous people) that there was greater depth and beauty to their ancient culture than was generally known.

I asked Dr M about the petitions.

'Those paintings are our Magna Carta,' he said. 'They promote the strength and beauty of our Yolngu culture to the world.'

He said Yothu Yindi was bringing together the skills of both *balanda* and Yolngu to try to create a new beginning. The band set up the Yothu Yindi Foundation in 1990 to encourage and maintain the traditional dance (*bunggul*), song (*manikay*), art and ceremony.

Some Yolngu people at the Garma Festival told me they could remember being hidden as children from white men with guns on horseback.

During the festival, classes were conducted by both visiting academics and learned locals on subjects ranging from bush foods and medicine to land management, bark paintings, the cultural significance of the yidaki (didjeridu) and the need for bilingual education.

It was not long after meeting Yothu Yindi that I got to know another great Indigenous musician, Kev Carmody. A few months after ending our management relationship with Lobby in 1988, the Painters & Dockers signed with Sydney-based manager Joe Hayes, who also handled the little-known Carmody. Joe's own record label Rutabagas had just released Carmody's first album, *Pillars of Society*, which drew heavily on a simple acoustic style.

We got the chance to sit down with our new stablemate and hear about his fascinating journey into music. He told us he had graduated from university in Brisbane by persuading lecturers to let him present his essays in song form.

In an era of big hair and complicated productions, his simple acoustic style was instantly appealing.

'That first album was acoustic because we didn't have enough money for anything else, but as I went on, I was always exploring sound,' Kev reflected. 'One of the things my grandfather told me was you have to learn to listen to the wind.

'What he was saying was, use your imagination, widen it out, be aware of things around you. You learn to listen in another way. That's the key to my music. Just opening up to that sensory perception of sound.'

Another feature of Kev's songs was their overtly political nature.

In the simple yet biting number 'Thou Shalt Not Steal' he sang of the hypocrisy of British settlers who brought Christianity to Indigenous Australians. These Bible-readers forbade them to steal while robbing them of the land that Indigenous people had inhabited for more than 60,000 years.

Kev went on to write with Paul Kelly one of the all-time great Australian songs 'From Little Things Big Things Grow'.

Another powerful black activist, the inimitable Gary Foley, who had toured Australia as guest of famed UK punk band The Clash, joined The Dockers one night backstage at the Paddo RSL in Sydney.

Little did I know I would spend fourteen years with a woman from his Gumbaynggirr clan. Gary's dad and my daughter's grandfather Roger were old mates.

37

IT'S MERPATI AND WE'LL FLY IF WE WANT TO
(1997)

The final resting place of the five journalists murdered at Balibo has always been surrounded in mystery.

Early on, the Indonesian and Australian governments said the remains had been sent to Jakarta soon after the journalists were killed. They said a quick ceremony was held and the remains were put in a single coffin and laid to rest in Jakarta's central cemetery.

The Stewart family never believed this, and my mum often said, 'It's probably just old chicken bones. Both governments just wanted to cover it up and move on as quickly as possible to keep us all quiet.'

Despite this, I agreed to go to Jakarta in 1997 to visit the grave site after a request from my editor, Alan Howe. He wanted a first-person piece on what it was like to see the grave. I had no idea his request would lead to such an eventful journey.

I flew to Darwin and stayed there for a week catching up with my girlfriend Donna Brown. I even talked her into coming to Jakarta with me. Before she could leave, she had to finish an art project she was working on for the Darwin Festival. It was a float for the annual street parade, created with the young people from the Kulaluck Indigenous community.

This Darwin mob lived in a little community near Nightcliff Beach, which was blighted by excessive drinking and domestic violence. One resident was the renowned Top End artist Prince, who listened to Roy Orbison from dawn to dusk.

The children flocked to Donna and eagerly helped build the float. The race was on as she had to complete the project before our flight to Jakarta, on the same day as the Darwin Parade. She worked furiously on last-minute additions to the float. It was eventually deemed finished and given a prime position near the front of the parade. The big problem came when the head of the statue on the float fell off as it was leaving Kulaluck and urgent repairs had to be made. I told Donna I would go the airport to get our tickets and she would have to hurry to make the flight.

At the airport, I watched the clock move quickly towards departure time. Exasperated, I had to plead with the steward in charge of closing the door to leave it open just for a little while longer until Donna could arrive. He gave me a few minutes and then said, 'Sorry mate, we've got to go.'

I was standing with my back against the door pleading for him to wait just a little longer when I saw Donna running up the gate. Somehow we managed to get her on board.

We flew to Kupang in West Timor to spend the night while waiting to meet our connecting flight to Jakarta on the infamous Indonesian domestic airline Merpati. I had wondered why the airline had the unofficial motto among Darwin locals: 'It's Merpati and we'll fly if we want to.' We soon found out.

When we fronted the airport counter in Kupang next morning, the attendant announced that the plane was overbooked.

'Hang on, mate, we have our seat allocation and everything,' I declared.

'I'm sorry sir, we have sixty bookings and only forty seats.'

I lost it big time and only agreed to calm down when the airline offered us another night's accommodation in Kupang and tickets on the next day's flight. Losing a day was bad for our schedule as it meant less time in Jakarta where I would go in search of my brother's supposed grave.

The next day we did get a plane, but it was the one that did the mail run. And so we went up and down delivering post and supplies to little islands along the way and did not reach Jakarta until late in the afternoon. I was left with about three hours in Jakarta to find the cemetery, and then the grave. We jumped in a cab to the Australian Embassy where I met a weary-looking official.

'Listen mate,' he said, 'the cemetery is miles away and you might need a day to get there.'

It seemed everything was being thrown at me to stop me from getting to the grave.

We got into another cab and I told the driver, 'Take me to the cemetery.' He said, 'No problem, sir,' and we pulled up at the cemetery about fifteen minutes later.

The lying bastards at the Australian Embassy had tried to give us the run-around—a pattern that started in 1975 and has never ended to this day.

Donna and I found the Christian section of the cemetery and were able to track down the grave by following the dates of burials. Even though we knew it probably contained none of the true remains, I did shed a tear. I think it was seeing Tony's name on the headstone with the words, 'Beloved son of Noel and June' that tipped me over the edge. It did not seem right that this stone marker with gold lettering marked the final resting place of a 21-year-old boy from North Caulfield.

After about half an hour at the grave, we ventured into Jakarta. It was a horrible place—or was it just my mood? We checked into a budget hotel so we could have a few hours' sleep before our midnight departure.

We lasted about half an hour in the room, which had condensation dripping down the walls and stained bedsheets swarming with bugs. Exhausted, we sat for hours at the airport waiting for our flight.

Our final problem was, we didn't have any money left for the re-entry tax at Darwin airport. A local surfer lent us some money, a rare act of kindness after being treated with contempt on a pretty miserable trip.

38

I LOVE TO ROCK
(1997)

A trip to the Northern Territory in 1997 saw me travel to the remote community of Maningrida with national youth radio network Triple J, which had organised for sound engineer Chris Thompson to record a compilation album of Indigenous acts from all over the Top End.

Alcohol was hard to find unless you fancied spending ten dollars for a warm can of beer. This was the first time I saw up close the devastating effects of white culture on Indigenous people and alcohol was a huge problem in Maningrida.

Sitting on the coast 500 kilometres east of Darwin, the community was usually sedate, but come 'barge day', pallets of beer would arrive by sea. Some locals would then have what they called a 'big drink' and many would subsequently go into the horrors. Old disputes re-emerged, domestic violence broke out and the place fell to pieces.

There was one takeaway food shop in town run by a couple of storekeepers from Perth who would sell crap to the community: deep-fried chicken and litre upon litre of Coke. Vegetables and fruit were super expensive.

The Triple J sessions in Maningrida recorded some of the best Indigenous talent in the Top End.

I met the fabulous Letterstick Band, one of the nation's best unrecognised rock bands, who are named after traditional wooden tools that carry carved messages between places and generations. On the beach at Maningrida the band's charismatic frontman, C. Maxwell told me what he was passionate about.

'I like to hunt dugong, I like to do our old dances and ceremonies but mostly, I love to rock,' the mischievous singer said.

Tragically, he and the band's bass player were killed five years later in a road accident.

Other long-time bands to record at that session included Broken English and My Boys The Good Boys.

A rather different Top End experience was when I stayed at the luxury five-star resort at Seven Spirit Bay on the Cobourg Peninsula. I went there to write a report on the newly opened complex for the *Sunday Herald Sun*. My fellow guests included Japanese newlyweds, stressed-out New York lawyers and rich folk from Southern Australia. Every meal was gourmet, the resort pool long and cold, and the surrounding sea teemed with fish, sharks and dolphins. My private bungalow was immaculate.

The resort is located near the abandoned settlement of Port Essington, 300 kilometres north-east of Darwin where British colonists tried to build their first town in what is now the Northern Territory, long before opting for Darwin.

Port Essington today has a creepy feel, an eerie memorial to one of the British Empire's more disastrous attempts at colonisation. The only remains of the settlement today are a row of huge chimney fireplaces which the whites built soon after their arrival to keep warm in winter. The place never actually gets cold but. In fact, it was boiling hot while we were there, even though it was July and supposedly winter in Australia. The British tried to raise sheep and grow wheat in the tropical landscape. Bad move. Port Essington was eventually abandoned for fear of starvation.

If only the whites had asked the blackfellas. The place teems with delicious and healthy bush tucker, marine life and animals. It would have been like starving to death in the middle of a supermarket.

* * *

My newspaper sent me back to the top of Australia for a visit to Bathurst Island in the Tiwi Islands, a forty-minute flight north of Darwin, where I learned how much the locals love their Aussie Rules footy.

I was met at the airstrip by two elders, who took me on a tour of their island. At first it was very formal between us, and the conversations were brief. When they took me to a beautiful old billabong, one of the blokes said, 'This is a very sacred place for us.'

I walked around studying this special place with some reverence until I noticed a small piece of artwork or writing on a rock. What would it say? What nugget of 60,000-year-old ancient wisdom would it impart?

I bent down to read it. It said, 'Good Old Collingwood Forever'.

'You guys like the footy, then?' I observed.

That broke the ice as they opened up about their favourite AFL players. One of the old guys was particularly concerned about a certain player and the extent of his recent groin condition.

Later in Melbourne, acclaimed Bathurst Island artist and mate Gordon came to town to promote a new exhibition of his fantastic work. He asked me to come to the opening night at a trendy Toorak art gallery. A refined art historian proceeded to deliver a long-winded speech, gushing about my friend's art pieces mounted on the walls. Gordon Gordon edged close to me and whispered, 'Paulie, get me out of here will ya, let's go to the MCG.'

'But mate, this is your big night,' I said.

'No, it's boring. Let's go.'

We snuck out, jumped in a taxi and were soon in the Outer at the MCG watching a Friday night football match.

Gordon used his mobile to ring his mob back home on Bathurst Island. 'Hey, can you see me? Can you see me?' he asked, waving his hand in the air.

I laughed. We were in a crowd of 60,000.

Another trip to The Top End saw me accompany *Australian Idol* winner and Indigenous singer Casey Donovan on a promotional tour for the Fred Hollows Foundation in 2005. A highlight was meeting actor Tom E Lewis (star of the film *The Chant of Jimmie Blacksmith*) who took us to his family's freshwater billabong. A magic spot.

39

WORKING WITH THE MOB
(2011)

In 2010 I went to work with Jesuit Social Services as a mentor for young people. I loved the work, but one of the best things about the job was that I got to sit next to the inimitable Aunty Pam Pedersen in the backroom of the Artful Dodgers Studios in Collingwood.

This woman is formidable and was still surfing and running marathons in her seventies. We used to spend most of our time laughing.

As daughter of the late great Sir Doug Nichols, legendary Aussie Rules footballer and Governor of South Australia, she is indeed Indigenous royalty. I loved hearing her stories about some of the visiting celebrities who would drop in to see her father when he was a religious pastor tending to his flock in the back lanes of Fitzroy.

'I can remember Louis Armstrong playing his trumpet in the lounge room and Harry Belafonte singing us a tune,' Aunty Pam told me. 'The Ink Spots were also visitors. I even had The Jackson 5 in my car one day and we broke down in Spring Street [in Melbourne] and the boys got out of the car and changed the tyre for me.'

I used to tell people that Michael Jackson learned the moonwalk by directing traffic for Aunty Pam.

She later invited me and our Artful Dodgers workmates Roger Pugh and Marianna Codnoglotto as her guests to a special presentation at the Carlton Football Club where the Club apologised to her family for its treatment of Sir Doug.

Carlton had turned its back on him when he had arrived at the club for a try-out because none of the trainers would rub down a blackfella. Instead, Nicholls went to Fitzroy, where he became one of the greats of the game, representing Victoria.

Aunty Pam was brilliant because instead of berating the club for its blatant racism, she calmly listed her father's great achievements as a champion footballer, runner and boxer.

She then said, 'See what you fellas missed out on?'

At the event I met former Carlton great Syd Jackson, who spent most of his career copping dreadful racist abuse from white football fans. Incredibly, when he was chosen for an international tour in 1968 he struggled to get a passport because there was no record of his birth. Authorities had taken Jackson from his parents at the age of three.

Another Indigenous role model I met very early in his career was the actor Aaron Pedersen. We struck up a friendship soon after he arrived in Melbourne from Alice Springs to work for the ABC as a television reporter.

Journalism soon took a backseat to acting and Aaron has since starred in numerous films and TV series such as the highly successful series *Mystery Road*. The last time I saw him was on the set of the fantastic Australian film *High Ground*. Produced by Maggie Miles, the film stars Aaron, Simon Baker, Jack Thompson, Maximillian Johnson, Jacob Junior Nayinggul and Witiyana Marika from Yothu Yindi.

My work with Jesuit Social Services took me to the Western Sydney working-class suburb of Mt Druitt, where I spent two years with the local Indigenous mob, a community-enterprise supermarket and cafe in nearby Doonside. I compered the family festival at Mt

Druitt's Holy Family Primary school on three occasions. I enlisted the services of the school bank from the services of the choir from St Ignatius College Riverview, one of Sydney's most exclusive schools.

My close association with the Melbourne Indigenous community paid dividends during my stint in the liver clinic at the Austin Hospital because I was looked after by the Koori unit. Largely staffed by Indigenous healthcare workers, the unit takes special care of Indigenous patients and luckily for me they took me in as someone with an Indigenous daughter. It made a huge difference to have an 'Aunt' from the community drop in for a chat and a cup of tea every now and then.

One regular visitor at my hospital bedside was Grant Hansen, who for many years hosted the popular *Marngrook Football Show,* which covered the game with an Indigenous focus. Marngrook was the game played before white settlement that involved kicking a stuffed possum skin and many believe it helped to inspire Aussie Rules.

I first met Grant when I reported on a tour of Canada by Archie Roach and a troupe of other Indigenous Australian musicians. Grant came along to sell didjeridus and explain his culture to the Canadians, and we spent the trip sharing rooms and many laughs.

A visionary, he took the *Marngrook Show* from community radio to become the highest-rating show on Indigenous television network NITV.

You get to know your real mates when you are dying in hospital. Grant was a pillar of support, telling me in my darkest moments that everything would be fine. We spent hours talking about his favourite band, the rockabilly outfit Ol' 55, but I won't hold that against him.

Life certainly takes unusual twists and turns. How was I to know that sitting next to Aunty Pam at the Jesuits would play an important role in my family's life?

When Donna and I split up, Aretha eventually came to live with me, and as the single parent of a young Koori girl I found Aunty Pam a wonderful supporter and adviser.

I admit that I am a pushy old stage dad, but I am so proud and delighted that Aretha has emerged as a leading voice for not only young Indigenous people, but all young people.

In this role, Aretha appeared on the ABC's prestigious *Q&A* program. She has also been asked to share her views in magazines, on radio and at public demonstrations. A photo of her with a clenched fist in the air while addressing a huge 'Sorry Day' rally in Melbourne was prominently displayed in the UK in *The Times* newspaper.

She is passionate about the media and the need for more diverse voices, cultures and faces on air. My mum and Grandma Jan would have been so proud. Aretha chose to study fine arts at Melbourne University and has emerged as a popular mural painter.

But that is enough about her. She used to be known as 'Paulie Stewart's daughter'. Now I'm 'Aretha's Dad'.

40

LEAVING ON A JET PLANE

Apart from playing with the Painters & Dockers and The Dili Allstars, and my Timor-Leste activist duties, I was still working as a journalist at the *Sunday Herald Sun* throughout the 1990s. As I had always intended, I was burning the candle at both ends.

As far as professions go, you would never go into newspapers for the money. It is certainly not the highest paid work, but the fringe benefits are pretty good. In fact, they are fantastic.

One perk is overseas travel.

While most music journalists chose to fly to places like London and Los Angeles for some brief face time with a star and a quick flight home, I managed to arrange some more unusual overseas assignments. Once again, I was guided by my fascination with outsiders.

Over the years, I travelled with Queensland boy band Indecent Obsession to South Africa; Archie Roach to Canada; Melbourne world music combo Not Drowning, Waving to Papua New Guinea; and The Wiggles on one of their first major US tours. I even got to follow Japanese punk band The Stalin around their homeland.

A very special trip was when I accompanied singing sisters Vika and Linda Bull in 1996 to Tonga in the South Pacific, where their mother was born. They had been invited to perform at a ceremony marking the King of Tonga's national weight loss competition. As part of a campaign against the nation's crippling levels of obesity, locals lined up to measure their weight loss over a set period.

Afterwards we were taken to a local feast, and I swear the tables were creaking under the weight of the food. There were crayfish, pigs, pippies, bananas, pineapples, fish, yams, rice and mangoes. I have never seen so much food.

I later had the great honour of being invited to the small island owned by the family of the sisters' beautiful mother Siniva, which was a vision of paradise in the Pacific. Siniva and the girls' Australian-born father Austen made the trip with us.

Vika and Linda are real troupers, and love a party. One Saturday night they appeared at a leading kava club in Nuku'alofa, the capital of Tonga. At these male-only establishments, the local guys would sit around drinking kava and singing loud and suggestive ditties while being served by young women. Something strange happened when midnight marked the start of the Holy Sabbath. These same guys started to sing the sweetest and most heartfelt gospel hymns you have ever heard.

The local church services were a joyous musical experience. Surely these were the voices of angels?

I would later visit Fiji and Vanuatu and find that they have their own spectacular Pacific choirs. The best hands down, though, were the men and women of the tiny Cook Islands whose population of fewer than 16,500 is blessed with some truly remarkable singers.

I broke down in tears at a church mass on its largest island, Rarotonga, when the choir began singing. Their voices struck at your very soul.

41

THE STALIN IN JAPAN
(1984)

In 1984, some bright spark at the Royal Melbourne Show decided to hire a major Japanese rock act. Super group Godiego—they sounded like Australia's Little River Band and were a huge drawcard in Asia. The only problem was, even though they had performed the theme song for the cult TV series *Monkey*, nobody had heard of them in Melbourne.

I was asked to interview them to drum up some much-needed interest. It was terribly embarrassing when they put these guys on a small stage in a rain-drenched paddock at the Melbourne Showgrounds.

The few drunken yobbos who made up their crowd started screaming abuse at these 'slant-eyed bastards'.

I had met their manager Sadayuki Kurawaka earlier in the year when he was arranging the band's tour. He was grateful for my interest. We got on well over a long lunch and he said if I ever got to Japan, I should look him up. He gave me his card, which I put in my wallet and forgot about.

Six months later I arrived in Tokyo after a holiday through Asia and things were looking bleak as I was flat broke. I recalled I had 'Waka's' number.

I tentatively rang him, hoping he would remember the journalist he spoke to from Australia, and that at best he might take me out for lunch.

The phone was answered by his secretary. I told her I was in town and keen to hook up with her boss. She said to ring back in an hour. When I did, she informed me that my car and driver were waiting for me at a certain hotel where my new best friend had also lined me up some accommodation. You beauty.

Waka then offered me a tour of Japan with another band, punk act The Stalin. The boys in The Stalin were funny guys. We did our best to communicate, but my Japanese was very limited.

Formed in June 1980, frontman Michiro Endo explained he had chosen the band's name because, 'Joseph Stalin is hated by most people in Japan, so it is very good for our image.'

As a Painter & Docker, I could relate to the strategy. I got instant credibility with the boys when I said I came from the same town as Nick Cave and The Birthday Party, who they were big fans of. They said they loved the song 'Ick the Tripper', which I had never heard of until I figured out they meant 'Nick The Stripper'.

The first morning of the tour we stopped at a Japanese roadhouse and I thought, 'Great, bacon and eggs and a coffee.'

Wrong.

The guys in the band all settled down to a breakfast of rice topped with a raw egg. I was dry retching with a hangover and passed on the food.

The Stalin later played at a huge music festival. What amazed me was the way the stage crew swapped over bands in ten minutes flat. No mucking around. At a similar event I attended in Jamaica, it was a good hour and a half for a 'quick turnover'. Mind you, the Rastas shuffling the instruments around on stage were also passing around huge spliffs.

I got back to Tokyo after the tour and was now completely broke. I sat at a railway station wondering what in the hell I was going to do. A Japanese guy approached me and pointed at my T-shirt, featuring Australian punk band The Saints.

'Very good band, I like a lot,' he enthused. We got talking about music and he asked me where I was staying. I explained I was a bit down on my luck, and he did not hesitate.

'You come to my parents' home with me.'

I didn't have a choice really. When we arrived, his parents were at the kitchen table eating. They saw me, looked horrified and raced from the room.

They soon returned with armloads of presents, a bottle of sake for my honourable father and an ornate tea set for my honourable mother. A scoundrel to the core, I ended up pawning these gifts to get more travel cash.

On another Asian trek, I hooked up with pop band CDB from the Melbourne suburb of Dandenong. It had members of Indian and Sri Lankan heritage, Andrew De Silva, Brad and Gary Pinto (who became stalwarts of the Melbourne music scene) and Danny Williams.

These guys were real sweethearts and had a huge following in Malaysia. They were lined up to do a big showcase for Sony BMG records at a nightclub in Kuala Lumpur where they got to share the dressing room with a posse of beautiful Malaysian, Thai and Filipino dancing girls.

Hang on a minute, though, these girls were just a bit too sculptured. You guessed it, they were all ladyboys, and more than happy to share facilities with their new friends from Australia.

Unfortunately, the boys never got much support in their own country, feeling alienated in the Australian music scene.

'We didn't grow up listening to AC/DC and Cold Chisel, more the likes of Marvin Gaye and Earth Wind & Fire,' said singer Andrew De Silva.

The lack of imagination and vision shown by Australian record companies has always amazed me. They would rather sell re-hashed rock 'n' roll back to Britain and the United States when there are huge markets just to our north hungry for a more multicultural sound.

42

HOOTERS
(1985)

US college radio stations fell in love with Australian post-punk bands in the 1980s. The Painters & Dockers had our first two albums released in the United States on Big Time Records, who had also released albums by the Hoodoo Gurus. The label invited me to do some promotional work if I could get myself stateside.

When my housemate Francis Duke heard that I was going, he said he would tag along and that after our duties in Los Angeles we should go to the giant Reggae Sunsplash festival in Jamaica.

I managed to scam two press passes to the festival. We started our trip staying at a sleazy dive on Hollywood's overrated Sunset Strip. I spent a couple of days doing interviews about The Dockers at local college radio stations before we flew into Miami enroute to Jamaica.

When we reached the capital Kingston, our flight stopped to pick up more passengers for the trip to Montego Bay, and some of the wildest-looking Rasta men you've ever seen came onboard. These guys, seriously, had dreadlocks down to their ankles. One had shaped his hair to resemble a large hookah pipe. Man, what were we in for?

You've got to love a city like Montego Bay, where arriving tourists are given a huge glass of rum at the airport. We found out that Americans treat Jamaica like Australians treat Bali, with marauding drunken football teams and wet T-shirt competitions—no respect for the local culture.

As you can imagine, many of the locals are not particularly fond of whites. On the beach a group of wealthy Americans were watching some locals play cricket. They asked about the rules and were told to, 'Fuck off, mon.'

By now, Francis and I had been joined by Australian mate Chris Herd, who had thrown in a university course in Ohio to come with us. The best thing he did was bring a cricket bat. The locals saw it and demanded to know where we were from.

'Australia,' I told the meanest-looking guy, a chap called Mr Excellence.

He smiled. 'We love the cricket, man. And we love the Australian players, Dennis Lillee, Rod Marsh, the Chappells and Max Walker. Legends, mon.'

'Now let's play some cricket.' Which we did for the next three hours.

The Americans watching us asked why we weren't sliding into the wickets like they did on baseball fields. We rolled our eyes along with our new Jamaican mates.

This was a beach Test match of epic proportions.

The huge Sunsplash festival couldn't have been more different from its counterparts in Australia. For a start, daily proceedings began at 9pm and went through to dawn because it was too hot during the day.

Rather than sell Coke and hot dogs, vendors did a brisk trade in fresh goat and coconuts. Reggae stars on the bill included smooth soul singer Gregory Isaacs, Bob Marley's children The Melody Makers, and a unique DJ called Yellowman, who was an albino Rasta.

* * *

Another time I was invited to Los Angeles to interview someone, it was music legend Neil Diamond, who had recently announced an Australian tour. After flying across the Pacific I was told I would get just fifteen minutes to do an interview.

To my surprise I was ushered into his personal office to find it was full of Australian Aboriginal art. He turned out to be a knockabout character, and we laughed about his wife's support of AFL team the Brisbane Lions.

The interview went for an hour. I returned to the hotel the record company had booked for me and decided on a dip in the hotel pool. A bevy of beautiful people were stretched out on loungers and I swear the girls were three-quarters silicone. You have never seen so many massive fake breasts. It was a big theme in LA. Bored, and not interested in their company, I asked the hotel concierge if there was a nearby Native American art gallery, or maybe a museum I could visit.

'No, we don't have one of those,' he scratched his head, pondering. 'We do have a Hooters just across the road, though.' His mental leap from an art gallery straight to a topless bar staggered me.

I usually got on pretty well with the musicians I interviewed, mainly due to the fact that as a working musician I knew first-hand the pressures and strains they were under. I understood that musicians need plenty of space on the road. The last thing you want is a busy-body journalist humbugging you twenty-four hours a day.

As part of my duties as music writer at the *Sunday Herald Sun* I was invited to Vancouver to interview top-selling hard rock act Nickelback.

The Nickelback boys were road-weary and sick of talking to the media as they had been savaged by some critics. They were a sullen lot as we sat down to talk about their upcoming Australian tour.

To set off proceedings I asked if they had ever played at the small Vancouver venue The Town Pump, adding that I had played there several times with my band. It was an instant icebreaker.

'It was where we did our first-ever gig,' said singer Chad. 'It wasn't a huge place but we had a lot of fun there.'

'I loved playing there,' added the drummer. We then had an in-depth conversation about the band's early days and Chad invited me to his house outside Vancouver.

Another overseas junket involved an exclusive interview with the big hair guitarist Brian May from Queen. The occasion was to announce that Queen's stage musical *We Will Rock You* would be coming to Australia.

We met in the garden of May's mansion in Surrey. There was one question I was dying to ask about the band's huge hit 'Bohemian Rhapsody': what the hell was it about?

'I could tell you, but then I would have to kill you,' he sniggered.

43

WANTOK NO. 1
(1991)

In years to come when people write up the Top 10 most groundbreaking Australian albums of all time, surely the list will include the innovative masterpiece *Tabaran* by Melbourne act Not Drowning, Waving. This unique album features the earthy sounds of Melanesia combined with western music and it is like nothing you have ever heard. The word *tabaran* is used by locals in the Rabaul region of Papua New Guinea and refers to a powerful spirit that has its own special dance.

Band leader David Bridie, who also fronted Australian act My Friend the Chocolate Cake and has had a successful solo career, has since spent considerable time and energy recording the music of the Pacific. I was lucky enough to join his band on one of their first trips to PNG, where one of the more unusual concerts of my life was held on a football field in Rabaul surrounded by volcanoes—some still active.

One of those volcanoes would wipe out the town three years later.

The Rabaul area was full of World War II relics, including tunnels the Japanese had dug into cliffs to protect their submarines from Allied planes. The locals told me the story of an old Japanese soldier who returned after the war and spent years searching the tunnels looking for the Rolls Royce he said he had driven for a General during the war. He insisted the car had been hidden in a cave when the Japanese pulled out.

The band recorded with local singer-songwriter George Telek, a huge star in his own right in PNG who I worked with hosting *Port Moresby Idol*. George's first band had been called The Unbelievers, a provocative title given the religious fervour of the country. He had been a wild boy in his youth but had calmed down, unlike some of the hardcore PNG mob who would scrape the enamel off their teeth so they could get a better hit from chewing the local narcotic, betel nut.

George and David have long been firm friends, or *wantoks* in pidgin English. *Wantok* comes from the words 'one talk' meaning kin or close friends who talk in the same language. Together, the pair have produced many a fine recording and they have done much to highlight the plight of West Papua, which like Timor-Leste has suffered from Indonesian occupation.

I hooked up with Not Downing, Waving in Port Moresby in my best St Kilda attire of black jeans, black shirt and black boots, and felt completely overdressed compared to the band in their thongs, singlets and shorts. I almost died of heat-stroke!

Port Moresby is the most violent city I have come across in all my travels, and that includes places like Soweto, Dili, Jerusalem, Sao Paulo, Kingston Town, Cairo, New York and Glasgow. Our hotel was surrounded by security guards wielding baseball bats who patrolled the grounds at night 'to keep the rascals out'.

* * *

My first ever trip outside Australia was to PNG in 1980. Some fellow cadet journalists headed off to Bali but because of what happened to Tony I was determined not to spend any of my tourist dollars in Indonesia. I ended up alone in the PNG capital, staying in a cheap hotel.

The first night I went down for dinner and sitting at a long table I noticed two rows of black girls smiling at me with amusement. Confused, I asked one the name of our hotel.

She giggled. I was in The Port Moresby Hostel For Single Working Girls, which occasionally took in tourists.

I soon found that the locals in PNG are a friendly bunch, but you have to be careful anywhere near a bar once the drinking starts.

I was befriended by a local artist, a celebrity in his country. I spent many hours with Lithigartha talking about world politics, history and philosophy, and he declared that I was his new wantok. He revealed that he was a firm believer in black magic and told me how he had seen large stones removed from people's heads and necks.

One day he informed me he was taking me to a *hangi*, a local barbecue. The hosts gave us each a big bottle of beer then proceeded to start the cook-up. They got a huge pig, slit its throat to drain its blood and wrapped it in foil. They dug an enormous hole and placed hot stones at the bottom, piling the pig on top and covering it with palm leaves. Then we waited. And waited. And waited.

To pass the time, I foolishly tried to match my hosts beer for beer. Big mistake. I was then offered a chance to sample some betel nut.

'Sure, why not?' I mused.

End result, I fainted flat on my face, much to the horror of my hosts, who carried me to the house's master bedroom to sleep it off. I slept all night while the host family camped around me on the floor, as they had given up their bed for the drunken visitor.

Another journalism jaunt to the Pacific in 1997 took me to the back-blocks of the Solomon Islands after I had heard about the work of English composer Anthony Copping.

He said he had first caught the South Pacific music bug on a trip to the area a decade earlier and he had become obsessed with recording the traditional sounds of the region, many of which were now sadly disappearing. He was supported by Solomon Islands guitarist and friend Pascal Oritaimae on an amazing quest that took in 300 islands,

200 performers, and a baffling number of different languages, given that some dialects were spoken in just one village.

They travelled mainly by log canoe and using old bush tracks. Not surprisingly, Copping developed a bad case of malaria visiting remote parts of PNG, West Papua, Vanuatu and the Solomons. In a real recording coup, he had managed to capture the vocals of one of the last remaining sorcerers in the Pacific.

'We never knew what songs we were going to be entrusted with and that was the thrill,' he explained to me. 'One of the women who sang a traditional song for us was ninety-two and as you work you are thinking this will be lost forever unless we record it. That gives you an enormous sense of responsibility.'

When he had finished his recordings, he returned to his studio to add his own musical interpretations.

'I wanted to retain the music's integrity but also to create something in harmony with the modern world,' he said.

His record company agreed to fly me to the Solomon Islands to witness his extraordinary efforts first-hand.

We spent a lot of time on the island of Guadalcanal, the site of heavy fighting in World War II. It is near Iron Bottom Sound, a part of the seabed named for all its warship wrecks.

One day I took myself to the massive sand dune on Guadalcanal that had been the site of one of World War II's bloodiest battles. Today, Guadalcanal is a quiet Pacific backwater but for six months from August 1942, the flower of Japanese and American youth battled it out for a few square kilometres where a crucial airstrip could be built.

The fighting was fierce and bloody. The Japanese lost 26,000 men; the Americans lost 1,600 and had 4,200 wounded. The American victory turned the tide of the Pacific War.

Villagers said they still dig up human remains and old weapons. As I stood on the desolate dune, I couldn't help but think of the thousands of young Americans and Japanese who had died there.

For what?

We moved on to explore other islands in the Solomons, nearly drowning one day when our motorised canoe was hit by huge seas and driving winds. The boat was way overcrowded and I was ready to jump out and try to swim to shore. At the last moment, there was a lull in the wind and we arrived safely at a small village. The locals were starving because their usual fish supplies had been devastated by Indonesian fishing boats with huge nets, but typically they were happy to share what little they had with us.

Unfortunately, Copping's album was too innovative for the Australian mainstream music scene and it fell between the cracks.

44

STRAWBERRY KISSES
(1992)

The 1990s Queensland boy band Indecent Obsession were not everyone's cup of tea. In some parts of Australia they had a devoted following of young girls, but most young blokes didn't like them. In fact, some detested them.

At Transformers, an infamously rough venue in Moorabbin in suburban Melbourne, they liked their music hard and fast. Indecent Obsession's sweet pop sound went totally against the vibe in the room the night I saw them in action there. There were yells of 'poofters' and 'Queensland fags', and the odd empty beer can was thrown by the annoyed locals.

It was a surprise, then, when they hit the jackpot and landed a huge record deal in South Africa. They had the honour of being the first white pop band in the world to play in the country after the easing of its apartheid-era cultural isolation in 1992. The band had enjoyed modest success in Australia with their debut tune 'Strawberry Kisses', but it was certainly no major hit.

I had heard they were off to South Africa for some appearances and rang their record company, Mushroom, insisting I should cover this historic visit.

Music guru and *Countdown* host Ian 'Molly' Meldrum managed the band. Realising it was a good yarn, he encouraged Mushroom to send me along for the ride.

When we landed in Johannesburg at about 5am I said to Mushroom representative Anne Gibson, 'Gee, wouldn't it be great if someone turned out to meet us.'

We walked into the airport to scenes of pandemonium as 2000 white teenage girls mobbed the band.

A vivid memory is a line of black policemen struggling to fight back the young female tidal wave. These girls had never had a Beatles or Stones or Bay City Rollers tour to go crazy at and they seemed intent on making up for it.

Indecent Obsession would go on to play massive stadium shows throughout the country, while Miss South Africa and other beauties hung out with the boys backstage.

I had developed an interest in the African National Congress (ANC), the black revolutionary movement that had fought the apartheid regime. Many people had pointed out to me the similarities between ANC leader Nelson Mandela and Timor-Leste's Xanana Gusmão. Both ratbag terrorists one day, much-admired Presidents the next.

The ANC had spent years fighting inhuman and brutal white injustice so I suggested to the guys in Indecent Obsession that they should meet the ANC and pay their respects. They had little idea who the ANC were but agreed anyway. I rang the ANC, who were keen to meet the visiting pop stars from Down Under. Later the band conducted workshops and invited ANC members to concerts. I rang Molly back in Australia and he was thrilled that I had pulled off such a meeting. Getting the ANC's backing proved vital and the tour was a great success.

I met a really nice girl who worked for Indecent Obsession's record company in Johannesburg. She was the token black employee on staff. We got talking and I asked her where she lived.

'Soweto,' she replied.

'It must be an interesting place,' I said.

'Would you like to have a look?' she offered.

'Sure, let's go.'

We drove to Soweto in her little car and went through some of the back streets lined with tin-roofed shanties.

She was widely respected in her community for having a prestigious job at a white firm. The locals would see me and tense up, but when they saw who I was with, they would visibly relax.

I will never forget the piece of graffiti on a Soweto wall that read 'One white, one bullet'.

We drove past Mandela's heavily fortified home and went to an outdoor stage where, I was told, the last performer of note had been black 1960s soul sensation Percy 'When A Man Loves A Woman' Sledge.

When I got back to central Johannesburg that night I was greeted by an anxious white staff member from the record company.

'We were worried about you. Where have you been?' he asked.

'Soweto,' I said.

'Where?' he asked again.

'Soweto,' I repeated.

'You are joking, right? You are lucky you weren't bashed, robbed or murdered,' he said. 'So what's it like, anyway?'

'What do you mean, "What is it like?"' I asked.

This chap said he had never been game to visit Soweto, a township of 1.3 million people, even though it was just forty-five minutes up the road.

I came back with a head full of ideas about cultural exchanges between black South Africa and Australia. But it was early days and people thought I was talking crazy. Nowadays it's nothing to see African bands touring Australia.

Nelson Mandela's debut trip to Australia, organised in part by my friend Jacqui Geia, was a truly awe-inspiring experience.

Mandela had only recently been released from jail where he had been held for decades and badly mistreated. His appearance at a Melbourne rally was like the arrival of a massive pop star, with the crowd going into a frenzy when he walked on stage. What would the great man say? Many expected him to vent his anger against white South Africans.

Instead, the man who had suffered so much at the hands of the apartheid authorities absolutely floored me and others when he called for black South Africans to forgive their white countrymen. Not only forgive them, but love them unconditionally.

A very special man indeed.

In 1986 I became involved with another liberation struggle facing as grim an outlook as East Timor, this one in the African nation of Namibia. After noticing a poster calling for help from a group called the South West Africa People's Organisation (SWAPO) I found their run-down campaign office near Flinders Street railway station in Melbourne, which was manned by a guy called Hadino Hishongwa. He urged me to help Namibia, which was being governed by the apartheid regime in nearby South Africa. I agreed to help him by organising a benefit concert.

First, we needed a venue. I approached the good-hearted Bruce Kane, the student activities officer at Melbourne University. He too was moved by the plight of Namibia and offered one of the student halls at the university. We thought we might be able to get a couple of bands together but the whole thing snowballed.

In the end, sixteen acts performed and ABC radio recorded the show. A live album called *SWAPO Benefit* was later released and it went to number one on the Australian independent charts.

Any sense of triumph was spoiled for me, though, when halfway through the night I was called to the admission desk to deal with a problem. Being manhandled by the bouncers were a bunch of local

Kooris. Security said they had been causing trouble and they were all being thrown out.

'What is the problem?' I asked one of them.

'You are full of shit, mate, you don't need to go to Africa to see oppressed blacks, what about all the problems we face?'

I had no comeback, he was dead right.

The whole SWAPO show taught me one extremely important lesson about running benefits and releasing fundraising albums. Accountability.

It is vital that every cent raised goes to the cause nominated. Never give anyone a whole stack of money unless they can prove where it is going.

That was the disappointing thing with the guy from SWAPO, who had been a founding member of the movement and would later serve as a government minister when the country finally gained independence. He was never really clear how the proceeds from the night were actually spent. All I know is that he took a holiday to Fiji not long after the concert, and for some reason bought himself a stack of duty-free white goods while he was there.

That is why it was great working with John Sinnott from Australia-East Timor Association (AETA) on various projects because he insisted every cent be accounted for.

Another miscalculation was when the Painters & Dockers were asked by some Australian-Irish wharfies to play a fundraiser for something called the Irish Benevolent Fund. We did the benefit show at the South Melbourne Town Hall on a Saint Patrick's Day for these so-called Irish community workers. The band was horrified when at the end of the show four balaclava-clad men stood at the front with garbage bags into which the crowd dropped wads of cash while they sang pro-IRA songs.

45

ONE-LEGGED RACE
(1997)

I was fortunate to be able to cover other stories overseas without an entertainment bent. On one assignment I was sent to Cambodia to report on the progress of the country's Paralympic team as it prepared for the upcoming Sydney 2000 Games.

I had been invited by a character named Chris Minko, who had played trumpet with Melbourne band Bachelors From Prague and later ran a workshop on the Port Melbourne wharves making trade union floats and stage props for parades and other events.

Flying into the Cambodian capital Phnom Penh, I was struck by a sinister vibe and a sense of desperation. Maybe it was the burnt-out buildings and the squalor that reminded me very much of Dili.

Amid the squalor, there were some absolutely beautiful old French colonial houses—real works of art. Cambodia's modern conflicts began when the giant US military machine started bombing the neutral country to flush out Vietcong rebels from neighbouring Vietnam. Naturally, many locals objected to this and the fanatical communist guerrillas the Khmer Rouge sprung up under the command of the infamous Pol Pot to challenge the pro-American forces. Pol Pot had developed his bloodthirsty Year Zero philosophy on the Left Bank in Paris with other intellectual radicals. When it was put into action, that philosophy turned into mass murder.

I was told by locals that when the Khmer Rouge took over, all members of the previous regime, plus lawyers, teachers, doctors, anyone with an education, and even people condemned for wearing spectacles, were thrown into camps with their whole families before being executed.

In the 350 places in the Cambodian countryside that became notorious as the Killing Fields, upwards of two million people were estimated to have been slaughtered in one of history's worst genocides.

Communist Vietnam eventually swooped in to liberate the people from this evil. The UN peacekeepers were helping to maintain an uneasy truce while I was there. The constant warfare had sown another deadly harvest, namely millions of unexploded landmines. The ugliest thing about these weapons is they have little military value and are used mainly to terrorise civilians. It is hard to believe that human beings actually designed many of these landmines to look like brightly-coloured toys so children would pick them up.

In Cambodia, you became blasé about seeing people with one limb. The hospitals were a shambles, crammed with landmine victims and their families, who would bring in all their worldly possessions. Pigs, goats and dogs wandered the corridors. It was chaos.

Remarkably, the best massage I've ever had was at a facility in Cambodia filled with landmine victims. I was not expecting much and was mainly hoping to help out a little by giving some work to a guy who had had his eyes and most of his face blown off. His sinewy fingers unlocked every stress knot in my back. I was soon fast asleep.

Most of the Paralympic team were landmine victims who had lost legs. They had been given artificial racing legs by the Australian Embassy and Endolite Asia, a hi-tech prosthetics company.

Athlete Nok Rotha told me he lost his leg to a landmine when he was searching for food for his family.

'I was in a Khmer Rouge army unit on the border near Thailand,' he said. 'We were starving and government troops left food cooking out in the bush surrounded by landmines. I was so hungry that I went to get food and stood on a mine.'

'Like everyone, I would love to win a gold medal in Sydney. I might not do it, but I certainly will be trying my hardest,' he said.

I reckon the guy already deserved one for enduring the challenges life had sent him.

46

BAD LAND, SAD LAND
(2000)

The life of a journalist has taken me to some of the most ostentatious and glamorous locations in the world, but I've also seen some of the darker places.

Timor-Leste has beautiful mountains covered by rainforests but people there will still point out old massacre sites like the massive cliffs where villagers were asked to embrace Indonesian rule, or jump. Many jumped.

Standing on top of those cliffs, looking down at the beautiful forest, it is chilling to imagine people choosing to jump, but to borrow from a famous Midnight Oils lyric, 'It's better to die on your feet than to live on your knees.'

It was just as eerie at Dili's Santa Cruz cemetery where in 1991 Indonesian troops opened fire on unarmed students and civilians in an act that shocked the world.

I came across one of the most sinister places I have ever visited during a trip to Germany to cover the World Expo in Hanover in 2000. I was in a group of junketing journalists being wined and dined throughout the Saxony region of Germany. We visited castles, art galleries, wineries and restaurants, and I really did feel like a pig at the trough after a couple of days as we were constantly served massive meals and countless local beers.

The tour guide told us that a highlight of our trip would be a visit to the German cultural city of Weimar. It was indeed a beautiful place, full of ornate churches and the home of playwright Johann Wolfgang von Goethe, who wrote his most famous piece, *Faust*, there.

Leaving Weimar, the tour guide announced she would briefly take us to the former Nazi concentration camp at Buchenwald, about ten kilometres to the north-west. She said we had a tight schedule but we could have a quick look around.

As the day was absolutely freezing, most of the journalists were back on the bus within five minutes but I felt I couldn't come all the way to Germany and just be dazzled by its cultural history while ignoring the horrors of its past.

I set off alone to explore the camp. I was dressed against the cold in boots, long johns, singlet, skivvy, trousers, jumper, thick coat, gloves, scarf and a heavy woollen cap. I was still freezing to the bone. I could only imagine the plight of the starving inmates who were made to wear flimsy pyjamas as they toiled all day in the snow. I wandered into one building and went down to the basement where I was confronted by a row of ovens.

In the silence I literally trembled, and it was not because of the cold.

This was not ancient history. These ovens were put to evil use just fifteen years before I was born, with the trauma of the Holocaust still vividly scarring the lives of some of my childhood neighbours in Melbourne. I returned to the bus an hour later to the annoyance of everyone else onboard.

Closer to home, I was invited two years later in 2002 to cover the annual jazz festival on Norfolk Island, off the coast of New South Wales. Like Buchenwald, it has an evil past. In Australia's early days, if a convict caused trouble, he was sent to Port Arthur in Tasmania. If you really crossed the line, it was a one-way trip to Norfolk Island.

Prisoners were kept in appalling conditions, including the infamous 'dumb rooms', which were so small you had to stand upright. Floggings were common. It was said that one of the few acts of kindness a prisoner could do for a fellow inmate was to piss on his back to help the lash marks heal.

Today, Norfolk Island is a mecca for retirees enjoying its relaxed pace and mild temperature. A highlight of my visit was lunch with 1970s singing icon Helen 'I Am Woman' Reddy, who was then the island's most famous resident. A huge international star after the 1971 release of her feminist anthem, she told me she was a firm believer in reincarnation and talked of her former lives, including the one in which she was a swashbuckling pirate.

I attended several concerts in the old prison. Sitting there on the opening night of the jazz festival, watching veteran Australian jazzman Don Burrows in action, I couldn't help but think of all the tortured souls who had graced this exact spot.

47

THE PRICS
(1989)

My work supporting Timorese independence had shown me what a powerful tool music could be. That is why I got involved with a troupe called the PRICS. Performers Releasing Information about Clean Syringes was the name chosen for an educational health collective based on an idea of two Victorian health workers, Terri Pryor and the inimitable Graham Stevens, a true visionary and dear friend. Graham and Terri had realised that young drug users were much more likely to listen to the messages of musicians than to any advice from police, priests or social workers.

They came up with the concept of creating a group of musicians to perform songs delivering the right messages to those most at risk of catching the HIV virus.

Terri rang me in 1989 and said, 'What should we call the act?'

I suggested The PRICS because (a) it was cheeky, (b) it explained our task, and (c) most importantly, it showed we did not take ourselves too seriously. That was the attitude that might cut through to the young people we were trying to reach. The group included Rebecca

Barnard, David Bridie, Kerri Simpson, Shelly Scow, Rob Craw, Tanya-Lee Davies, Josie Jason, Chris O'Connor, Richard Gray, Paul Winterbine, Michael Hohnen, myself, and the late greats Peter Jones and Janine Hall.

Later members would include Shane O'Mara, Helen Mountfort and Michael Barclay.

The Victorian Government funded the project, sending us to perform at halfway houses and youth detention centres throughout the State and into NSW. These shows involved playing a number of songs, doing creative safe sex workshops and outlining safe drug use. Some of the institutions we performed at were interesting to say the least.

Sadly, many of the detainees at the youth detention facilities were young Pacific Islanders (aged about fifteen, but looking twenty-five) and Indigenous youth. I remember performing in front of one of these groups and having several young Islanders run their fingers across their throats, mouthing, 'You're dead, arsehole,' whenever their minders looked away.

It was an eye-opener mixing with these kids. When you heard that some had committed rape or murder you felt utter disdain for them, until you learned that many had also been raped or abused by their own parents or carers.

After one session of hearing the stories of their childhoods, I rang Mum in tears to thank her for the loving care she had always shown me. The PRICS released an album called *Covered*, in 1992, and another collection two years later in conjunction with the Triple J network.

Graham Stevens, a provocative but loveable gay loudmouth, hired The Dockers to appear at the music events Rockin' the Docks and Rockin' the Rails, which were part of a government campaign against excessive drinking called Rage Without Alcohol.

Rockin' the Docks saw the band board a hovercraft to play at various piers around Port Phillip Bay, with fans gathering at the piers.

I don't know how we got so drunk considering it was supposed to be a dry event discouraging alcohol abuse. Maybe it was something to do with the vodka in the lunch-time orange juice on the hovercraft.

The day came to a climax at the spiritual home of the real Painters and Dockers, the historic Station Pier in Port Melbourne. By the time we arrived, the crowd had been drinking in the hot afternoon sun for hours, and fans started wildly slam-dancing. Police moved in to try to calm them down and a full-scale riot was only narrowly avoided.

Rockin' the Rails was similar, except this time, we played on a train that stopped at suburban stations. We were accompanied at the first of these rail gigs by big hair 1980s act Geisha.

I was drunk again.

One performance at Camberwell Station went crazy, with some members of the enormous crowd getting onto an old tin roof which was on the verge of collapsing. The organisers pleaded with the compere Molly Meldrum to get us to calm down. Molly, crazy bastard that he is, encouraged the crowd to greater acts of anarchy. This was rock 'n' roll, after all. Rather than do a slow ballad, Molly started the band off in an over-the-top version of the 1970s Supernaut hit, 'I Like It Both Ways'. We pulled out of the station to scenes of absolute mayhem.

We did another day of Rockin' the Rails with Paul Kelly and The Coloured Girls, which was fun right from the word go. Our departure from Flinders Street station was delayed because one of the Coloured Girls told organiser Linda Carroll that band member Derek Smalls was missing.

The call boomed out on the station's loudspeakers as staff anxiously scoured the platform for him.

'Derek Smalls, Derek Smalls, please board the train immediately.'

Ten minutes passed. Still no sign of the musician. But hang on, why did that name ring a bell?

Then it hit us. Derek Smalls was the fictional bass player in the rock 'n' roll spoof movie *Spinal Tap*. He would not be joining our party for some time.

After Rockin' the Rails, Stevens employed us to perform our song 'Safe Sex' in the annual Moomba Festival parade down the main street of Melbourne. I don't think the organisers of this traditional family event were banking on a noisy rendition of a song encouraging the use of condoms, but we were trying to get our HIV message to the young people at risk.

Wanting to give it an authentic feel, we dressed in pyjamas and played on a huge double bed surrounded by lingerie-clad girls from the St Kilda-based Prostitutes Collective of Victoria. I can still remember the look on the face of Premier John Cain as we cruised past the VIP stand outside the Melbourne Town Hall.

'What the f—?'

It was good mate and Triple J producer Chris Thompson who asked me to attend another meeting with some musicians who were trying to help a particular group of children. These children had all struggled because of their parents' drug habits or even their deaths caused by overdoses. The first meeting was at the home of convenor Jane Rowe, who wanted to set up a fundraising organisation.

Rowe believed with a passion that every child deserved the opportunity to break out of their parents' destructive cycle of addiction. In 1998 she recruited her friend, the veteran guitarist Spencer P Jones, to help with the project.

Spencer made a name for himself in music circles with cowboy punks The Johnnys, the hard and heavy Beasts of Bourbon and his own solo material. He also played sidekick to some of Australia's biggest stars including Paul Kelly, Renee Geyer and Tex Perkins.

The founding members of this new organisation included me, Spencer, my PRICS colleague Rebecca Barnard, youth worker Jay Jordens, community lawyer Simon Northeast and Triple J producers Chris Thompson and Michael Pavlich. Rowe named her new organisation Mirabel after a character in a childhood story who cared for neglected children. The Mirabel Foundation has gone on to raise large amounts of money to provide shelter and support for children, a helping hand for struggling grandparents and even the odd Christmas present.

One of Jane's fundraising initiatives was the publication of two cookbooks *Rock Chefs for Mirabel* and *Laughing Stock*, in which musicians and comics shared their favourite recipes.

It was an honour being part of the Mirabel family. Around that time I was also invited onto the inaugural board of Ausmusic, the peak music industry advisory group, by its chief executive, the former federal Labor MP, Pete Steedman. Steedman was a lovable ratbag who had upset some MPs by wearing his leather coat into Parliament. Ausmusic pushed to get more home-grown music on the radio and supported emerging musicians. I was the token alternative music representative and would sit back listening to the board heavyweights, wondering what the hell they were on about.

Whenever asked for my ideas I just said, 'You should buy communal sound systems for bands to share. That would keep costs down and let them do more shows.'

They would nod their heads in agreement and move straight on to the next issue. The shared sound systems never appeared, but the free board lunches were great.

48

THIS IS SERIOUS
(1986)

Ever seen a band that leaves you gobsmacked? For me, it was the Melbourne musical terrorists This Is Serious Mum, or TISM.

The Dockers had just supported the Hoodoo Gurus before a full house at The Palace in St Kilda and I felt indestructible. I headed off to late-night venue The User's Club in Carlton for some celebratory beers.

About 3am, six or seven guys walked on stage wearing balaclavas. They started reading copies of *The Age* newspaper and nonchalantly singing songs like 'Defecate On My Face'.

It was yobbo culture at its most basic, combined with high prose, philosophy, mad rants and political statements. Perhaps the best part of TISM was their utter disdain for music journalists.

Their outfits included Ku Klux Klan hoods, giant balloon headdresses and T-shirts saying 'Choose Smack' instead of the 'Choose Life' slogan made popular in the 1980s. Their eccentric lead singer Ron Hitler-Barassi—real name Peter Minack—would often end up in his undies as the crowd ripped his clothes off.

One of the best compliments the Painters & Dockers received was the persistent rumour that we were actually TISM in disguise. I think this came about because one of the early reviews of the band said, 'These guys are shithouse, just like the Painters & Dockers but in masks.' People actually believed this rumour.

It was years later that Hitler-Barassi told me of my role in TISM's birth. My mum June had worked at Camberwell High School with an old friend of mine, Terri Rowe. Terri was married to Peter Minack's brother Gerard, a roadie with TISM who moonlighted as a prominent financial commentator. Because I was writing about music for the *Sunday Herald Sun*, Rowe gave Mum a cassette for me. I was intrigued by the label—'Defecate On My Face'—and when I popped it into a cassette player the song was a ripper. I passed the tape on to Michael Lynch, who worked alongside The Dockers' first management team.

It was years later that Peter Minack told me that tape I passed on had kickstarted their career. Michael Lynch apparently loved both the song and the band and started getting them paid gigs. TISM went on to become a major drawcard around Australia.

49

ELVIS WAS A GENTLEMAN
(1999)

Some of the best stories journalists ever hear just drop into their laps. One of mine was the occasion that Elvis Presley toured Australia in 1999. Yes, he was dead at the time, but he appeared on a big screen supported by his former backing band and his three black back-up singers, The Sweet Inspirations. It was a testament to Elvis' eternal popularity that televised images of The King could still pack out theatres. Journalists were flown to Adelaide to interview his former bandmates at the start of the tour.

The press conference was a pretty laid-back affair as Elvis was not taking questions. I went to my hotel room but was soon bored so decided to go for a wander. I stumbled across The Sweet Inspirations, who were half-heartedly playing the pokies downstairs. There wasn't another journalist in sight. I introduced myself and when they agreed that I could join them I bought a round of drinks and sat down.

'What was The King really like?' I asked.

'Well,' said Myrna Smith, the most outspoken of the three women, 'for a start, Elvis hated to be called The King.'

She said he would never let anyone address him like that.

'Elvis would point to the heavens and say, "There is only one King". He really looked after us, no one was allowed to swear or cuss around us.'

'Except him, of course,' laughed another of the trio.

Between sips of her Long Island Iced Tea, Smith added that Presley was a very generous man.

'One night he gave me a baby blue Cadillac as a present,' she recalled. 'You see, once during a show he offered to give me a ring off his own finger. I refused to take it, saying I was a lady and he was a married man after all.

'Well Elvis said he didn't want the ring and threw it into the crowd. He felt so bad about dissing me that the next night he had the whole carpark behind the venue filled with Cadillacs. He asked me what my favourite colour was.

'I said baby blue, then I was dumbstruck when he took out a huge set of keys and picked one and said "This is your car".'

The three said they thought it hilarious when Elvis started to dress like a black gangster.

'Elvis was funny, he enjoyed all those black movies of the 1960s, particularly the pimp movie *Super Fly*,' said Myrna. 'He even bought all these pimp clothes, but he looked so ridiculous dressed like that.'

The backing singer said Presley slept all day and roamed all night.

'He would often take us to the movies at 3am, where he would have booked out the whole cinema.'

She said he preferred gospel music to the newer bands of the early 1970s.

'I can remember one time Led Zeppelin came around to say hello and Elvis had to ask someone who they were. Still, Elvis was really like a brother to us,' said Smith, 'and, of course, I think his music will live forever.'

I later visited Memphis with my buddy Paulie Greene, a rubbish remover by day and Elvis impersonator by night. He'd always wanted to go to Memphis and this became possible after he won big-time punting on a horse race. Paulie's wife Cathy didn't like to fly so he asked me to come and I'm sure glad I did.

We went to Memphis during Elvis Week in August 2010, when Presley look-alikes from around the world gathered to pay homage. On the first night we entered a crowded lift at the prestigious Peacock Hotel and I was the only person not dressed as The King.

There was a African-American Elvis, an Asian Elvis, an Indian Elvis, a Brazilian Elvis and my friend Paulie, an Australian Elvis.

The Indian Elvis looked at me in my plain clothes and got a lot of laughs by asking the assembled Elvis', 'So who's the freak?'

I went to bed early but Paulie struck up a conversation at the hotel bar with one of Elvis' former bodyguards. They got on like a house on fire and the bodyguard ended up lending him a couple of rings that he said Elvis had given him. Paulie came up to our room about 5.30am and gave me one of the rings, which I proudly wore for a few days.

While he was sleeping it off I got up early and decided to track down a local gospel service I had heard about. I jumped on a tram for the suburbs of Memphis.

Before too long I saw from the tram a huge church, so I jumped off and followed a stream of people wearing their Sunday best. I knew I would be one of the few white faces in the congregation, not that it mattered, as the locals made me feel right at home especially when they found out I was Australian. The service was remarkable. The singing was sensational, everyone looked fantastic and audience participation was encouraged. At one stage the preacher jumped up and down on a huge double bed in front of the altar shouting, 'Drive lust out, drive lust out'.

He urged us to hug our neighbours in the church. I turned to the gorgeous girl standing next to me and thought, 'This is not driving lust out, it's driving it in.'

Later, Paulie and I visited Graceland and placed on his grave a Gumbaynggirr angel, painted by my mother-in-law Aunty Janice Brown, a massive Elvis fan.

We made a pilgrimage to the small town of Tupelo, the Bethlehem of rock 'n' roll, and saw the tiny two-bedroom dirt-floor cabin where Elvis was born. We even went to the hardware shop where the rocker bought his first guitar.

As part of this visit, I talked Paulie into a side trip to Richmond, Virginia, to visit the Museum of the Confederacy. I had long been fascinated by the fact that one of the last actions of the US Civil War took place in Williamstown in Melbourne, when the Confederate raider the *Shenandoah* arrived in port in 1865. In Richmond we saw the ship's original flag and read its captain's logbook. I even arranged for an expert on the ship, Sam Craghead, to visit Melbourne the following year to talk on the subject. We also visited Craig's Hotel in Ballarat where the captain and officers of the Shenandoah had attended a ball held in their honour by Ballarat gold tycoons.

The popularity of Elvis' posthumous tour of Australia was evidence that rock stars simply don't die any more. In fact, I got to play guitar on stage once with all-time great Jimi Hendrix in front of a crowd of thousands, despite the fact he too had been dead for years.

I was invited to Seattle in 2000 for the opening of a museum called the Experience Music Project, where I joined the master guitarist on stage with a virtual reality headset. Every now and then Jimi would turn to me and nod when it was my turn to play.

The museum was not far from the tiny bar where grunge super trio Nirvana cut their chops. The bar was designed by Frank Gehry and funded by Microsoft billionaire co-founder Paul Allen, a massive Hendrix fan.

Apparently, Allen has a room with hundreds of brand new guitars and every night he twangs away trying to sound like Jimi but no matter how much money he has, he can't cut it. I love that. Dirt-poor Jimi is still the master as you can't buy genius.

50

SAINT NICK
(1980–2007)

The man many would consider Australia's version of Elvis is Nick Cave. He was one of the first people I ever interviewed for the *Sun News-Pictorial* in 1980 and right from the get-go he showed he was a cut above the rest: smart, charismatic and very hard-working. I loved the way he made himself a mythical personality.

He once told a journalist he'd been born with a tail and had to have it surgically removed. Another time he claimed he had a twin brother who died at birth, as Elvis did.

The best story he helped spread was that the good folk of Warracknabeal, the small Victorian town where he was born, were building a huge statue of him sitting on a horse and wearing only a loincloth. Several English news organisations wrote about this but those who bothered to contact the town's mayor found that he knew nothing about it.

Cave backed up his make-believe with great song-writing and a magnetic stage presence.

I thought he would go a long way after that first interview when he was singing with Melbourne Goth band The Birthday Party and lived in a small flat in Robe Street, St Kilda.

The piece I wrote was one of the first mainstream stories about Cave but he amazed me and the photographer Neale Duckworth by tenaciously refusing to take part unless he could choose the photo that would accompany the story. This was unheard of, given that most artists would bend over backwards to get their picture in the paper, and Cave did not just ask for the right to veto the photo, he demanded it.

Who was this upstart? Obviously someone with a big career in mind.

Cave ended up choosing a striking shot of himself with a brooding look and massive teased hair. The next time I interviewed him he walked into the old Phoenix Hotel on Flinders Street, the favourite watering hole of football and racing reporters. He was in a lime green suit and a pair of elf boots. The crusty old hacks did a double take.

'Who the fuck is that clown?' hissed one as we found our table to do the interview.

I also met Cave and other Birthday Party members at the Richmond Recorders studio when they made their *Kicking Against The Pricks* album as they borrowed some Dockers equipment for the recording.

In 2007, a retrospective on Cave's career opened at the Victorian Arts Centre. For my first story since my transplant, I interviewed him for the *Sunday Herald Sun*. I had a head full of pills but it all went well until I overstepped the mark. He had actually just said, 'This is a good interview, great questions,' when I pushed my luck.

'So, Nick, you have done a song with Kylie, what about doing one with The Wiggles?'

'I spoke too soon,' he said with a mocking tone.

Drawing on more than 800 items donated by Cave and curated by the Arts Centre's Janine Barnard, the exhibition included lyric books, posters, photographs and personal items from his office and library.

During our interview I reminded him that he had come a long way since his Robe Street days and recalled how he had shocked me and the photographer during that first interview by demanding to choose the photo.

'Did I do that? If only I still had that power,' he said with a wry smile. 'The primary importance to me has always been the creative process. I am obsessed by it and have taken it more seriously than anything else.'

Cave admitted he had created an aura around himself by telling music journalists fantastic tales, conceding that he had invented the tail story.

'I am no spin doctor. That was just my playful nature,' he said. 'It usually happens when I get a journalist who I think would believe anything. Yes, I did say I was born with a tail and my mum keeps it in an old pickle jar.'

He chuckled about the horse statue story.

'I told one English journalist there were plans to build a revolving restaurant in the mouth of the horse.'

Think about it ... that's a hell of a big statue.

I told him about my interview with US blues great Screaming Jay Hawkins, who had accompanied Cave on an Australian tour.

'I love Nick Cave's music but the guy and his band dress like street bums,' Hawkins had said.

'I take his point,' said the lanky singer-songwriter, who was now dressed immaculately in black open shirt, black suit and black boots.

'I could tell you stories about Screaming Jay that would curl your hair,' he laughed. 'Let me put it this way, no one wanted to sit next to him on a plane because, and I am not joking, every day he would boast about how many people had covered his song "I Put A Spell On You".'

Cave admitted that he and his band had used hard drugs at Richmond Recorders.

'Make no mistake, though, we were there to make music first and foremost,' he said. 'We weren't arseing about. If we wanted to just take drugs we could have stayed home and taken them in Robe Street.'

He said he had little interest in Australian politics.

'I mean, who do you choose between, it is hard to tell the two apart,' he said. 'If I ever find the energy to vote, I do it in England.'

I told him I had stood next to the future Prime Minister Malcolm Turnbull at one of Cave's concerts on Sydney's Cockatoo Island and the politician had declared himself a huge fan.

'I would ask him to cease and desist,' said Cave.

* * *

My good friend Paddy Donovan, then of *The Age*, gave me some sound advice when I told him I was about to interview Rolling Stones guitarist Keith Richards.

'Mate, make sure you record it.'

That was the plan but things didn't quite work out. I had my questions in hand and tape recorder ready to go but when the moment came to talk to the rock idol, I was babysitting five kids. My sisters had left me in charge of the family brood at a holiday house near Rye beach with the words, 'It's your turn, Paulie.'

'But I am about to interview Keith Richards,' I pleaded.

'Well say hello from us,' said Annie as they headed off.

The fact I was speaking to one of the world's biggest rock stars didn't mean shit to them, so I found myself in charge of five little rascals; Jessica, Patrick, Frances, Dominic and Cassie; all running amok in our holiday shack. I went into a bedroom, shoved my behind against the door and began the interview. I was flustered and blurted out my first question to Keith, without remembering to turn on the tape recorder.

'Mate, you must have done millions of these interviews but does Australia really stand out from other countries or is it all just one blur?'

The guitarist didn't miss a beat and began singing down the line.

'There was a redback on the toilet seat when I was there last night. I didn't see him in the dark but boy I felt his bite.'

I was stunned. 'You mean, you know "Redback on the Toilet Seat"?'

'Man, everyone knows that song,' he said.

If only I had recorded it, added some backing music and released it as Keith Sings 'Redback on the Toilet Seat', I could have made a bloody fortune.

Keith said one of the things he liked about performing in Australia was that, 'I get to yell out "Show Us Your Map Of Tassie".'

This was tabloid gold. I appreciated the effort he went to.

Unfortunately George Harrison was not so accommodating. I attended a press conference at the Sydney Opera House in 1983 when the former Beatle was helping to promote the autobiography of the Fab Four's publicist Derek Taylor, *Fifty Years Adrift*.

Harrison seemed totally disillusioned in a room crowded with eager journalists and cut a lonely figure in the middle of the maelstrom. Taylor appealed to the journalists to ask him about his book but the first question from the media pack was, 'Will The Beatles ever play again, George?'

He took a deep sigh and just looked out the window.

A more animated Beatle was Pete Best, Ringo Starr's drumming predecessor. I had arranged a lunch interview with him in Melbourne's Southbank and I earned a lifetime of brownie points with my editor Alan Howe, a massive Beatles fan, by taking him along. Best told us how The Beatles had done their early rehearsals in his mother's kitchen. According to John Lennon, Best was only in the band because he had provided that rehearsal space and a drum kit. He was sacked after just eighteen months but instead of being bitter about it, Best was actually grateful to have been allowed a private life.

'It was a blessing in disguise,' he said. 'I get to tour the world talking about my time with them and have an all-star band on the strength of being a former Beatle.'

English 1960s rock star Eric Burdon shared with me his own 'fandom' story. He said he was a devotee of black American diva Nina Simone and decided early in his career to cover one of her songs, 'Don't Let Me Be Misunderstood' with his band The Animals. His rock version of the song was a major hit.

Burdon said he later went to see Simone in concert in Europe and made his way backstage to pay his compliments. When they were introduced, she leapt at him across the band room with her minders having to stop her from hitting him.

'You're the white motherfucker who stole my song,' she barked.

Another fiery woman was celebrated civil rights activist, academic and author Angela Davis. I sat opposite her in an Ethiopian restaurant in Footscray when she was in Melbourne on a speaking tour in 2016. Jesuit Social Services, where I was working, had asked if any staff would like to attend a lunch in her honour. I jumped at the chance. She was a prominent figure in the 1960s and beyond, working with the Communist Party of the USA and the Black Panther Party.

Some of Melbourne's most prominent women attended the lunch but somehow I found myself sitting directly opposite the famed activist. Trying to make conversation, I said it was sad that black rock 'n' roll pioneer Chuck Berry had recently died.

'That motherfucker never invented nothing,' she hissed. 'Everyone knows it was Sister Rosetta Tharpe who came up with that rock guitar sound long before him.'

A passionate woman for sure.

Towards the end of the lunch, an African guy came into the restaurant and said something under his breath to one of the women at our table, which made her cry. Without missing a beat the then-72-year-old Davis whipped off her shoe and wielding the pointy end as a weapon challenged the guy to a fight. He left quick smart.

Another diva I interviewed was the sultry singer Eartha Kitt, who had starred as Catwoman in the *Batman* TV series. Eartha treated me like a cat toying with a mouse.

I also had an unusual chat with blind Motown star Stevie Wonder. He was a delight to talk to, but I noticed in his Melbourne motel room a very nervous black guy pacing up and down.

'Who is that?' I asked a record company employee.

'That's Stevie's eyes, the guy who accompanies him when he goes driving.'

It turns out Stevie loves getting behind the wheel. No wonder his sidekick looked stressed.

Visiting rock stars always claim to enjoy an Australian trip. Flattering your hosts helps to drum up ticket sales. I had to admire the honesty of rock's self-proclaimed Prince Of Darkness, Ozzy Osbourne, about why he was looking forward to a trip Down Under. Was it the Opera House? The Great Barrier Reef? Kakadu? What was the main attraction in Australia?

'I'm in Alcoholics Anonymous now and I went to a few meetings in Sydney on my last trip,' he said. 'I met some really lovely people there. You get a nice type of person at AA meetings in Australia.'

He freely admitted to three decades of rock 'n' roll excess.

To be honest, a lot of rock stars turn out to be pretty boring when you talk to them, as they are often arrogant and self-important. To them you are just some newspaper hack from the bottom end of the world.

On the other hand, the gravel-voiced pianist Tom Waits took our chat very seriously. He rang me at home twice after our interview to clarify his answers.

Then there was Gene Simmons of 1970s glam rockers Kiss, who said, 'Paul, I look forward to coming back to Australia to catch up with your mother and sisters ... again.'

Dickhead.

Simmons spent most of his interviews boasting about the thousands of women he had slept with, which always struck me as odd given how ugly he was under the Kiss make-up and hair.

Fellow reporter Nik Garifilakis toured with Simmons on a

speaking tour of Australia and told me later, 'Never work with your heroes.'

I learned that lesson about interviewing your heroes firsthand when I got a chance to talk to Johnny Rotten (real name John Lydon) from the Sex Pistols when he was touring in 1984 with his band Public Image Limited. The guy was an arsehole. I know it is very punk to spit on stage but to spit on the wall of your expensive hotel room in the middle of an interview just seemed silly.

The worst person I reckon I ever interviewed was Canadian jazz diva Diana Krall, a legend in her own mind. What a piece of work she was!

It was quite common to take work experience students on interviews and they were always keen to accompany me to meet some visiting star. The stars were usually happy to talk to the youngsters and many found their naivety so refreshing they would spend the whole session just talking to them. Not Diana Krall.

I took along a young girl from Wonthaggi in Gippsland, who was beside herself with excitement. The record company representative had no problem with her sitting in, but Krall had other ideas. When she walked into the interview room she screamed, 'Who is this?'

I explained it was a girl on work experience. Krall lost it.

'Who said she could come in? I want her out now,' she demanded.

The teenager fled the room in tears and Krall won herself one scathing write-up.

Oddly enough, the one-hit wonders tend to be more arrogant than the veterans. Talking to blues legend B.B. King, I told him how a young Australian band had recently told me they could only play two nights in a row because 'they got too tired'.

King, one of the most influential musicians of the modern era, smiled and said, 'Man, I've been on the road for forty years.'

He told me that he had toured so often that when his new house was built, he had the bedroom designed like a Holiday Inn motel room.

'It is the only way I can find the toilet during the night,' he confessed.

I made a fool of myself by asking another blues great Bo Diddley 'How is Lucille?' The look he gave me as he said, 'That's what B.B. King calls his guitar,' was withering enough to make me do my homework in the future.

A sobering encounter was with Marc Hunter of the New Zealand band Dragon, whose hits included 'April Sun In Cuba' and 'Are You Old Enough?'

He had just been diagnosed with cancer and was already showing signs of the wretched disease. He died far too young at forty-four, even though he had assured me during our chat that flying saucers would arrive in time to cure him.

51

BEST DAY ON THE JOB EVER
(1996)

It was my favourite day as a journalist. The Godfather of Soul, James Brown was touring Australia when his promoter rang me, pleading for a story to generate public attention. The singer had been in trouble with law enforcement agencies in the United States and the bad publicity was hurting ticket sales.

I had recently met AFL great Nicky Winmar, who was working with Donna on an Indigenous health project, and the St Kilda player had mentioned he was a massive James Brown fan and would love some tickets.

A flash went off in my head.

I rang the promoter and said I would do a story if Brown agreed to do a snap for the paper with Winmar. Brown is a famous black rights activist and I asked the promoter to tell him that Nicky was also a champion for his people. I sent him the iconic photo of Winmar proudly raising his jumper during a 1993 Collingwood versus St Kilda game to show the crowd the colour of his skin, explaining that Winmar's defiant gesture had been a turning point in the football Code's battle against racist abuse.

Winmar was one of the first Indigenous players in the AFL to speak out against racial taunts. His stance provoked a furious backlash from the more brain-dead parts of the football world, but the controversy helped to push the league to introduce anti-racism rules.

Brown, of course, was the author of the 1960s anthem 'Say It Loud, I'm Black And I'm Proud'.

The promoter got straight back to me and said, 'Mr Brown would like to meet that brother and shake his hand.'

James Brown enjoyed phenomenal chart success over his long career, with a staggering ninety-one entries in the Billboard Hot 100, including seven in the Top 10. This compares favourably even with Elvis, who had 108 Hot 100 songs.

Brown always insisted on being addressed formally. If any reporter referred to him as 'James' he immediately walked out, or cancelled the interview. It was Mr Brown, and *only* Mr Brown. I can remember one journalist saying to me, 'Who does this guy think he is?'

I replied, 'He's the undisputed Godfather of Soul, mate, you call him whatever he wants, you idiot.'

Even the members of his own band referred to him as Mr Brown. They also had to dress immaculately and be note-perfect each and every performance.

I arranged a time for Mr Brown to meet Nicky Winmar on Wednesday 24 April 1996. In the bowels of the Rod Laver Arena in Melbourne I introduced the pair and produced a football as a photo prop. Despite being on a crutch with a leg injury, Winmar proceeded to have a kick with the Godfather of Soul while I stood and watched. Surreal.

A photo of the pair appeared prominently in the *Sunday Herald Sun*, the biggest selling newspaper in the state. Ticket sales went through the roof and a grateful Winmar got to see his idol live in action. A terrific result all round.

Years later, I had my own fan thrill during a Painters & Dockers show at the St Kilda RSL in Acland Street when Winmar surprised me by suddenly appearing on stage to join me in singing 'Die Yuppie Die'.

52

THIS IS THE PLACE FOR A SONG
(2005)

During his reign as editor of the *Sunday Herald Sun*, Alan Howe went out of his way to promote Australian music. He was good friends with some of the country's rock icons, including Russell Morris, Jim Keays of The Masters Apprentices and Darryl Cotton of Zoot.

Vlad Juric, of the Painters & Dockers, said it was seeing Zoot perform 'Eleanor Rigby' that inspired him to buy a guitar.

Through Alan, I got to hang out with these music legends, who were surprisingly normal, friendly types.

Howe also organised a fundraising concert at the Sidney Myer Music Bowl for victims of the 2004 Beslan school siege in Russia, in which children were caught up in a terrorist attack. He asked me to help assemble the line-up. Artists who donated their time included Ross Wilson, Deborah Conway, Kate Ceberano, Vanessa Amorosi, Stephen Cummings, The Dili Allstars and several expat Russian musicians.

The success of the event got Alan thinking about other musical projects we could arrange. The first CD we worked on together was for children's welfare group Kids Under Cover. It was an unusual album featuring twenty different versions of the great 1971 single 'I'll

Be Gone' by the Australian band Spectrum, ranging from rock and reggae versions to folk, techno and disco.

One of the better covers, and the favourite of the tune's writer Mike Rudd, was the death metal version by local band Blood Duster. The Dili Allstars did our version in Tetum, with Paulo on lead vocals.

Another of Alan's real passions was the Immigration Museum, which he helped to set up in the Old Customs House, a grand building on a site in Flinders Street not far from where John Batman first arrived on the banks of the Yarra in 1835 and declared the formation of a city.

We decided to produce an album to raise funds for the museum and called it *This Is The Place For A Song*, playing on Batman's famous comment, 'this is the place for a village'.

It featured fourteen well-known Australian rock songs by fourteen different cultures.

Gil Santos, Colin Badger and I produced the album while the sound engineer was former Sacred Cowboys guitarist Terry Doolan, whose day job was with the national broadcaster SBS, running the studio in Federation Square.

Amongst the tunes we had Hungarian gypsies Vardos doing Kylie Minogue's hit 'I Should Be So Lucky', South American act Inka Marka doing the Seekers' classic 'The Carnival Is Over', Vietnamese musician Neil Ta and family doing a version of the Russell Morris classic 'Wings Of An Eagle', Japanese punk trio Mach Pelican doing Australian Crawl's 'Beautiful People', and African band Musiki Manjaro doing Men At Work's 'Who Can It Be Now?'

Quite a few of the original artists returned to the studio to work on these new versions with the multicultural musicians. They included Ross Wilson, Judith Durham from The Seekers, Billy Miller from The Ferrets and the late Greg Ham from Men At Work.

The album was nominated for a Fine Arts Award from the Australian Record Industry Association (ARIA) and Gil and I were flown to an award ceremony at the prestigious Sydney Conservatorium of Music.

Afterwards we mingled at a slap-up party with the other nominees and winners, who were much better educated musicians and composers. We joined a conversation with one group and I was asked, 'So where is your next show?'

'Our next gig is at the Espy.'

'Is that the Opera House just outside Munich?' one inquired.

'No mate, that's the Esplanade Hotel in St Kilda,' I replied much to their bewilderment.

53

THE YOUNG RUPERTS
(1990)

I have played with many a combo over the past forty years or so, but I have never rehearsed as hard as I did when appearing with the *Herald Sun's* in-house band The Young Ruperts.

We played several shows, but the big daddy of them all was the one in 1990 celebrating the 150th anniversary of the *Herald,* one of the papers that merged to form the *Herald Sun.* The company hired a large floating stage on the Yarra River at Southbank and laid on a free bar for the evening. Some bright spark had also decreed that it was employees-only, so partners were not invited. That inevitably meant a free-for-all of bacchanalian excess.

The crowd was so pumped and well-lubricated we could have performed 'Happy Birthday' fifteen times and still got a standing ovation. The sight of Rupert Murdoch's rather conservative sister Janet Calvert-Jones standing beside the stage rocking out to the band was priceless.

Later, some executives were in big trouble as it emerged they had re-entered the nearby *Herald Sun* offices and been caught doing some horizontal folk dancing on their desks with work colleagues. It was a hell of a night.

As a side note, despite working at his papers for thirty years I had only one encounter with Chairman Rupert Murdoch.

I walked into the Herald and Weekly Times building one day in my usual colourful attire and was spotted by the Chairman, who approached Gordon—one of the security guards—after my entrance and said, 'Please tell me I don't employ that guy?'

'Yeah, that's Paulie, he has worked here for years,' said my old pal, much to the dismay of the world's most powerful media magnate.

Another interesting outfit I have worked with is Epic Brass, which was pulled together by Jack Howard, a trumpeter with Midnight Oil and Hunters & Collectors, to pay tribute to Australian rock songs featuring brass instruments. Singers brought on board included Deborah Conway, Sean Kelly of Models, Ron Peno of Died Pretty, Steve Lucas of X, Fiona Lee Maynard, Penny Ikinger and Helen Cattanach Of Moler.

A real buzz for me was the night one of my heroes, Midnight Oil drummer Rob Hirst joined the line-up for a version of The Dockers' 'Die Yuppie Die'.

Another great series of gigs was with radio personality, marriage celebrant and top bloke Johnny von Goes in his AFL Grand Final footy shows, his Valentines Day gigs at Oakleigh Tonight, and at several Triple R barbecue days.

I later did some work as a guide on the rock 'n' roll bus run by the Arts Centre Melbourne. Run by music enthusiasts Mary Mihelakos and Bruce Milne, the tour takes fans to some of Melbourne's more iconic sites, reinforcing what a great musical city it is. Bruce begins each tour by saying his biggest musical claim to fame is that his mum wrote the lyrics to the much-loved theme song for Australian children's TV show *Play School*.

The bus ride is always a lot of fun and we get to point out various places along the route including St Kilda's Seaview Ballroom and Esplanade hotel, Molly Meldrum's house in Richmond, Richmond Recorders, the house where punk film *Dogs In Space* was shot, the Tote pub in Collingwood and the Old Greek Theatre in Richmond.

54

SOME GIGS YOU JUST HAVE TO DO
(2006)

Lobby Loyde is the only man I have shared breakfast with who talked non-stop, polished off eight fried eggs and smoked a cigar, all at the same time. Then again, there was nothing ordinary about John Baslington Loyde.

I was lucky enough to be managed by Lobby for five years and even luckier to call him a friend.

My first glimpse of Lobby was him playing guitar with his band Coloured Balls, the act of choice for Melbourne's intimidating youth cult the Sharpies in the 1970s. His hard, fast and very loud guitar playing was a magnet to the Sharpies. If Billy Thorpe was the heart of early Australian rock 'n' roll, then Lobby was its soul.

Born in Longreach, Queensland, Lobby spent most of his life in Melbourne and is often credited with inventing pub rock in Australia. He would recall playing four gigs a night in the early years, but Lobby was never in it for stardom. To him, it was all about the music. Black, white, rich or poor, he said there were just two types of people: musical enthusiasts, and the rest.

He detested the music industry's bean counters as 'seamy, suspect people that really don't give a rat's arse about the music'.

Angus Young of AC/DC said Lobby was one of his band's major inspirations. Angry Anderson of Rose Tattoo said, 'More than anyone else, Lobby helped create the Australian guitar sound.'

Lobby was a true eccentric and loved talking about alien technology and the latest weapons being built by the US military. He was a natural storyteller and I have lost count of the times Lobby would hold court, with the band listening in awe to one of his fanciful rock 'n' roll tales.

In 2006, Lobby was found to have inoperable throat cancer and The Dockers were invited to play at a huge benefit concert for him that August at The Palace nightclub in St Kilda.

I had already been diagnosed with severe liver damage but there was no way I was going to miss it, despite the fact I had turned yellow and was fast losing my energy.

We were asked to do two songs at the benefit and arranged a rehearsal at a South Melbourne studio. On hand to greet us was Billy Thorpe, the nuggetty Australian rock legend, who walked into our room with a Marshall amp over each shoulder.

'Where do you guys want these?' asked Billy, who seemed in perfect health. I had got to know him a few years earlier when I suggested to Alan Howe, my editor at the *Sunday Herald Sun*, that we hold a special competition.

The newspaper ran a Have Billy Thorpe Play in Your Backyard competition, which drew thousands of entries. The backyard gig was covered by all the TV networks, with news helicopters hovering overhead. Billy rocked the suburban house to its foundations.

It was great to see Lobby's benefit packed out with 2000 fans and he was beaming, particularly as his wife Deb and most of his five children were there. I was feeling particularly knackered because of my illness, so fellow Docker Mick Morris kindly collected me from my mum's house, where I had moved to give Donna a break from caring for me.

I still managed to get off to a bad start by missing a step as I walked into the VIP lounge and falling flat on my face.

Backstage, I found myself talking in a small group with Lobby, Billy Thorpe, Ian Rilen and Jimmy Barnes. Six months later while lying in the Austin Hospital I realised that since that conversation, Barnes had had open-heart surgery; Lobby, Billy and Ian had all died; and I was going to join them if I did not get a new liver.

Yes, it's a long road to the top if you want to rock 'n' roll and a lot of people don't survive the journey.

55

CRY ME A LIVER
(2006)

Come 2006, and I learned there was indeed a price to pay for my hectic lifestyle of rock 'n' roll, journalism and activism. I should not really have been surprised but it did shock me when I was told by my doctor that I needed a life-saving liver transplant.

I knew I had a problem with my liver as a doctor had told me in the late 1980s that I had contracted hepatitis C and it would have an impact later in life. At the time, I asked him if I should quit drinking and he told me to switch to light beer. I took that to mean things weren't so bad, so I kept drinking at my normal pace: full bore.

Now the hour had arrived to face my past. Luckily, I did not have to do it alone.

I have to acknowledge my A-Team for keeping me going during my illness, giving me positive vibes, dispensing medicine and nursing me without complaint. Over a torrid eighteen months from early 2006, many people took days off work to take me to hospital, or undertook such glamorous pursuits as cleaning the vomit and shit from my bed clothes and pyjamas.

Mum would often drive halfway across town to drop off soup and other meals, despite her own advancing years. She also nursed me at her place and had to deal with my constant whingeing. Some days we would just sit and talk for hours, which I realise now was one of the few good things to come out of my ordeal.

With my mortality looming over us, Mum and I had some fantastic discussions about the things that really matter in life, which usually revolved around family and love. We had always been able to talk openly. When I was in my twenties she was intrigued to hear about an adventure I had had at an S&M club, and to see the whip marks on my back.

'That sounds fascinating,' she said. 'But don't tell your father.'

Credit must also go to Donna Brown for keeping me fed and clean while also caring for Aretha, who was five years old when my liver problem was diagnosed.

Walking to the local shops now took me almost an hour instead of a few minutes but the sicker I got, the more I assured everyone I was fine.

Then there was my brother Dr Greg 'Pugsley' Stewart, who was nicknamed by Dad after the fat little kid in *The Addams Family*. The irony is that Greg is a lifelong health fanatic, swimming whenever he can and staying very trim.

People often tell me, 'I met your younger brother,' and I always say through gritted teeth, 'I'm six years younger.'

A country GP, Greg has had a lot of experience with patients who have burned the candle at both ends, including many with bad livers. He says his life was shaped by his medical internship in India and several years working with Indigenous communities around Katherine in the Northern Territory. He was also greatly affected by Tony's death, given that they were only two years apart. He has regularly volunteered at health clinics in Timor-Leste and unlike his big-noting little brother, he does it all on the quiet.

When I was in trouble, Greg dropped everything to take me to hospital or mow my lawns, and it was a real blessing to have a doctor in the family who could explain in terms I would understand the baffling details of my treatment and medical condition.

I don't think I have ever fought with anybody as much as I have with my big sister Annie. Close in age, we had some great tussles when we were young over who could use Dad's radio at night. But when things got deadly serious, she kept me positive. A professional storyteller, Annie encouraged me to write about what I was going through, even jotting down what I dictated when I was too ill to use the laptop. Some of those musings became the basis for this book. Reminiscing was fun, gave me something to do and was fantastic therapy while I lay hoping for a new liver to arrive.

Dad nicknamed my younger sister Janie, 'The Biter'. Biter took me to hospitals, nursed me, and looked after my daughters, all while being incredibly busy with her own children and her work as a consultant on issues of sustainability and corporate responsibility. Janie also became a close friend of one of my best mates, Peter Wilson, when they both lived in Tokyo in the 1980s.

The accepted wisdom was that Jane and Greg were the sensible, productive professionals while Annie and I were the ratbag party kids.

I've often wondered whether my family would have been such a close-knit bunch if Tony hadn't died so young.

My A-Team also included Greg's wife and fellow GP, Beth Quinn, Jane's partner Peter Broadbent, and my daughters, nieces and nephews; Jessica, Frances, Esther, Cassandra, Dominic, Patrick, Anna, Julia and Aretha. Plus heaps of blended family, including Arianne, Coco and Bridget.

Each in their own way helped me battle liver disease and I have been overwhelmed, embarrassed and humbled by their efforts.

An ordeal like mine is also a really effective test of your broader circle of relationships. It turned out that I had been blessed with Natalie, Beau, some genuinely loving friends, including my oldest female mate, Rosanne Michie. Her parents used to play tennis with mine and I can never remember a time when she wasn't considered family. I have still not forgiven my sisters and Mum for watching me play in the St Mary's Tennis Club under-thirteen singles grand final and supporting the winner ... Rosanne. After my transplant she went out of her way to take me for walks on the beach and cheer me up.

I was shocked at how many messages of support I received from pals around the world.

Timor-Leste's President José Ramos-Horta, Robert Thomson, the New York-based second-in-charge at News Corporation, Midnight Oils frontman Peter Garrett and Mark Forbes, the Jakarta correspondent of *The Age* all took time to wish me well.

56

LIVER MATES

Sickness is really the great leveller. I was amazed at the immediate and tight bond I formed with other patients at the Austin Hospital liver clinic. Complete strangers became instant friends.

One day I was wheeled into a four-bed ward where my companions were three little old ladies who were just basically waiting to die.

'Great, this is going to be fun,' I thought sourly.

It turned out that these three women all had remarkable stories about their lives, loves and struggles. One told me she was a long-time fan of Australian country music act The Hawking Brothers and used to follow them from gig to gig. The four of us spent an afternoon singing Elvis songs together.

In another ward, I got a smile and a sympathetic nod from an Ethiopian patient who must have had at least twenty people in our room trying to comfort him. We both laughed when the final visitor left and he let out a huge sigh.

I would never have met people like this if I had been healthy, let alone come to value so much the medical workers who tended to me. I have met hundreds of them during more than a decade of visits, check-ups and procedures.

I now know the corridors of the Austin Hospital in Heidelberg like the back of my hand, having paced them when restless and wide awake at night. One night, a security guard found me wandering the empty twelfth floor in a state of confusion. When he gruffly asked what I was doing there, I said, 'My two sisters have brought me in a cake and we are having a tea party.'

'Okay mate,' he said gently, instantly turning from a burly security guard into a caring health worker. 'Let's go back to your ward now, your sisters have called and said the tea party has been delayed.'

I did have a number of interesting religious experiences in the hospital as one of the few ways to get out of the liver ward was to attend the Sunday religious service. Each week was a different religion. I'm not fussy so I attended the Roman Catholic, Greek Orthodox, Presbyterian, Methodist, Buddhist, Islamic and Jewish services. Funny how similar they all are.

One day I found myself sobbing aloud when I joined a bunch of really old ladies singing 'The Lord Is My Shepherd'. They were all frail and unwell, but sang with such hope and faith that I just lost it and tears streamed down my face.

At the height of my illness, I had the sleeping patterns of a vampire, snoozing by day with disturbing dreams and fully alert at night. My arms were purple from the hundreds and hundreds of blood tests and needles. For a Saturday night treat I would pretend that my condition was worse than it really was so I would get some extra morphine tablets and a glass of cordial.

My main pastime was remembering the good times. The nurses must have thought I was mad because in the middle of the night I would occasionally burst out laughing recalling some of the zanier moments.

I had drips giving me blood products, medicines, sustenance and I do not even know what else. One painful result of a malfunctioning liver is ascites, or the accumulation of liquid in spaces between the organs, resulting in a hard, swollen abdomen, so the doctors had to drain me every now and then. I had X-rays, ultrasounds, blood sugar tests, needles, swabs, my fill of hospital food, sleepless sweaty nights and constant cramps.

On bad days I managed to write just fifty words, on others none at all. Some days I could manage a little walk, but at other times I could barely raise my head off the pillow. I was getting sicker and sometimes could not stomach my medication, throwing it up.

One of the worst things about lying awake contemplating how I had got there, was that I knew I had nobody to blame but myself. There were a few years in the 1980s when I basically lived off cheap champagne and finger food. I didn't drink like a fish, more like a killer whale.

But the real reason I needed a new liver was that I had contracted hep C by using shared needles 'shooting up' heroin. I didn't do it for months, I didn't do it thirty, twenty or even ten times. I did it three times.

Why? Because my friend was doing it, and I was blind drunk. What an idiot I was.

This particular mate had suffered a terrible leg injury playing football and been put onto really strong painkillers which were the end of him.

I also have to admit that a group of guys I hung out with, all Rolling Stones fanatics, fell in love with Keith Richards, and wanted to copy his infamous 'wasted junkie' persona.

I quickly found heroin to be totally masturbational. When you are on it you don't need to interact with anyone else and you have your own selfish high. The trouble is that it doesn't last long and you soon crave more. After dabbling a few times, I can remember it came to a Friday night where six guys gathered in a lounge room for a blast. My friend Ross Greene and I both declined.

As the four others dozed it off we looked at each other and said, 'What the hell are we doing here? It's Friday night, let's go and meet some girls.' We got off the couch and hit the nearest nightclub.

Heroin went on to kill many people I knew and leave others brain dead. My own relationship with that insidious drug was very short, but it still cost me big time.

I had lived like there was no tomorrow, but tomorrow came.

After eighteen months waiting for a new liver, I was close to the end of my reserves. It was weird to realise that I was basically waiting for someone else to die so I could live.

Why had I lived such a kamikaze lifestyle? I had had a great job and a fantastic time on stage feeding off the buzz of a thousand crowds. I had enjoyed years of free overseas jaunts, had loved working on causes I cared deeply about, and I got paid for talking to rock legends and watching interesting new musical acts. To top it all off I had two gorgeous daughters, Frances and Aretha, a loving family and more friends than I deserved.

Lying in my hospital bed surrounded by beeping medical equipment, things became clearer. I realised that I have had a gnawing feeling of angst and sorrow since the age of fifteen.

The message I had taken from Tony's death was that life could be over before you knew you were even living it. Without being conscious of it, I had decided long ago to live each day as though it were my last.

Now each day really could be my last.

Doctors warned me that even if I did get the call to rush to the operating room, success was no certainty. If a liver did arrive, a huge team of doctors and nurses would spend at least twelve hours operating and I was in very poor shape to go through that sort of physical trauma. In a best-case scenario I would then spend days sleeping heavily and face long bouts of intensive care.

I knew the tension of the surgery would be hell for my family but it would be a lot easier for me than for them. I would either wake up or I wouldn't.

57

TRIPPY
(2007)

By 12 August 2007, eighteen months after my initial diagnosis with liver disease, things were looking bleak. A priest was called to my bed at the Austin to help me prepare to meet my maker. I could not really take in what he was saying because I was so shaken by his arrival. This was what happened in the death scene in movies. When he left, I was as low as I had ever been.

The following day, an unbelievable saga unfolded. Others have told me it was just a lucky coincidence, but I put it down to divine intervention.

In fact, I consider it a life-changing miracle.

I woke in the hospital late at night to find a little nun in a blue and white habit sitting on the end of my bed. I thought I was hallucinating again.

But no, she really was there, a smiling woman in her early twenties. She had no needles or medicine for me, so I realised that she was a palliative care worker employed to assist those crossing over to the other side. She said her name was Sister Helena and gently urged me to make peace with myself and accept what might be about to happen. As I became fully awake, I noticed that she was dark-skinned.

'Where are you from Sister?' I asked.

'A little country called Timor-Leste,' she said.

I shot up straight in bed. 'You are joking with me, right? Is this *Funniest Home Videos* or something?'

My sister Annie had left a bright Timor-Leste scarf around my bedhead as a good luck talisman for me, and I thought my visitor might have noticed that and was playing with me.

'No, what are you talking about?' she said.

'I'm very interested in Timor-Leste. I play in a band with some guys from there,' I replied.

'Not The Dili Allstars?' she asked.

I was gobsmacked.

Sister Helena settled in on my bed for a long chat. She explained that she came from Oecusse, a Timor-Leste enclave that is surrounded by West Timorese territory, and her order of nuns had sent her to work in Australia.

I told her about Tony and we talked about some of the aid I had helped to get to Timor-Leste, including to her hometown. My spirits soared remembering good times in a sunny place a long way from the liver ward.

She asked why I was in the hospital.

'I need a new liver, Sister. I have been waiting eighteen long months and they might not give me one, even if they do get one that matches me. Things are looking bad.'

She sat quietly for a while and then said, 'I'll help you get a new one.'

I thought she must have been dipping into the altar wine a bit early that day.

She said she would ring the nuns in Timor-Leste to get them all to pray.

'That's right, Sister, we have to pray for Timor-Leste,' I said.

'No, not Timor. We pray for you, Paulie. We will pray for you.'

I started to get very emotional as I couldn't believe that this stranger would go to so much trouble.

'But there's one thing,' she said. 'If we do get you a new liver you must help the women and children in Timor-Leste.'

'Sure, Sister, sure,' I said, seriously doubting that anybody's prayers would save me, or that I would ever need to keep my promise.

When she left, though, I was more optimistic than I had been for months. Surely the fact that she was from Timor-Leste was an omen? It was too out there to be a coincidence.

First thing next morning, my sister Janie was visiting when my usual nurse rushed into the room all excited.

'No breakfast for you Paulie, we have a liver for you.'

The funny thing is that even though I had been waiting for that news for more than 500 days, I was not at all surprised after Sister Helena's visit.

I was ecstatic.

But then a hiccup. My doctor walked in looking flustered and said, 'Well, the liver arrived and unfortunately we have just worked out that you are not actually compatible with it. But would you believe, another one arrived straight away and it is a perfect match. Getting two at once really never happens.'

I was to undergo surgery straight away. Jane called our family and Donna to tell them the news. As I was wheeled downstairs for the surgery, my excitement and relief were jumbled up with the realisation that I was about to be given an anaesthetic from which I might never wake up.

I asked Jane to call my pal Peter Wilson in London and hand me the mobile. He had been working as a foreign correspondent in the UK for years but I knew he wouldn't mind being woken in the middle of the night.

I told him what was happening and that this was it. We knew this could be our last conversation. I finished the call saying that if I didn't make it, I would save him a spot wherever I ended up: either at an outdoor table with a good view in heaven, or two seats at the bar in the other place. I thought I was being hilarious but it freaked him out. He told me he loved me, then he spent the night staring up at the ceiling and wondering what news the next call would bring.

58

I'M ALIVE
(2007)

Slowly I started coming out of the fog. Waking up from twelve hours of surgery is not like flicking on a switch. It is flashes of half-consciousness and garbled conversations followed by three mind-altering days floating in a morphine bubble.

I eventually realised that I had made it, which was as big a surprise to me as it was to anyone else. The relief on the faces of my loved ones told me how close I had come to the end.

It struck me that being a white Australian was a major gift as the same condition would probably have killed me if I had been born in Timor-Leste, or as a blackfella in the Top End.

I know nothing about the person whose liver is still keeping me alive but I am eternally grateful that they and their family had agreed to be part of the organ donation program.

My re-emergence into the land of clarity was an unusual episode as I came to in the liver ward's intensive care unit and found Elvis standing at my bedside. Yep, you read that right ... Elvis.

The Elvis in question was old pal Paulie Greene, who had been on his way to a ceremony at the Melbourne General Cemetery to mark the anniversary of the death of The King of Rock 'n' Roll. He dropped in at the Austin Hospital in full Elvis regalia on a whim to check on my progress, his stretch limo waiting outside. Paulie Greene's arrival caused a sensation. As he walked through reception, worn-down patients suddenly started smiling, people in wheelchairs rushed to him and nurses and doctors made sure to say hello. He was swamped by people wanting selfies. In fact, the happiness that he spread was a marvel to behold. Hospitals should definitely start employing Elvis impersonators.

After such an intense operation, the doctors didn't want me lying around, so within hours of regaining full consciousness I was walking the corridors, wheeling along an intravenous drip hanging from a large metal frame.

After eighteen months of hardly eating, I was suddenly ravenous. Food had never looked, nor tasted so good.

I was given a list of twenty-four pills that I had to take every day. 'I will never get it together to remember which ones to take,' I pleaded with the nurse.

'Well, you will just have to,' she replied, calmly refusing to buy into my anxiety.

I was sent home to a new regime that I found confusing and a little overwhelming, but I was determined to do two things: keep my promise to Sister Helena, and respect the incredible gift of a new liver.

Fellow rockers Roland S Howard (The Birthday Party) and Spencer P Jones (The Johnnys) are among the many people who have not survived their liver problems, and I knew how amazingly lucky I was to get this second chance.

Recent recipients of a liver transplant can often recite their latest blood test results and medical procedures and keep a close eye on how long their new livers are likely to last. That all bamboozled me so my attitude was that I would turn up for whatever tests were required, take my prescribed medication, and get on with life.

It was hard at first to give up drinking. When I went back to work at the *Sunday Herald Sun* in March 2008, I trooped along to the pub with my journalist mates as usual but always stuck to lemon squash.

My most startling discovery was just how boring boozy conversations are when you are sober. After decades of thinking that my drunken banter was hilarious and amazingly astute, I suddenly realised that it was just repetitive blather.

Things were soon grim on the work front. Alan Howe had moved on from running the newspaper and we had entered a more soulless and slimmed-down regime relying heavily on celebrity stories and public relations-driven gumph. The coverage of music and popular culture was to be limited to Kylie Minogue's short pants and John Farnham's latest health problems, and it was made clear to me in a quite unpleasant way that my "old-fashioned" style of journalism and my interest in causes such as Timor-Leste and Indigenous rights were surplus to requirements.

Six months after my return, when I was still not quite back on my feet, I was shown the door and found myself unemployed for the first time in my life. Relying on a disability pension was no fun but the glory days of Australian newspapers had gone and being a newspaper journalist made me as employable as a horseshoe maker. I had a crack at anything that came my way, including a brief stint writing press releases for the Australian Cancer Research Foundation.

Amid my money worries, I heard that the City of Port Phillip, which encompassed St Kilda, was running an essay competition with a healthy $2000 first prize. I needed that money.

At the risk of sounding vain, I knew I was in for a strong chance as soon as I started writing. It was a bizarre experience. Somehow I listened to an inner voice that told me what to write. Stories of St Kilda and my family's life in the area came out in short, sharp sentences.

I won the prize from a large field and that money kept the wolf from the door for a spell.

59

'I WANT TO MAKE A MOVIE ABOUT YOUR BROTHER'
(2008)

I had heard this line several times over the years, so I was a little sceptical when I first met leading Australian filmmaker Robert Connolly. He immediately impressed me when he said he wanted to meet the Timorese community in Melbourne to get them heavily involved in his film. I told him the best way would be to go to Gil's place in Endeavour Hills on the outskirts of Melbourne for a community barbecue and spend some time with them.

What helped to win over my siblings and me, was that Rob also made sure he spent time with Mum to get her side of the tale of the Balibo Five. No federal politician, or Channel 7 executive had ever given her that opportunity.

For his *Balibo* movie, Rob recruited veteran Australian actor Anthony LaPaglia, American-Guatemalan newcomer Oscar Isaac, and some of the cream of Australia's young acting talent, including several cast members from the recent ratings smash *Underbelly*. Australia-based Timorese actress Bea Viegas was chosen to play the female lead.

Filming began in Dili in June 2008, and the film was released the following year at the opening night of the Melbourne International Film Festival at Victorian Arts Centre's Hamer Hall.

President Ramos-Horta attended and in an address before the film, he alleged that the Balibo Five were tortured and killed by Indonesian forces. The screening was a sober experience for the Stewarts, and the sobbing of my daughter Frances echoed through the venue as the film came to its confronting end. It was hard to attend the after-party with everyone in a buoyant mood while my family was once again deeply affected by the retelling of the story.

The actor playing Tony was Mark Leonard Winter, who went from making our film in the tropics to freezing Tasmania where he starred in *Van Diemen's Land*. Mark also spent time with Mum, which we greatly appreciated. The only problem was that nobody had warned me that with his 1970s sideburns the actor was a dead ringer for my brother.

When work began on the movie, I was invited to Timor-Leste to present the first Balibo Prize for Journalist of the Year, that country's equivalent of Australia's Walkley Awards. My speech was not well-received because I told the assembled Timorese politicians and VIP guests that rather than buying expensive cars for themselves, they should give more funding to their local artists and musicians.

The two guests I took to the event, local musicians Mali and Osmay from The Galaxy Band, had to buy shoes so they could get in. I was booed for suggesting they be given more support.

I was mid-speech when in walked Mark and the rest of the *Balibo* cast and crew. Anyone who knows me well will tell you that I am not often stuck for words but on that occasion, I was struck dumb.

"That's Tony, what the f—?"

Mark's physical similarity to my brother was matched by the phenomenal effort he made to understand Tony and imagine what he had gone through.

There is a favourite family photo of all five Stewart children in our backyard in the 1960s. Mark told me that for the scene in the movie where Tony was just about to be killed, he had that photo strapped next to the camera. He figured it could have been one of the last images that went through Tony's mind.

I had somehow ended up with Tony's favourite pair of red Doc Martens boots. They were too small for me so three times I had put them out in the rubbish, only to go back and retrieve them as I just couldn't throw them out. I gave them to Mark and guess what … they fitted him perfectly. In the movie, he retraced the final moments of my brother's life wearing those boots. Surreal.

Rob Connolly asked for help with the soundtrack so I drafted in Gil, who recruited some Timorese musicians. One of them was the Bob Dylan of Timor-Leste, Ego Lemos, whose song Balibo was a highlight. The soundtrack album featured a musical score by Lisa Gerrard and two songs by The Dili Allstars: 'Liberdade' and a reworked version of the Graham Parker song, 'Hey Lord Don't Ask Me Questions'.

Later that year, the film was feted by another peak music industry body, the Australian Recording Industry Association. Rob rang to ask if I could go to the ARIA awards in Sydney to pick up the prize for Best Original Soundtrack album.

'Let me think about it … yeah, I can do that,' I quickly replied.

I gave the ARIA to Gil and today it sits in pride of place in his lounge room.

The film was supposed to screen at the 2009 Jakarta International Film Festival but it was banned by Indonesia's film censors. Foreign Minister Marty Natalegawa said the ban was to avoid a 'negative global perception of Indonesia'.

The film had a much better reception in South America than in Indonesia, and it was chosen to screen at the 2010 São Paulo International Film Festival in Brazil. Gil and I were determined to go to Brazil to garner support for Timor-Leste. As Brazil was another former Portuguese colony, we figured there would be a lot of interest in the film.

We approached an Australian power company in Brazil, who agreed to fly us over provided we used its banner as a backdrop whenever we performed. We did a couple of acoustic shows after screenings of the movie, which went on to win the Audience Award for Best Foreign Feature Film.

I wasn't the only member of my extended family affected by Tony's murder, of course. One cousin, the late playwright Aidan Fennessy, was moved to write a stage production about the Balibo Five entitled *National Interest*. The play focused on Mum and her reaction to the tragedy. It was performed in Perth and Melbourne in 2012 and received enthusiastic reviews.

After I got back Mum's health and morale were in decline and I called President Ramos-Horta to ask whether there was anything he could do that might give her a lift. A few weeks later when I was in Dili, he presented me with a posthumous medal of merit for Tony. It was a small act of compassion that meant an awful lot to Mum and the rest of our family.

60

COMPASS
(2009)

I was so thrilled to be alive after my surgery, and I was convinced my recovery was due to divine intervention. In fact, many a friend and family member teased me about my belief that the little nun had saved me. I understood their scepticism but pointed out that they weren't the one who had been dying in Ward 8 at the Austin and had come close to being given the last rites.

I was so convinced about this miracle that I contacted the ABC television's religious program *Compass*. After hearing my story, the ABC agreed to send a film team along with Gil and me on our next Timor visit. A Sydney-based Timor-Leste supporter gave us thirty-five guitars to distribute and Sydney musician Gabby Winterfield helped me to string them. Gabby was later to find worldwide success fronting the psychedelic act Jagwar Ma.

More help came from my niece Cass' husband Rob Jones, who helped me pack the guitars into his ute to get to the airport. When we reached Dili, ABC crew in tow, Gil and I gave most of the instruments to artists who rehearsed at the city's main arts complex, Arte Moris, and we dropped off a couple to some blind musicians.

On a later trip, Gil and I were asked to deliver three huge suitcases of donated items which turned out to be women's hair products. A customs official at Dili Airport gave his colleague a knowing look and whispered, 'Ladyboys.'

We took the products to a local market, spread them out over two tables and told the women shoppers to 'take what you want, it's all free'. Pandemonium broke out and for the rest of the week we were pointed out as 'the hair product guys'.

The most important part of the guitar-delivering trip was going to meet the Alma Sisters at the urging of Timor-Leste's Ambassador to Australia, His Excellency Abel Guterres we took the Compass crew to visit the Alma Nuns in Dili.

'They look after the poorest of the poor, Paulie,' he explained. 'Disabled and abandoned children. Please just drop in and say hello.'

I was only too happy to meet them because I had promised Siser Helena at the Austin that I would help the women and children in Timor-Leste.

At the nuns' facility near Dili International School we found five sisters looking after about thirty children with disabilities. They were thrilled with the two guitars we gave them.

One of the younger nuns, Sister Yustina, asked if we would like to come along on a visit to children in nearby villages. The first thing we noticed was that she got around on a small motor scooter, the only form of transport the nuns had. We followed her with the ABC film crew and were quickly struck by the poverty we encountered. In some places if you owned more than a few chickens you were the wealthiest person in the village.

Led by experienced journalist Mark Edmondson, the ABC crew interviewed old friend—now President—José Ramos-Horta.

The result of our trip was the *Compass* episode 'Balibo, My Brother & Me'. After the episode aired in August 2009, I was asked to appear on the ABC television quiz show *Spicks and Specks,* where I met the inimitable English comedian Francesca Martinez.

Born with cerebral palsy, Francesca says she has often been yelled at by people in the street who think she is drunk, but she has turned her misfortune into a series of comic routines. She had the *Spicks and Specks* audience in hysterics when she said sex was always very quick with her boyfriend as, 'With my shaky hand, by the time I put the condom on him it's all over.'

Francesca helped me out by agreeing to pose in a T-shirt promoting an education campaign for ActionAid, an international charity for women and girls living in poverty.

The charity's executive director in Australia was Archie Law, who happened to have been the drummer in the 1980s band Huxton Creepers, and he gave me some short-term work recruiting celebrities to promote ActionAid's campaign.

61

NUN OF THE ABOVE

Meeting the nuns in Timor-Leste inspired Gil and me to help them with their amazing work. I talked them up in Australia, telling anyone who would listen that just when you are ready to write off the Catholic Church, you come across the little Alma nuns. And I do mean little because when you meet them, they all seem to be under five foot tall.

They take on the thankless job of caring for children with disabilities in a country that lacks many basic support services. The children, many of them orphans, have massive physical and intellectual challenges and the nuns have to keep a close eye on them as they can tend to wander off.

In all my time with the nuns I have never heard one complain and they seem to be permanently smiling.

One little Sister, the formidable Rezi, used to get up every morning and walk ten kilometres to the village of a little girl to massage her impaired legs, and then walk the ten kilometres home. I couldn't believe one person would do this for another. There is no money, fame or glory in it but because Sister Rezi pays her such attention, the rest of the village treats the little girl with more respect.

You can imagine some of the big heads I have dealt with during my career writing about pop stars (hello Diana Krall!). So I do find the utter humility of the Alma nuns to be a wondrous thing. These women are not in the least interested in the latest fashions, cosmetics and jewellery. Instead, they have uncluttered lives filled with spirituality, love and compassion.

Gil and I decided the first thing the sisters needed was some better transport. We launched an appeal to buy a new van as the five nuns in Dili had one motor scooter between them and no way to move their children around.

When stories of the nuns' work appeared in the *Sunday Herald Sun* and *The Age*, donations rolled in. I told to Sister Ely, the head nun in Timor-Leste, that our campaign had gone really well and we had raised 'eighty'.

She said, 'Eighty dollars? That is fantastic, Paulie, we can buy extra rice, medicine and some blankets.'

When I said, 'No Sister, not eighty dollars—$80,000,' she stared at me silently as if trying to compute what I was saying. She took some convincing and then broke down in tears.

I told my friends The Wiggles about the work of the nuns and they gave me a free shipment of Wiggles clothes and other merchandise for the sisters.

Val Eimutis, a former producer at Triple R radio station who went on to become a bigwig at the Toll transport group, helped us to get the gear up there in record time. Hundreds of Timorese kids are now running around in their Dorothy the Dinosaur shoes. That is not as trivial as it sounds because the tough plastic boots are great at protecting them from tropical diseases that can prey on bare feet.

After we bought the van, a Melbourne-based supporter Annie Dunn helped the nuns build two classrooms and start a school. Sister Ely told me that some Chinese troops drove past their complex one day and saw the two new schoolrooms being constructed. They stopped and a young captain asked what was happening.

'I explained that Australian supporters had offered to build us two classrooms to assist our children's education,' she said.

He wrote something in a pad and left. The next day the Chinese troops returned with several truckloads of equipment and men, and told the nuns they were going to build two classrooms as well.

I said, 'Hey Sister, that is great, it is like having two boyfriends and playing them off against each other.'

Without missing a beat, she smiled and nodded, 'Exactly.'

The nuns are not so straight. I ventured back to Timor-Leste to meet them again with a young female friend Esra Ozege, who I had met after speaking about Timor-Leste at a breakfast for some National Australia Bank employees.

She approached me after my talk and said, 'Next time you go to see those nuns, I'm coming with you.'

I never thought she would follow through but she did.

I just love going up to work with the nuns and introducing them to people who will help them. They give me 'soul juice' and it was while flying back from one of those visits that I realised something huge was happening to me.

In the 1980s it was all sex, drugs and rock 'n' roll, now I was hanging out with nuns.

I was lucky that after all my angst and self-destructive behaviour, I had found a healthy and productive way to cope with my anger. My new passion was to find ways to raise money for them and I soon learned that if I was collecting money for the nuns, I needed to work with a registered charity to provide accountability and valuable tax breaks.

That is how I came across Jesuit Mission, the religious order's international aid organisation. Gil and I began channelling money we raised for the nuns through the North Sydney-based Jesuit Mission.

Sadly, I was really blowing my Satanist credentials.

62

THE TRANSPLANTS
(2011)

Even though I had received a new liver, I still needed to go back to the Austin for regular check-ups.

It is an interesting fact that the waiting room in a liver clinic is a great place for ageing rock musicians to meet. After curious glances and stuttering introductions, I met several fellow musicians at the clinic where we discovered we shared similar stories and were all grateful to still be alive.

A group of us decided in 2011 that we wanted to 'put something back in' and thank the families of organ donors, so we would form a band to do exactly that. Called The Transplants, we did a number of shows to thank the unknown Australians and their families whose generosity had kept us alive.

By 2022 I was celebrating fifteen years with my new liver and still feeling incredibly grateful.

That is fifteen years with my daughters, fifteen years travelling back to Timor-Leste, fifteen years of falling in love, and fifteen years of playing music; fifteen years that I wasn't supposed to have.

Other musicians thankful for their second chance included guitarist and singer Shane Laffy, singer Jo Fraser, sax player Steve Dagg and Indigenous rapper Little G. We were joined in The Transplants by supporting musicians Colin and Michael Badger on guitar, keyboard player John Grant and drummer Bob Cleary.

I recruited the broadcaster turned politician Derryn Hinch, who had had his own liver transplant. Someone asked if Hinch could actually sing and I said, 'Who cares? It's Derryn Hinch.'

When he performed with us at the Caravan Music Club in the Melbourne suburb of Oakleigh in February 2012, Hinch was wonderfully accommodating, delivering his surprisingly good version of the Joe Cocker song 'You Are So Beautiful' without any fuss, and then joining the rest of us for a rousing rendition of The Dockers' singalong anthem 'You're Going Home In The Back Of A Divi Van'.

I was thrilled when word came through that we had another potential recruit, one of Australia's biggest ever musical stars, Judith Durham of The Seekers. Durham wanted to join The Transplants in honour of her friend Dr M Yunupingu, the Yothu Yindi frontman who died of kidney disease.

I still can't believe I have shared a stage with her. It is easy in the Kylie Minogue era to forget just how big Durham and her band were. In the 1960s they vied with the Beatles and the Rolling Stones at the top of the UK charts and they still hold the record for the biggest crowd at Melbourne's Sidney Myer Music Bowl, an estimated 200,000 people way back in 1967.

Another character who asked to meet The Transplants was American rock pioneer Bobby Rydell, who received a new liver and a new kidney in 2012 at the age of seventy.

One of the first US teen idols, he first hit the record charts in 1959 and had hits including 'Wild One' and 'Volare'. Bobby was honest enough to admit that a massive vodka addiction had destroyed his liver.

63

MENTORING THE FLYBZ

When I met Fablice 'Fab' Manirakiza and Ira 'G Storm' Amin they were refugees with big dreams sitting in a corner at the Artful Dodgers Studios in Collingwood. Fablice, seventeen, was the first to approach me.

'Sir, I heard you have played music for some time now?' he ventured.

'Yeah, I've played in a few bands, mate, but please don't call me sir.'

'That's great, sir. We're into music, too. We want to make hip-hop. We call ourselves Flybz and we have already made an album, but we are a little disappointed,' he said.

'Why's that, pal? And please don't call me sir.'

'Well, sir, we thought we were recording our lyrics with our best English but afterwards the producer said he loved our music, but he wanted to know which language we were using. He didn't know we were singing in English.'

He said he and his fourteen-year-old nephew, G Storm, had been sent to the Artful Dodgers by the Multicultural Arts Victoria, which had simply not known what to do with them.

At the time, I was trying to drum up some last-minute publicity for Just Cycle, a charity cycling event that Jesuit Social Services was holding at the Rochford winery in the Yarra Valley. I noticed that Victoria's former Premier Steve Bracks was taking part and using our Timor connection, I persuaded him to do a publicity photo. I then offered the Flybz (pronounced fly-beez) a great opportunity.

'Boys, I have got a deal for you,' I said. 'If you can get to the Williamstown Botanic Gardens at 8am tomorrow for a picture with former Victorian Premier Steve Bracks then I will know you're fair dinkum and you can appear at this event.'

I truly never thought they would get their act together to make the early morning trip from their home in Springvale—a forty kilometre drive, or two and a half hours by public transport.

Lo and behold, there they were, on time and ready to go. Their picture with Bracks appeared in the *Herald Sun* the next day. This changed everything.

The boys realised I could introduce them to a brand-new audience and a brand-new Australia.

I realised that, unlike a lot of the young folk I had been working with, these lads were polite, super-keen and, most importantly, reliable. Getting any young person up, ready and on time is not as easy as it sounds. That first media stunt set the tone of how we would work together: think big and go for it.

Gradually, the boys started to share their story with me and I was gobsmacked at what they had been through. Working with them made me feel alive again and it put to bed the cynic in me. To hear their stories of struggle and their joy at simply being in Australia washed my soul. I began to feel a strange new lust for life in their company. Quoting that great philosopher Kylie Minogue, I never realised 'I should be so lucky'.

The two boys and I went on to perform workshops at close to 250 schools around Australia and Timor-Leste over the next six years. Along the way, they moved from being people I was paid to work with, to being family who got to meet my brother and sisters, nieces, nephews and friends.

By the end of our days together, we were an entertainment machine that never left a school without the students dancing their arses off and mobbing us as we made our way out of the school gates.

The boys told me they came from Burundi and even though I thought I could place most countries around the globe, I had to admit I had never heard of it. It turns out Burundi is a tiny country in central Africa between Rwanda and Tanzania. Like better-known Rwanda, it had suffered decades of horrific civil war and mass killings.

Fablice and G Storm said they spoke Swahili, Kirundi, Kinyarwanda and French, but they were determined to perform proficiently in their new language English.

'In Australia nothing is beyond us,' Fablice predicted.

I soon started taking the boys out to experience my Melbourne. Our first adventure was the annual Reclink Community Cup Aussie Rules football game, a charity event originally set up by St Kilda's Sacred Heart Mission, where rock musicians line up as the Rockdogs for a grudge match against a team of radio station DJs, the Megahertz.

It was a case of 'from footy things, big things grow'.

Keen to make a name for themselves as hip-hoppers, the lads readily agreed to attend the match in 2011 after organiser Jason Evans said they could perform a few numbers after the game, which in the past has drawn crowds of up to 23,000.

Unfortunately, when we arrived at Elsternwick Park, Jason told us that too many bands and musicians had been arranged so there was not enough time for a Flybz appearance. He said though that the boys could act as boundary umpires if they liked. They were disappointed but good sports, agreeing to run the boundary.

I was impressed by their enthusiasm. Jason put his head around the door of the dressing room as they changed into their umpire outfits and asked us if we were all set.

'Proceedings start in five minutes so get ready.'

As I walked them onto the ground, the boys said the only problem that might arise is that they had never actually been to an Australian Rules game.

With the starting whistle about to blow, G Storm added innocently, 'What is a boundary umpire?'

'Oh, great guys, there is a huge crowd here who will string you up if you make a mistake and you're saying you don't know the rules?'

So moments before the big game I found myself blurting out the basics.

'If the ball crosses the line, blow your whistle. Grab the ball, throw it over your shoulder and run, just run all day to make sure you are near the boundary line if the ball crosses over.'

Like most things the Flybz did, their enthusiasm won them many fans, including much-loved game caller Tony Biggs, who acknowledged in his commentary the great job 'the boys from Burundi' were doing.

The boys joined in the post-match celebrations and even managed to get a photo with winning Rockdogs captain Dan Sultan.

Things got even more interesting a few days later when Rockdogs coach Paul Kelly rang me to say he had been impressed by the boys and asked if they would like to join in a kick-to-kick session he has with some friends each Sunday morning.

When I told them, they were keen to play even though they had no idea who Kelly was. They rocked up for a kick and gradually got to know Australia's No. 1 singer-songwriter. When G Storm went to school next day and told them he had been playing kick-to-kick with this guy called Paul Kelly, his teachers thought he was lying until he showed them a selfie with the musician.

I suggested that they should record one of Kelly's songs. Fablice replied (and this is why I love these guys), 'No, we don't want to do one of his songs, we want him to do one of ours.'

Now that's balls.

I couldn't believe it when Kelly agreed to co-write a song with Fablice and yours truly. We had a session at Artful Dodgers that produced the hip-hop song 'Child Soldier', based on the boys' early lives in Africa.

Kelly sang the chorus. A fantastic Melbourne musician who performs under the name Pataphysics added some soulful trumpet and the song was produced and engineered by Killing Heidi's Jesse Hooper. Triple J and community radio ran the song and it aired on the ABC TV show *Rage*.

I also convinced the ABC to record an episode of its *My:24* documentary series about the Flybz's lives.

The Victorian Football League contacted me to invite them to be the half-time entertainment at their Grand Final at the Docklands stadium and even asked them back for a repeat performance a year later.

The Flybz finally got to perform at a Community Cup concert three years after their initial disappointment when I invited them to join the Painters & Dockers on stage for a song.

Just before we played, the crowd erupted when three streakers dashed across the field. G Storm was flabbergasted. 'This is crazy. Forget about hip-hop, I love this rock 'n' roll.'

The Flybz's personal stories had a profound effect on me and on every audience I ever saw them talk to. Their tales are the reason I wake up most days grateful that I was born in Australia.

Soon after meeting them, I got them telling their stories at schools, finishing off with a number of hip-hop tunes. It quickly proved a winning formula.

They were also a great double act, with Fablice supplying the light, funny stories, and G Storm recalling some of the darker moments of their childhood in the refugee camps. They learned first-hand how to hit an audience with the horrors of war before making them laugh hysterically at their early misadventures in Australia. Classrooms and lecture theatres full of students and teachers were spellbound by their stories. They had never heard anything like it.

'When I was eight, my parents were killed,' Fablice would recall. 'When I was eleven, the soldiers came to my school and told all the tall boys in the class to stand up. I was one of the tall boys and they gave me a gun and some bullets and told me to march towards the sound of the guns and to kill anyone I met on the way. Luckily for me, when we got to the front lines, I was chosen to go and buy some food and I told my officers I needed to go pee,' he said.

'Anyway, when we got to the food store I ran away and hid in the jungle. I wasn't scared being with the wild animals because it was way better than being a child soldier.

'I hid for a few days, then stopped a taxi and the driver thought I was a drug dealer with money, so I got him to drive me back home to where my sister worked. Once there I went and got the fare money off her. That was the end of my army days. Thank God I never shot or killed anyone.'

Cool rapper G Storm would surprise the students at private schools by telling them how much he admired their school uniforms.

'When I was a boy, all I ever wanted was a school tie and jacket,' he said. 'We had nothing like that. You guys are so lucky. School was not so easy for me. In Burundi, we had to walk ten kilometres to get there and then ten kilometres back every single day and I was always, always hungry.'

You could hear the classroom clock ticking in the silence.

'Once, my mum got sick and was taken to hospital and I had to fend for myself, so I lived by eating mud and rats.'

Even the big Maori boys at Liverpool High School in Western Sydney were blown away by this story.

'I thought you said "mud and rats",' one of the tougher-looking boys yelled out with a confused tone.

'I did,' said G Storm nonchalantly.

Fablice outlined how his mother belonged to the Hutu tribe while his father was from the enemy Tutsis. Both were killed in the devastating civil war in the former German and later Belgian colony.

'When Mum and Dad died, I lived like a wild boy on the streets, taking drugs and drinking. Sniffing petrol. My life was very hard,' said Fablice. 'I was on my own and things were very bad.'

After escaping the military in 2003, he fled to a refugee camp over the border in Tanzania to reunite with his eldest sister. She, too, was a former child soldier who had escaped the civil war and was now living with her baby and eight-year-old son G Storm in the refugee camp.

'I thought being a child soldier was hard but being in the refugee camp was much worse,' Fablice said. 'We had one bucket to use for drinking and cleaning.'

With conditions in the camp deteriorating and no chance of safely returning to their homeland, the family were accepted as refugees to Australia in 2007. Fablice laughs when recounting his arrival in his new home.

'I knew absolutely nothing about Australia,' he says. 'All I knew was that on a box of matches I saw the word Australia and a kangaroo. I thought the whole country would be full of big red kangaroos.'

Fablice said there was a lot of jealousy in the camp from those without refugee visas.

'The people who weren't chosen to go overseas started spreading rumours to scare us,' he said. 'They said that in Australia white people ate black people.'

'When we arrived at Tullamarine airport there was a guy holding a piece of paper with my sister's name on it and I freaked out and told my family here was the guy that was going to eat us. We all started running until someone stopped us and said, "No he won't eat you, he will drive you to your accommodation".'

The boys said they could not believe the abundance of food and opportunities in Australia.

'We only ever ate meat on Christmas Day but here you can have it all the time,' marvelled G Storm.

Fablice said the duo couldn't believe it when their home suburb Dandenong had a so-called hard rubbish day.

'A guy was showing us around and we said how trustworthy Australians were to leave their things out on the street. He said, no, it was just rubbish and they were throwing it all out. We were amazed and by the end of that week we had ten televisions.'

I loved their wonderment at being in Australia.

They would say things like, 'Hey Paulie, have you seen that show

Q&A on the ABC? Did you know you can make fun of a politician in Australia to their actual face and they don't take your family away in the middle of the night?'

They were mystified by the attitude of many young Australians.

'Why do the young people here complain? This place is paradise,' said G Storm.

Fablice arrived without speaking a word of English but went on to become an accomplished speaker and won the Arts and Fashion Award at the Victorian Government's Young Achiever of The Year Awards in 2016.

The Flybz have always been very interested in finding out more about Australia's First Peoples. I constantly told them if any white person abused them and said, 'You don't belong here mate,' they should turn around and say, 'Neither do you.'

You have never seen anyone happier than Fablice when I took him to a huge protest against Australia Day.

'This is so great,' he said with wide eyes.

'Why?' I asked, puzzled.

'Well, if this was Burundi, the police would turn up soon and start shooting live bullets into the crowd.'

After establishing ourselves in Victorian schools, the boys and I ventured up to Sydney. One of the workshops we did there was at prestigious St Ignatius' College Riverview, which has educated many of Australia's top business leaders and politicians.

When I watched the Flybz perform to 1300 students at the school assembly, the guy sitting next to me on the stage just loved the boys, saying, 'These guys are great.'

The chap beside him was just as enthusiastic. A teacher was later surprised that I had not recognised my neighbours.

'That was John Eales, the most successful captain in the history of Australian rugby and another former Wallaby, David Giffin,' he said.

A South Australian tour quickly followed where the boys' story made it on to the local ABC TV show *The 7.30 Report*. We also did extensive tours of Western Australia thanks to the support of Mark Antulov, the Principal of Prendiville Catholic College in Perth.

* * *

Some might find it an odd way to mark the fortieth anniversary of my brother's murder at Balbo but I lined up the Flybz to do a hip-hop tour of Timor-Leste. Once again, the ever-reliable Gil Santos joined me and the Flybzs on the trip. Typically, Gil lined up accommodation, a sound system and transport for our arrival. We played at pubs, clubs, schools and outdoor venues and even in the waiting yard at Dr Dan Murphy's free medical clinic in Dili. We had run into our old friend Dr Dan in a bar and he asked us to come down to his clinic to do some tunes for the patients.

As we performed at the clinic, we were surrounded by patients who had to wait hours as a limited number of staff battled all kinds of diseases with limited drugs and equipment. The clinic treats many of Timor-Leste's young mums and in a country where women have an average of seven children, it's a very busy place. Sadly, Dr Dan passed away in 2020 but the fine work of his Bairo Pite Clinic continues.

As we played the first tune, a figure emerged from the crowd. It was a very old man in traditional garb with snow-white hair, a weather-beaten face and a wicked, toothless grin. We were all spellbound. The old guy looked around, smiled and then lifted one leg up, dipped a shoulder and busted out his best moves in time to the beat. The crowd just lost it. Smiles returned to downcast faces, people laughed and squealed, and happiness reigned for a few precious minutes. It was magic. I confess I teared up.

Our first show was due to be held at an exclusive Dili club for white expats and aid workers but Gil was having none of that. He shifted the event to an outdoor stage and made entry free so poor families could attend as well. He then lined up six support acts and invited the local HIV prevention agency to use the concert to spread their vital message. In the end, close to 4000 punters turned up and the concert was broadcast live on national television.

The acts included November's Children, a young Timorese hip-hop posse who knew all the latest beats and songs from the United States. Ah, the internet.

The Flybz were treated like hip-hop superstars everywhere we went. Early in the trip, Fablice told me that Dili felt oddly familiar.

'You have talked to us so much about Timor-Leste, Paulie, but this is just like my country Burundi, just with more dogs.'

A memorable appearance was at the opening of a new episode of the series featuring Timor-Leste's first female superhero, where the Flybz met Ramos-Horta, later posing for photos with him.

Feto Fantastiku—The Female Superhero Peacebuilder is a series created by youth worker and actress Jacinta de Sousa Pereira who plays the title role. Her unique film and TV spots have made her famous in her homeland as she spreads her message on women's rights.

It is fitting that her male sidekick is a character called Simple Man.

Jacinta told us that she campaigns against gangs and domestic violence.

'Sadly, Timor-Leste is afflicted by violence,' she said. 'When an argument breaks out, people do not talk to each other, they immediately start hitting each other. There is domestic violence every day and it is children who suffer the most.'

She said she encouraged people to resolve their conflicts peacefully.

Of her fame, she said with a blush, 'People increasingly recognise me in the street. Children shout out "Feto Fantastiku" when they see me, either that or the catchphrase from our broadcast: "Attack the problem, not the person!"'

I reckon Mum and my brother Tony would have loved Feto Fantastiku, and the old hip-hopper at Doctor Dan's bringing a smile to the faces of destitute patients.

64

GIVING PEOPLE A VOICE
(2011–onwards)

Julie Edwards, the head of Jesuit Social Services, has long been recognised as a progressive chief executive but she deserves particular credit for putting up with me.

I did have her laughing when I confessed that I might have confused students at Xavier College during an early appearance with the Flybz.

After our presentation we were asked a number of questions by the students. One asked my opinion of the founder of the Jesuits, St Ignatius of Loyola. Speaking on the run, I shared with the large audience a quote that I thought came from St Ignatius about facing adversity and never giving up.

'Well boys, St Ignatius reminded us there is always a cause for hope,' I said, feeling quite chuffed with myself. I was on a roll.

'As St Ignatius said: "In the velvet darkness of the blackest night there is always that burning light … over at the Frankenstein place."'

As soon as the words had left my mouth, I turned pale, realising I had quoted not the founder of the Jesuits but the transsexual character Frank-N-Furter from *The Rocky Horror Picture Show*. Oops.

Some bosses might have lost patience but Julie stuck with me and I was also backed to the hilt by my amazing manager Marianna Codognotto, and we began to see the Just Voices program pay dividends.

It really took off after former tax office worker Danielle Sherry joined the team at the Artful Dodgers. She brought a new level of organisation and professionalism to Just Voices, allowing us to encourage more young people to share their stories. Bookings rolled in, thanks largely to Danielle, a funny, kind and super-efficient operator.

Some might think of us as chalk and cheese (the old rocker and the former tax worker) but we proved to be an awesome combination, lining up and delivering more than 500 performances by our young speakers and musicians to tens of thousands of students.

The program grew to include soulful hip-hopper Adrian Eagle, Afghan asylum seeker turned law student Nahid, West Papuan refugee Jefry, and Sammy, a formerly homeless talented young hip-hop artist from the south-eastern suburbs of Melbourne. We also worked with rising Indigenous artists, including spoken word artist Jonathan 'Caution' Binge, singer-songwriters Aaron B and Olivia Meg, guitar wiz Elijah Augustine, dancer and didjeridu player Brent Watkins, and singers Monica Caro and Lawrence Austin.

Danielle and I were proud of the fact that anyone could approach us and we would stage an appropriate workshop.

One of the more unusual requests was from twelve female politicians from Bangladesh who wanted help keeping their young people from being recruited by hardline Islamic jihadists. No problem. We gave them a two-hour workshop on how art and music could be used to counter this growing danger. After that gig we figured nothing was beyond us.

I was walking through Southern Cross railway station in central Melbourne on the way to work one morning when I passed two Sudanese buskers.

What first interested me was that they were both playing acoustic guitars, whereas most young Africans I had met were into electronic hip-hop loops and beats. As I walked away, the taller one started to sing, and his voice stopped me in my tracks.

I walked back to listen to the rest of the song then said, 'Buddy, you can really sing. You guys have to record this stuff.'

They looked at me sceptically, clearly wondering what this strange old bloke was trying to get out of them.

I stood there long enough to convince them to come and visit the Artful Dodgers. Clement, the taller one, and his cousin Angelo, eventually turned up at the studio and when they met the Flybyz and other young Africans who were enjoying the facilities, they were hooked. They became regulars at the facility and refined their act. Performing as The Travellers, they did shows at prestigious hotels, the Melbourne Town Hall and the Melbourne Cricket Ground, a bit of a step up from busking on platform nine at Southern Cross.

One of our absolute stars has been a Sudanese single mum who walked into the studio one day and said she wanted to talk to 'this guy Paulie'.

'That would be me,' I replied, impressed by her self-confidence.

'My name is Agum,' she said, 'and I am a superstar but no one knows me yet.'

When I first asked Agum about telling her stories in schools she said there was no way she could do it as her English was too bad. She has since emerged as such a seasoned performer and we have not been able to keep up with the requests for her to speak.

At one time unemployed and homeless, Agum also works as chief cultural officer at the Werribee Open Range Zoo, surrounded by the animals she loved seeing in the wild as a child.

One of the workshop leaders I most enjoyed working with was my Dili Allstars band mate Zeca Mesquita, a master percussionist and grandson of a *criado*. We have both been pleasantly surprised to visit some schools and find that they are already flying both the Timor-Leste and Aboriginal flags. You have come a long way, Australia.

At times I have shared my own story with students through the Just Voices program, something that I now realise has been incredibly therapeutic for me.

65

DOCKING ON
(2009–20)

Lying in Ward 8 of the Austin Hospital on and off for eighteen months on mind-altering drugs, my thoughts took to daydreaming. I relived Painters & Dockers shows and even though it seemed unlikely that I would ever get back on stage, the thought of doing one more helped to keep me going. I saw more clearly than ever how much fun it had been, not just for me but for many others, too.

So after my successful transplant, I was overjoyed to get a call from rock journalist Paddy Donovan in 2009 to say the Painters & Dockers were to be inducted into *The Age* newspaper's EG Awards Hall of Fame (now run by Music Victoria). It was a huge honour and recognition for all those hours we had spent on the road touring Australia, playing show after show.

This was our first major gig in years, with our best-known line-up—minus the late Phil Nelson—taking to the stage at the Prince of Wales hotel in St Kilda. There was a lot of love in the room that night.

Tickets had sold out quickly and 1000 people jammed into the iconic Fitzroy Street venue but when organisers asked us to do a second night, they were told that I could physically manage one performance but not two.

The best part of the night was seeing so many familiar faces in the crowd. Sure they were a little older and heavier than at that first gig in Port Melbourne twenty-six years earlier, and perhaps some were balding, but our mob turned out in droves. It was a wonderful reunion and I must say that my new liver and I put on a great gig.

A few years later we were asked to play again as the headline act after the Community Cup footy game at Elsternwick Park.

In front of a huge crowd, we were joined by the brass section of soul outfit Saskwatch, go-go dancers from the Rockdogs' cheer squad, and the Flybz. The theme artist of the day was Lou Reed and we opened the show with a blistering version of the Velvet Underground classic 'White Light/White Heat'. I managed to track down an awesome outfit to wear: a rather fetching green German Lederhosen.

Word got out and other offers came flooding in. More shows were booked in Brisbane, Adelaide, Hobart, Warrnambool, Sydney and Perth. We even got a gig at the acclaimed Meredith Music Festival in 2012. Later on we supported one of our favourite bands, Sunnyboys, at a Melbourne Zoo twilight gig with the Salvation Army brass band as special guests.

We were also asked to host the TV show *Rage* for the first time and I was invited to compere an episode of the top-rating show *Classic Countdown*.

It was just like the early days of The Dockers as we found ourselves causing mayhem and mischief without even knowing it.

That was also the case when Queensland band Violent Soho was threatened with ejection from a domestic airline flight because one of its members was wearing a Dockers T-shirt that read 'Eat Shit Die'. The name of our 1990 single was somehow deemed a threat under Australia's new anti-terrorism laws.

66

FORCE OF DESTINY
(2015)

Acclaimed actor David Wenham is one of many who considers the late director Paul Cox a giant of Australian cinema.

'He is unique, and we need him,' said Wenham. 'He is completely an auteur, because everything you see and hear on the screen has got Paul's fingerprints all over it.'

I first met Cox on ABC radio's *The Conversation Hour*, hosted by Waleed Aly. Cox walked into the studio, kissed me on the lips and said, 'Hello my liver brother.'

I totally understood where he was coming from as you do feel a special bond with other transplant recipients.

Cox had his transplant at the age of sixty-nine in 2009 after suffering cancer, and became romantically involved with another organ recipient he met in the hospital, Rosie Igusti. The experience inspired his last film *Force of Destiny*, which was released less than a year before he died in June 2016. The film's producer happened to be Maggie Miles from Burrundi Pictures, who I'd seen years before at Yothu Yindi's Garma Festival in the Northern Territory.

Ahead of the film's release, Maggie created a series of micro-docs with transplant recipients to promote the film and raise awareness about organ donation. After hearing about me from people at the Austin Hospital's liver unit, she contacted me in late 2014 to ask if she could base one of the clips on my story.

I was happy to help, and in the studio Maggie and I struck up an instant bond over our Northern Territory experiences, realising that we had many Top End friends in common. I was particularly interested to hear that she was single.

Maggie then asked me to interview Cox on stage during an event at Melbourne's Wheeler Centre aligned with the release of *Force of Destiny*.

My chat with Cox went well and I learnt later that Maggie was keen to stay in touch and perhaps even catch up after the event, but I stupidly gave her the impression that I wasn't interested and headed off to meet Fablice in a café in a nearby laneway.

I didn't bother telling Fablice anything about my discussion with Cox, instead I was raving about this intriguing woman who had organised the event. I mentioned that Maggie and her former partner had had a company that was involved in an iconic series of film clips for Yothu Yindi, including the clip for the song 'Treaty', prompting Fablice to declare an astonishing coincidence.

'We used to hear that song in the refugee camp,' he said. 'I didn't even know it was from Australia.'

I added that the production company had been called Burrundi Pictures. Burundi is the name of Fablice's homeland, at which he grabbed my arm and said, 'It's a sign from God. You gotta go after that woman.'

I laughed because I was already coming to the same conclusion, and as I threw my head back, I swear, I saw Maggie along the laneway reading a book as she walked.

She was so absorbed in the book as she walked along, I had to call out twice to get her attention and wave her over.

When I introduced them, Fablice told her that he could not believe my tall story about her company being called Burrundi Pictures. Maggie showed him an old Burrundi business card, which left Fablice shaking his head and muttering cryptically about signs from God.

Maybe he was right. Maggie and I are still together seven years later.

Maggie divulged later that she was also thinking of me as I called her over, but was trying to distract herself with the book. And that book Maggie was reading? It was a book on the power of dreams, which started with a quote from Carl Jung's *The Red Book*. As I called out, she was reading, 'Nothing happens in which you are not entangled in a secret manner; for everything has ordered itself around you and plays your innermost.' Maggie was raised in the village of Broughton Astley in the English Midlands but has now worked extensively through the Top End.

Force of Destiny indeed.

67

ALMA NUNS TOUR
(2018)

When you have had a liver transplant you have to keep an eye on your health, cut out the grog and take a cupboard-full of medicines for the rest of your life. Another consequence for me was a stern warning by my doctors to think twice about ever going back to Timor-Leste.

The drugs I have to take to lower my immune system and stop my body rejecting the new organ put me at risk of catching diseases like malaria and dengue fever, which of course are rife in Timor-Leste.

I became obsessed with dousing myself in insect repellant to keep the mozzies away, but I was still determined to continue my work with the nuns. My eighteen-year-old copy boy self would have been thrilled to know that I would eventually be wearing long pants every day.

It startles me now to think I have been back to Timor-Leste five times since my transplant but the risk has certainly paid off. Focussing on the plight of children with disabilities gave me an enormous sense of purpose, and somehow seemed to gradually ease the anger that had always burned inside me about my brother's murder. Compared to the challenges facing these children and the Alma nuns, my own problems seemed trivial.

Twice I accompanied the nuns as they did the rounds visiting remote rural villages and helping the poor, disabled and elderly. In 2017, Maggie and I dispensed another load of Wiggles merchandise donated by the entertainers. We were amused to find there was even one school in the rugged interior of the country where Wiggles outfits had become the official school uniform.

Word about my activities spread and many Australian visitors dropped into the nuns' Dili headquarters to say hello and offer support, while the nuns also made some trips to Australia.

The first visit I helped with was a 2013 fundraising mission to Melbourne by Sister Ely and her young offsider Sister Anastasia. I had used my own money to buy their plane tickets and realised at the airport that we had to go shopping straight away when they had arrived in sandals and thin skirts and we had a week of school visits in the rural areas around Ballarat, the old gold-mining boomtown north-west of Melbourne that is always chilly in winter.

Forty minutes after greeting them at the airport we were discussing the merits of different kinds of woollen underwear.

The nuns stayed at my sister Annie's house in Daylesford, about five kilometres from Ballarat, where they met Mum. I knew Sister Ely from Dili but when I first met the twenty-something Anastasia, I was worried she might not have the confidence to carry off the school appearances I was planning through the Just Voices program.

Far from it.

Sister Anastasia was a natural, with a beaming smile, a quick laugh and the ability to pick up a guitar and deliver a song to win over any room.

Five years later she was the senior member when she returned with the more reserved newcomer Sister Gertrudis. I took them to Sydney for a week of workshops followed by a week in country Victoria and Melbourne.

The words 'rest', 'relax' and 'day off' just don't feature in their lives. They would rise each day at 4am ready for action and brush off my blurry-eyed pleas for them to go back to bed.

'It's okay, Paulie, you get some sleep. We will just say some prayers for a while.'

I would try to get some shut-eye but touring with the nuns ended up being harder work than two weeks on the road with Billy Idol or Midnight Oil.

The two loved spending time with Aretha's grandmother, Aunty Janice Brown—especially in her lovingly tended back garden.

They even managed a dinner with prominent supporter and Wiggles manager Paul Field and his wife Pauline. That was a funny night as he took us to a famous Sydney steakhouse where I ordered a mouth-watering T-bone. The nuns politely followed my lead but then became embarrassed when they saw a waiter walk by carrying huge steaks.

'What is the matter, Sister Anastasia?' I asked.

'Paulie, there is so much meat on those plates. That would last a whole week at the orphanage.'

They changed their order to chicken satay appetisers, which were still big meals for them.

The two nuns and I powered through presentations at six schools. Saint Ignatius' College Riverview in Sydney, Loyola Senior High School in Mt Druitt, Star of the Sea in Brighton, Sacred Heart College in Geelong, Siena College in Camberwell, and Xavier College in Kew.

Sister Anastasia explained to the students that the Alma nuns differed from many other religious orders.

'We live, sleep, eat and play with the disabled children we look after,' she said. 'There is no divide between us. I am convinced all these children are gifts from God. They are my little brothers and sisters.'

She said many of the children were simply handed over by parents who could not cope.

In Melbourne, the nuns were interviewed on ABC Radio and took part in a benefit concert at the Mission to Seafarers welfare charity that was dominated by acts from the Artful Dodgers Studios and Elvis impersonator Paulie Greene.

In 2019 we were planning to bring the nuns back to Australia and to send more shipments of goods to them when the COVID-19 pandemic shut things down.

No bug was going to stop this partnership, though.

Despite her own daily hurdles and dangers, Sister Anastasia started texting me frantically when the virus began to spread.

'Are you okay, Paulie? We are worried about you.'

The usually unflappable little nun was anxious to check on my health. I was fine, locked down in the comfortable isolation of Melbourne. She was the one facing a real crisis and a scary future. She was the one living in lockdown with hundreds of abandoned children with disabilities in a facility with only the most basic equipment and resources, and limited food and medical supplies. She laughed and told me the only good thing to come from the pandemic was that she had picked up some new skills during lockdown.

'I have played so much indoor soccer with the children that I will be able to play professionally for sure once this is all over,' she said.

She added that a better use of lockdown time for the nuns would be to practice their English, and asked if I could help. I offered to do lessons via Zoom to help ease the lockdown boredom for the nuns and from that moment things took off.

Word of our idea got out and two dozen Australians ended up Zooming in for voluntary workshops in English, art, yoga, storytelling, medical issues, and African culture and wildlife.

Students from St Ignatius College in Geelong, who had been forced to defer a planned 2021 visit to the Jesuit school in Timor-Leste, jumped at the chance to stay in touch with their Timorese friends. Thanks to Alicia Deak, a coordinator at the school, the students took on a weekly English class by Zoom and the nuns just loved it.

Sister Anastasia admitted her team were frightened and at times ran out of supplies, but she remained incredibly upbeat.

'Please tell all of my friends in Australia to take care of themselves,' she said. 'For me, Melbourne is now my second home because of its people's kindness and love they have given us. When the virus ends,

I want to come back and go to the races at Flemington. That is my dream. I love horse racing.'

Timor-Leste now runs in my family's blood so it was important to me to introduce my daughters to the country. Both grew up attending Timor-Leste benefits, parties and family events. My eldest daughter Frances has always been reluctant to go there, saying she would find it too unsettling to visit the country where her uncle was murdered. I did, however, take my younger daughter Aretha to Timor-Leste in 2019.

As Aretha had been voted the first ever female Prime Minister in the Australian Indigenous Youth Parliament, I lined up several meetings for her with young Timorese women activists and leaders.

They began their first meeting by coming up with the resolution: 'No old white guys in the room', and promptly threw me out.

That's cool, I thought. The sisters are doing it for themselves.

We met up with Melbourne musician Darcy Fitzgerald, who was managing the Beachside Hotel in Dili. I had been to Timor-Leste twenty-five times and Darcy had been there for only two months, so it probably says something about each of us that he acted as our interpreter.

Eddie de Pina, a friend from the 1980s resistance struggle, drove the three of us up to Balibo. Born in Timor, he fled the 1975 civil war to Australia with his family when he was ten years old. He finished his education in Perth and returned to Timor-Leste amid the turmoil of 1999 to help rebuild his country.

Driving us up into the hills, he explained how he had set up the St Bakhita Centre in the village of Eraulo, forty-five kilometres inland from coastal Dili.

Named for a Sudanese saint, Josephine Bakhita, the centre supports 2500 local residents with services ranging from water and sewage projects to funeral assistance and an ambulance service.

Eddie insists he is 'just a truck driver', but I have long known that he is a natural fixer who can sort out any problem. Unlike some others with big government titles, he gets things done, so I have often turned to him for help and advice.

Shame he barracks for the West Coast Eagles.

We ended the trip back with Darcy at the Beachside Hotel. Its owner, Australian Michael Smith, also runs the Sun Theatre, an art deco movie palace in Yarraville in Melbourne's inner west. Smith and the theatre's manager Krissa Jansson go out of their way to promote Timor-Leste as a travel destination.

68

COVID DOCKERS
(2020)

Like everybody else, I saw my world go nutty at the start of 2020 thanks to the arrival of COVID-19. It broke out as The Dockers were finishing a February tour of supporting our friends the Sunnyboys. We knew we might not be able to play again for a while so we recorded our last gig, at the Forum in Flinders St, Melbourne, and released it as a live album, *You Know You Want To*.

This followed eight previous albums: *Love Planet, Bucket, Kiss My Art, Touch One Touch All, Advance Australia Where, Overt and Deliberate, Nervous 90s* and *The Things That Matter*.

There were also plenty of singles, and tracks on compilation albums and EPs, including *Hickory Dickory Dock*. In 2022 we will re-release our first ever EP, the four-track *Kill, Kill, Kill* with several songs that have only previously been released on vinyl.

Not a bad effort for a band that was supposed to play one gig thirty-nine years earlier.

Amidst the lockdowns, my bond with Timor continued when The Dockers worked with our old pals the Maritime Union of Australia through the union movement's foreign aid program.

We did a live concert with online access to raise money for victims of the devastating floods that hit Timor-Leste in late 2020. My favourite part of the show was when ten Timorese fruit pickers who had been working in Victoria joined us for a rousing rendition of 'Liberdade'. It was gratifying to find they knew the words by heart.

A year later when lockdown boredom was really pissing me off, I had an unexpected high with news that I had been awarded an Order of Australia Medal for services to the community and the performing arts. I felt embarrassed, given my shady rock 'n' roll past, but embraced it as something that might help me to promote the work of the Alma nuns.

Any good work that I have done has depended on the support of others, whether it was my bandmates in the Painters & Dockers, the Dili Allstars, the PRICS and The Transplants, the young refugees and others in the Just Voices program, the tireless activists for Timor or those wonderful nuns.

And for all my sins I have been lucky enough to love and be loved by an amazing line-up of family, friends.

Asked by the organisers of the Honours to make a statement, I said the following:

Firstly, I would like to thank the unknown Australian who decided to donate their organs thirteen years ago because their liver has kept me alive and kept me 'Docking'.

I would also like to thank the Alma nuns who have allowed me to work with them this past decade. It has been a wonderfully soothing and loving way to cope with the murder of my brother at Balibo in 1975.

The Order of Australia Medal also belongs to my brother Gil Santos for showing me in the early days of our fight for Timorese independence that in some cases, guitars are more effective than guns.

A big thank you to all members of the Painters & Dockers who have performed countless benefit concerts around the nation.

I am so proud of the fact that we are still going, and that we have always been a people's band—anyone can get up and perform with us.

69

FULL CIRCLE
(2021)

I was feeling pretty good about myself and then bang, once again I nearly died.

In September 2021, I organised an online fundraiser to buy a motorbike for Sister Anastasia, as the nuns had lost all forms of transport during recent floods, but I overdid things. The stress and long hours brought on another bout of my old enemy encephalopathy, the nastiest side effect of liver disease. I was watching television at my sister Annie's house in Daylesford and feeling exhausted, then suddenly I was waking up in the Austin Hospital five days later. My brother, Dr Greg, warned Maggie and my sisters that this could be it.

Finding myself surrounded once again by liver patients who were literally groaning and screaming with pain was even harder to take than it had been the first time back in 2006–07. I promised myself then and there that if I ever got out, I would finish the book I had been working on since my first spells in the Austin, and folks, if you've got this far, thanks for reading it..

It is coming up to half a century since my brother's death, the event that forever changed the lives of my family and so many others.

Truth be told, I thought at the time that the deaths at Balibo would soon be forgotten by everyone except the bereaved families. How was I to know that the incident would propel me through the rest of my life?

Without it, I might never have been that angry young man who found solace in punk rock, worked for thirty-five years as a journalist, was part of the team who received an ARIA Award for the *Balibo* film soundtrack album, worked for a decade with young people in crisis and formed a loving bond with a little group of nuns.

I have never gotten over the grief my mum suffered all her life because of Balibo. It was an open wound for her and it was hard watching her deal with it.

To date, no one has ever been charged with my brother's death, or paid any sort of price for the crime.

My mum never hated the people of Indonesia and often said Tony's killer was probably just some poor boy who had joined the army to try to feed his family.

Years later I received a letter out of the blue from an Indonesian mother.

'Every night when my family prays to Allah we include your brother,' she wrote. 'Please when praying to your God, remember our son who was sent to fight in East Timor but was never heard from again.'

Wow!

I had a bit of a revelation on my most recent visit to Timor-Leste when I asked Sister Anastasia about something I had noticed.

'Sister, you look different to other Timorese women,' I said. 'Which village are you actually from?'

'Paulie, I'm not from East Timor. The majority of us are Indonesians and we come from all over the place … Java, Papua, Flores, Sumatra, Sulawesi, Bali, West Timor.'

The penny dropped that I had done a 360-degree turn.

For many years I had loathed Indonesians and blamed them for my brother's death. Now I realised that I had been working alongside them: they were the same inspirational nuns who had helped me channel my fury into something positive, allowing me to help myself by helping other people.

Later I visited the sisters' headquarters in Malang, Indonesia, and as I stood there at a small rural airport waiting to be collected, I thought, 'At least these nuns don't know of my wicked rock 'n' roll past.'

A van then pulled into the airport carpark blasting music. Hang on a minute, I thought, this sounds familiar. Yep, it was The Dockers playing one of our punchiest songs, 'In My Mind'.

The van screeched to a halt, the door flung open, and four nuns waved for me to jump in.

'Come on, this is our favourite song,' said the driver.

At their headquarters I was humbled to see the hundreds of impaired and abandoned children in their loving care.

'These children don't care about which country the nuns come from,' I thought to myself. 'They just want a cuddle.'

PAULIE'S 15 GREATEST GIGS

Being the music writer on a major newspaper meant I was lucky enough to see many great shows. Lying in hospital waiting for a new liver I thought that a great way to ease the boredom would be to name my Top 15 shows. They span thirty-five years.

1. Kenny Rogers (Melbourne Sports and Entertainment Centre), 1985
The country music great played family videos during his show and insisted each member of the crowd bring along a can of food for the poor of Melbourne.

The highlight was when a guy from the working-class suburb of Spotswood was picked by Kenny to get up on stage and help him sing his classic 'Lucille'. Now this guy couldn't sing for shit but the passion with which he delivered the tune had me weeping in my seat. It was heartbreaking.

I swear there were crowd members in wheelchairs who got up and walked towards the stage at the end of the show.

2. X (Chasers Nightclub, South Yarra), 1984
Fronted by the awe-inspiring bassist Ian Rilen, with Steve Lucas on guitar and the gorgeous redhead Cathy Green on drums, X were a primal rock 'n' roll assault machine. What a night.

The stage was filled with teenage girls sitting transfixed by Rilen. The rest of the crowd included every low-life punk and ghoul in Melbourne. It felt like there had been a nuclear meltdown and a band had crawled out of the rubble to play.

They did an over-the-top version of their song 'Dirty Degenerate Boy' which contains the confrontational lines, 'I ain't got no money, I can't pay my rent, last week's dole cheque, up my arm it went'.

When it came to dirty, filthy rock 'n' roll, X was the real deal.

3. Stevie Wonder (Crown Casino, Melbourne), 1997

Henry Maas from Bachelors from Prague and I stood rebuking our fellow audience members for staying in their seats and not dancing. How could they not move to such magic?

The Master Blaster belted out some phenomenal funk tunes. Sadly, many in the crowd were more interested in getting back to gambling. The downside of putting on a sensational show in a casino.

4. Grace Jones (Palais Theatre, St Kilda), 1981

The eccentric former model took to the stage in a gorilla outfit and encouraged fans to climb on stage and simulate cunnilingus on her. The crowd went berserk.

I met her at the concert afterparty where she ate a peach and somehow made it look erotic. For someone who seemed so tall and slender on stage, she was tiny.

5. Eminem, Red Hot Chili Peppers, Metallica and James Brown (Seattle Center), 2000

The most diverse show I have ever seen was held to open a museum paying tribute to Jimi Hendrix. I had never heard of Eminem and he performed early in the blazing afternoon sun, with the crowd of white trash boys singing along to his raps. I thought this guy was going to be huge.

The more mainstream Chili Peppers were dynamic, as were Metallica, who made heavy metal mainstream. The night climaxed with yet another musical contrast when James Brown appeared with a seventreen-strong backing band.

It was impossible not to dance your arse off.

6. Split Enz (Palais Theatre, St Kilda), 1980

I was always a big fan of these Kiwi lunatics ever since seeing them perform a song called 'Maybe' on *Countdown* with their bent lyrics and whacky haircuts and clothes.

The Palais concert marked the release of their breakthrough album *True Colours,* which made them mainstream superstars. It was exciting to be there for the start of the Finn brothers' amazing journey.

The support act was the Australian combo The Reels, authors of the classic tune 'Quasimodo's Dream'.

7. Cesária Évora (Arts Centre Melbourne), 2008

Touring Portugal with The Dili Allstars was a massive musical education as I discovered *fado* music and heard the tunes of a singer they called The Barefoot Diva.

Hailing from Cape Verde off the coast of Africa, Cesária Évora was a massive drawcard in Portugal. She never wore shoes on stage, in a show of solidarity with the poor people she grew up with.

When she came to Melbourne, I couldn't find anyone who wanted my spare ticket, so I went alone. Évora's melancholic performance was unforgettable.

8. Ian Dury and the Blockheads (Festival Hall, West Melbourne), 1981

I hated it when all the punk musicians started taking themselves seriously.

That is why I love Ian Dury, who contracted polio as a child and defied the notion that stars had to be healthy and good looking. His songs mixed punk with traditional dance hall tunes, funk, soul and pub rock, and were delivered with wicked lyrics and remarkable musicianship.

This show was great, although afterwards I asked a guy for a cigarette light and he sent me sprawling along the footpath with one punch. The night had been so much fun that I honestly didn't care.

9. Archie Roach and Ruby Hunter, Kev Carmody and Tiddas (Vancouver), 1995

This trio of acts went to Canada to bond with their Native American cousins and share their stories and music.

The late Archie Roach was the king of Australian soul music and often performed with his late wife, the tiny powerhouse Ruby Hunter. As tour publicist, it was my job—one of the hardest I ever had—to wake them up for breakfast radio interviews.

Being a true professional, Archie rose to the occasion, charming DJs and listeners alike even though one DJ started his interview, 'So Archie, they took the kids away, that must have been a real bummer?'

Kev Carmody's song 'From Little Things Big Things Grow', which he co-wrote with Paul Kelly, is one of the most moving tunes in Australian music history, telling the story of the walk-off led by Vincent Lingiari at Wave Hill in the Northern Territory.

The rendition of the song he delivered in Vancouver, backed by the girls from Tiddas, had me in tears.

10. Paul Kelly and The Coloured Girls (Deakin University, Geelong), 1987

This was a band at the height of its powers, with each member intuitively knowing what their bandmates were about to play. Kelly put on a great performance and the prowess of his band really stood out.

As the support act, The Dockers stood at the side of the stage in awe—a remarkable learning experience. For me, this was the most dazzling line-up Kelly ever assembled.

11. Not Drowning, Waving (Rabaul, Papua New Guinea), 1988

Volcanoes ringed a football ground packed with locals listening in wonder to the music being created by their fair-skinned visitors.

Little kids ran amok, having the time of their lives at the front of the stage. It was unlike any other concert I'd attended.

Magic.

12. Sammy Davis Jr. (Hilton Hotel, East Melbourne), 1985

Dad was a huge fan and I managed to wrangle us some tickets to a gig that was an intimate affair in a small cabaret room.

Sammy had just had his second hip replacement but this didn't stop the remarkable showman, who really was the whole package—dancing, singing and telling jokes.

I have never seen anyone before or since who could match him for sheer entertainment skills.

13. Pinetop Perkins (B.B. King Blues Club and Grill, New York City), 2002

I saw this old blues pianist by accident in a bar off Times Square and just couldn't leave when I found out he was eighty-nine years old.

The legendary Mississippi blues man was still touring and playing every week with the passion of a teenager. It was an accomplished performance by a seasoned player. A very well-seasoned player.

14. Seu Jorge (Melbourne Recital Centre), 2015

I knew very little about this samba-influenced Brazilian when I ventured out to see him, other than the fact that he had performed Portuguese-language covers of David Bowie hits in the Wes Anderson film *The Life Aquatic with Steve Zissou*.

He mesmerised the audience with an acoustic tribute to the Ziggy Stardust-era of the glam king.

15. Warumpi Band (Big Day Out, Royal Melbourne Showgrounds), 1999

One of Australia's most underrated outfits, this band was fronted by the late George Rrurrambu Burarrwanga, who was part Bon Scott, part Mick Jagger.

He had the crowd screaming for more and his band was on fire, ripping through classics 'My Island Home' and 'Blackfella/Whitefella'.

George was inspired that day and clearly enjoyed performing for a crowd of Southerners.

Published by Melbourne Books
Level 9, 100 Collins Street,
Melbourne, VIC 3000
Australia
www.melbournebooks.com.au
info@melbournebooks.com.au

Copyright © Paul M Stewart (Paulie) 2022

All rights reserved. No part of this publication may be reproduced, stored in a retrieval system, or transmitted in any form or any means electronic, mechanical, photocopying, recording or otherwise without the prior permission of the publisher.

Every attempt has been made to locate the copyright holders for material quoted and images printed in this book. Any person or organisation that may have been overlooked or misattributed may contact the publisher for correction in any future printing.

Title: Paulie Stewart: All the Rage
Author: Paulie Stewart
Publisher: David Tenenbaum
ISBN: 9781877096334

 A catalogue record for this book is available from the National Library of Australia

Front cover image: Photo: Mary Boukouvalas
Back cover image: The other side of the coin.
Photo: unknown

Other Melbourne Books music titles:

Astonishing Rock Trivia
John Tait
Captain Matchbox & Beyond: The Music & Mayhem of Mic & Jim Conway
Catherine Fleming, John Tait, and Mic and Jim Conway
Chalet Monet: Inside the Home of Dame Joan Sutherland and Richard Bonynge
Richard Bonynge
Cold Chisel: Wild Colonial Boys
Michael Lawrence
Daddy Who?: The Inside Story of the Rise and Demise of Australia's Greatest Rock Band
Craig Horne
Hear Me Talking to Ya
Bob Sedergreen
Mick Thomas: These Are the Days
Mick Thomas
Midnight Oil: The Power and The Passion
Michael Lawrence
Nine Parts Water, One Part Sand: Kim Salmon and the Formula for Grunge
Douglas Galbraith
Noise in My Head: Voices from the Ugly Australian Underground
Jimi Kritzler
Roots: How Melbourne Became the Live Music Capital of the World
Craig Horne
Sound As Ever: A Celebration of the Greatest Decade in Australian Music (1990-1999)
Jane Gazzo and Andrew P Street
Sunbury: Australia's Greatest Rock Festival
Peter Evans
Tait's Modern Guide to Record Collecting
John Tait
Techno Shuffle: Rave Culture and The Melbourne Underground
Paul Fleckney
The Ballroom: The Melbourne Punk and Post-Punk Scene
Dolores San Miguel
The Dingoes' Lament
John Bois
The Remarkable Mr Morrison: The Virtuosity and Versatility of Australia's Master Musician
Mervyn E. Collins
The Seekers
Graham Simpson and Christopher Patrick
The Seekers: Behind the Curtain
Bruce Woodley AO
This Will Explain Everything
Jeff Duff
Wangaratta Festival of Jazz & Blues 30 Years
Adrian Jackson and Andra Jackson
Whatever Happened to Diana Trask
Diana Trask

www.melbournebooks.com.au

www.ingramcontent.com/pod-product-compliance
Lightning Source LLC
Chambersburg PA
CBHW032032150426
43194CB00006B/249